Varieties of Economic Inequality

Recently, the issue of inequality has regained attention in economic and political debates. Although this interest is welcome, the debate is still mostly focused on income or wealth distribution, which is an important aspect but does not present a complete view of inequality. Most of the theoretical and empirical studies produced by economists concern personal income distribution or factor income distribution. This is more evident in the studies of the evolution and characteristics of contemporary capitalism and globalisation.

Varieties of Economic Inequality considers both theoretical perspectives and empirical evidence of aspects such as income, gender, race, technology, power, region, education and class. Ultimately, this text rejects the idea of supposed long-run constant factor shares, the positive effects of inequality and the greater importance of absolute level of income compared to its unequal distribution, and instead reveals the structural inequalities that exist within societies.

This book advocates a move away from the focusing on inequality at the level of the individual and suggests policy for eradicating these various forms of inequality. It is suitable for those who study political economy, social inequality as well as economic theory and philosophy.

Sebastiano Fadda is Professor in the Department of Economics, Roma Tre University, Italy. He teaches advanced labour economics, and economic growth.

Pasquale Tridico is Professor in the Department of Economics, Roma Tre University, Italy. He is lecturer in labour economics and in economic policy. He is also Jean Monnet Chair in European Economic Studies.

Routledge Advances in Heterodox Economics
Edited by Wolfram Elsner,
University of Bremen
and
Peter Kriesler,
University of New South Wales

Over the past two decades, the intellectual agendas of heterodox economists have taken a decidedly pluralist turn. Leading thinkers have begun to move beyond the established paradigms of Austrian, feminist, Institutional-evolutionary, Marxian, Post Keynesian, radical, social, and Sraffian economics—opening up new lines of analysis, criticism, and dialogue among dissenting schools of thought. This cross-fertilization of ideas is creating a new generation of scholarship in which novel combinations of heterodox ideas are being brought to bear on important contemporary and historical problems.

Routledge advances in heterodox economics aims to promote this new scholarship by publishing innovative books in heterodox economic theory, policy, philosophy, intellectual history, institutional history, and pedagogy. Syntheses or critical engagement of two or more heterodox traditions are especially encouraged.

For a complete list of titles in this series, please visit www.routledge.com.

This series was previously published by The University of Michigan Press and the following books are available (please contact UMP for more information):

Varieties of Economic Inequality

Edited by
Sebastiano Fadda and Pasquale Tridico

LONDON AND NEW YORK

First published 2016
by Routledge
2 Park Square, Milton Park, Abingdon, Oxon OX14 4RN

and by Routledge
711 Third Avenue, New York, NY 10017

Routledge is an imprint of the Taylor & Francis Group, an informa business

British Library Cataloguing in Publication Data
A catalogue record for this book is available from the British Library

Library of Congress Cataloging in Publication Data
Names: Fadda, Sebastiano, editor. | Tridico, Pasquale, 1975– editor.
Title: Varieties of economic inequality / edited by Sebastiano Fadda and
Pasquale Tridico.
Description: Abingdon, Oxon ; New York, NY : Routledge, 2016.
Identifiers: LCCN 2015036972| ISBN 9781138928015 (hardback) |
ISBN 9781315682099 (ebook)
Subjects: LCSH: Income distribution. | Equality – Economic aspects. |
Distributive justice. | Social justice.
Classification: LCC HB523 .V37 2016 | DDC 339.2–dc23
LC record available at http://lccn.loc.gov/2015036972

ISBN: 978-1-138-92801-5 (hbk)
ISBN: 978-1-315-68209-9 (ebk)

Typeset in Times New Roman
by HWA Text and Data Management, London

Contents

Figures

Tables

Contributors

Valeria Cirillo, Sapienza University of Rome
Marcella Corsi, Sapienza University of Rome
Charlie Dannreuther, University of Leeds
Pasquale De Muro, Roma Tre University
Carlo D'Ippoliti, Sapienza University of Rome
Sebastiano Fadda, Roma Tre University
Svenja Flechtner, European University of Flensburg
Enrico Marelli, University of Brescia
Stephan Panther, European University of Flensburg
Francesco Pastore, Seconda University of Naples and IZA Bonn
Cristiano Perugini, University of Perugia
Fabrizio Pompei, University of Perugia
Marcello Signorelli, University of Perugia
Pasquale Tridico, Roma Tre University
Jacek Wallusch, Institute of Cliometrics and Transition Studies, Poznań
Beata Woźniak-Jęchorek, Poznań University of Economics

Acknowledgements

This book is an outcome of the contributions presented at the 2014 Summer School of the European Association for Evolutionary Political Economy (EAEPE) by Professors, experts in the field of inequality. The EAEPE Summer School was, as usual, held in Rome at the Roma Tre University and local organizers were Pasquale Tridico and Sebastiano Fadda, editors of this book.

Pasquale Tridico, Jean Monnet Chair in European Economic Studies, wishes also to acknowledge the support of the Jean Monnet Programme, Key Activty 1 (Project Number: 542598-LLP-1-2013-IT-JMC-CH).

Introduction

Bridging theories and evidences of varieties of inequality

Sebastiano Fadda and Pasquale Tridico

Recently, the issue of inequality has regained attention in the economic and political debate. Although we should welcome this interest, the debate is still mostly focused on income and/or wealth distribution, which is a very important but rather narrow view of inequality. Even if in the last decades, some scholars have introduced more comprehensive and multidimensional approaches to economic inequality, most of the theoretical and empirical studies produced by economists concern personal income distribution or factor income distribution. This is more evident in the studies of the evolution and characteristics of contemporary capitalism and globalization.

The proposed book is divided in two parts. The first part concerns the theoretical aspects of inequality, its foundations from a broad perspective: income, gender, racial, technology, power, regional, educational and class inequalities – all aspects analysed in this book. Inequality of living standards, well-being, opportunities and freedoms can't be adequately represented in terms of income and should, therefore, be analysed and tackled in a multidimensional perspective. The second part deals with empirical evidence and policy suggestions coming directly from the theorethical framework built in the first part: evidence of gender inequality, income, class, power, politics, technology, etc will be examined, and relevant policy suggestions will be advocated.

The book questions the grounds on which it may be argued that it's not worth worrying too much about unequal income distribution. From an ontological point of view, if we take a subjective ontology of inequality we have to question whether the world is made of individuals or states or markets. So rather than asserting that individuals are unequal we have to also understand how describing society as made up of individuals may perpetuate inequality further. From an economic point of view the book rejects the idea of supposed long-run constant factor shares, the positive effects of inequality and the greater importance of absolute level of income compared to its unequal distribution. From a theoretical point of view, we aim to combine a functional and bridging analysis of incomes with a gender approach and other types of analyses that reveal structural inequality within the society.

The very foundation of the problem of inequality, from an economic point of view, is the concept of social welfare. According to the utilitarian approach, social welfare is the sum of individual welfare. Social welfare improvements are not possible (or would not be "Pareto efficient") by re-distributing resources from one individual to another, because a "Pareto" improvement is only a situation in which it is possible to make someone better off, without making someone else worse off. On the other hand, an egalitarian approach would consider re-distribution of resources to avoid the situation where an individual could become richer by taking advantage of the fact that the other is in poor health or in poor education, or is disabled (Sen, 1973). In this latter approach, the application of the Rawls' criterion would be the best policy; the aim is not individual welfare but the level of welfare in the society. If one individual (A) has a lower level of welfare than another (B), and if B can be made better off by re-distributing resources from A, then the Rawls criterion of justice requires that B should have sufficiently more income to make B's utility equal to A's. In Rawlsian thinking, inequalities have to be adjusted following two principles: 1) offices and positions must be open to everyone under conditions of *fair equality of opportunity*; 2) they have to be of greatest benefits for the least-advantaged members of the society (Rawls 1971: 303). To be applied, these criteria require more than meritocracy. 'Fair equality of opportunity' requires not only that positions are distributed on the basis of merit, but also that all have equal opportunity, in terms of education, health, etc., to acquire those skills on the basis of which merit is assessed. The application of these principles would, in the end, produce much greater advantages for the society as a whole.

Another way to look at the problem of inequality is through social peace and cohesion. Sen (1973) saw inequality as strictly linked to the concept of rebellion and indeed the two phenomena are linked in both ways. Inequality causes rebellion, but it may happen that income inequality may increase after a rebellion where it brings power to a specific apparatus or a nomenclature or a social class; this has happened many times in history when, for instance, rebellions were led by army generals or by elites of nobles. In several transition economies, inequality increased after a "rebellion" which brought to power oligarchs. In particular, in the former Soviet Union inequality increased dramatically after the 1991 August Coup which deposed Soviet president Mikhail Gorbachev and dissolved the USSR (Tridico, 2010). In some African countries, such as Congo, Sudan, etc. the same happened: rebellions, carried out by generals and warlords, deposed previous authoritarian or less authoritarian regimes, but such a change brought about an increase in inequality. Nowadays, economists try to capture a causality nexus (inequality à rebellion à inequality) through the use of some modern governance indicators such as political stability. The link between political stability and inequality is demonstrated in numerous empirical works such as Alesina and Perrotti (1996) and Easterly (2001), where it emerges that income inequality increases during political instability.

An interesting explanation of inequality in the Americas is put forward by Sokoloff and Engerman (2000), who, in order to explain inequality in wealth, human capital and political power, suggest an institutional explanation, historically founded, which lies in the initial roots of the factors of endowment of the respective colonies. In general, political institutions set up by the Spaniards and Portuguese in Latin America were different from the ones set up by the British in North America. Moreover, the latter sent educated people and skilled work forces, along with the lords, to the New World, and these started to build their own future; while the Spaniards and the Portuguese did not encourage massive migration from the motherland but sent landlords who basically exploited slaves from Africa.

One of the first cross-country works on inequality was made by Kuznets (1955). He showed that in the early stage of economic growth income tends to be unequally distributed among individuals. In the early stage of a growth process, over time, the distribution of income worsens. In the later stages, national income starts to be more equally distributed. Hence, inequality declines in the end, after the country has accomplished the "U"-shaped trajectory. Several later empirical studies confirmed this relationship (Chenery and Syrquin, 1975; Ahluwalia, 1976). The reason for such a relationship was attributed to structural changes, which at the beginning of the "transition" bring about job losses and inequalities. However, in the last three decades, income inequality, in particular among rich countries, has increased. This is in strong contradiction to the Kuznets curve (1955). Piketty (2014) already noticed this; and in his recent book, he rejects the idea of the Kuznets' bell curve. On the contrary he proposes a horizontal "S" curve.

The implicit trade-off behind the Kuznets curve (economic growth/ inequality) and the idea that an increase in inequality is sometimes necessary for a rapid growth has been often criticized (Atkinson, 1999). An alternative hypothesis to explain why income inequality differs among countries is put forward by Milanovic (1994), who shows that inequality decreases in richer societies because social attitudes towards inequality change as those societies get richer, and inequality is less tolerated. Birdsall and Sabot (1994) showed, contrary to the Kuznets hypothesis, that inequality may be a constraint for growth and, if inequality is lowered, then a country could have a GDP per capita 8.2 per cent higher than a country with income inequality 1 standard deviation higher.

A similar hypothesis is suggested by Voitchovsky (2005: 273) who, however, stresses *the shape* of the distribution and suggests that inequality at the top end of the distribution is positively associated with growth, while inequality lower down the distribution is negatively related to subsequent growth. Moreover, empirical evidence in cross-countries analysis, from Latin American to East Asian Countries, would pose the question as to why Latin America has high inequality and low growth and, on the contrary, why East Asia has high growth and low inequality. Birdsall and Sabot (1994) suggest that it is a matter of policies and social attitude towards inequality. In Latin America, dictators, generals and the ruling classes acted, for a long time after WWII, with little respect for the poorest part of their society, implementing fiscal and trade policies that provided few benefits to the poor. On the contrary, in East Asia the ruling classes were more aware of social needs, and implemented policies such as land reforms, public housing, public investments in rural infrastructures and public education which had a positive effect on both growth and income distribution; better educated people can get a better job and earn more; public investment in the rural sector can bring farmer productivity and income higher; public housing and other social services can increase the purchasing power of people, and so forth.

In the last three decades, since 1980, the world changed, the structure of rich economies was reshaped, and in most advanced economies the huge technological progress created strong and long waves of transformations. Since the end of 1970s, the political changes created the basis also for a new paradigm of political economy, first in USA and in UK, and later in most advanced and emerging economies.

This new paradigm, which can be called "financial capitalism" is characterized by the strong dependency of economies on the financial sector, by the globalization and intensification of international trade and capital mobility, and by the "flexibilization" of labour markets. From an economic policy perspective, the change resulted in the withdrawal of the state from the economy (i.e., the minimization of its economic intervention) and the dominance of supply-side policies (i.e., labour flexibility, tax competition for firms and capital, etc.).

In this context, we argue, income inequality increased because labour, which is the most important source for income, is seen by the supply-side approach, as a cost to be compressed rather than as a fundamental part of aggregate demand to expand. In the age of financial capitalism, characterized by the intensification of globalization and financialization, labour–capital relations are changing, and in most of the cases labour represents the weaker part. From one side, within the conflict between labour and capital, trade unions lost power, and labour market institutions such as labour protection against firing, unemployment subsidies, substitution rate for unemployment subsidies, etc., weakened. From one side, labour flexibility, atypical labour contracts and temporary works created unstable jobs and, therefore, unstable consumption.

Moreover, within the new paradigm of political economy mentioned before, the welfare state represents another cost to be compressed. In order to foster firms competitiveness and economic growth social spending needs to be reduced, advocates of the so called "efficiency thesis" argue. In fact, most of the countries are experiencing a retrenchment of the welfare state or at least a stabilization of the expenses which corresponds, in the age of globalization and of ageing, to a per capita reduction in real terms. However, the efficiency thesis is challenged by "the compensation thesis", which argues that because globalization increases inequality, welfare state expenditure needs to increase. In other words, globalization pressured governments to expand welfare expenditures in order to compensate for the domestic "losers" of the globalization process. Some countries chose this second approach to cope with the challenges of globalization and in fact, in the past decades increased welfare spending.

The structure of the book

This book focuses on inequality. However, contrary to most books in this field, inequality will be explored from a broad perspective and from different approaches, not only income inequality and not only an economic approach to inequality. The book has the objective to explore first, the political implications of choosing a particular ontology of inequality. The positivist objectivist paradigm of neoclassical economics, that sees inequality corrected by the market, will be challenged. Second, it aims at showing that the exclusive focus on income and wealth has some relevant drawbacks: it leads to neglect of non-income economic inequalities that cause other, not less severe and intolerable, social injustices, and that interplay with income inequality; it limits economic analysis to the space of commodities, contributing to reproduce the scourge of "commodity fetishism" and its role in capitalism; it leads to a policy debate on inequality that is concentrated on conventional and short-sighted monetary income redistribution, such as basic or minimum income. Third, the book will highlight the "gendered inequality regimes" leading to a systematic sub-ordination of women or even more all kind of feminine coded activities in modern capitalist systems. Finally, the book deals with some fundamental issues concerning income inequality and welfare state within the age of globalization and financialization.

The book is opened by a conceptually broad article by De Muro, who argues that although we must welcome and support the renewed interest in inequality – that reconnects contemporary "economics" to classical "political economy" – we should, however, also notice that unfortunately the debate is still mostly focused on income and/or wealth distribution, i.e. "how the pie is sliced", which is a very important but rather narrow view of economic inequality. Even if in the last decades some scholars have introduced and developed more comprehensive and multidimensional approaches to economic inequality most of the past and current debate, as well as the theoretical and empirical studies produced by economists, concern personal income distribution or factor (functional income distribution). This is more evident in the studies of the evolution and characteristics of contemporary capitalism and globalization. Following an important work of Amartya Sen, this chapter aims at showing that, notwithstanding their importance and role, the exclusive focus on income and wealth has some relevant drawbacks, and it suggests that a broader approach is needed.

Chapter 2 poses a challenging question: what causes and how to curb income inequality. Fadda argues that knowledge of the causes of inequality is required in order to choose appropriate measures to reduce it. But the question itself of whether it is proper or not to take measures against income inequality is to a certain extent influenced by what is thought to be at the root of inequality. The aim of this chapter is to suggest measures to curb income inequality, and this implies the idea that inequality is for some reasons "bad" and not the natural consequence of a good working of a competitive economic system. But precisely this view has to be put under question in the first place. Nevertheless, even if inequality was thought as simply mirroring the correct working of a competitive system, it would still be possible to encourage measures to restrain it on the ground of ethical or social reasons.

In Chapter 3, Cirillo Corsi and D'Ippoliti (in Gender Class and the Crisis) take a gender perspective to analyse the economic crisis. They look at the most recent micro-data available at the European level, the European Union Statistics on Income and Living Conditions (EU-SILC), containing information on European men's and women's incomes in 2012. As it turns out, the crisis and the policy response to it have impoverished several European households and increased income inequality in Europe. However, there is no strong evidence, the authors show, to support or reject the narrative on the gendered impact of the crisis yet. As a consequence, it may be necessary to wait for further evidence before taking the two-stage narrative for granted, while stronger emphasis on pre-existing structural gender equality may be warranted.

Chapter 4 closes the first theoretical part of the book: this chapter discusses political and economic consequences of unequally distributed wealth, income and economic power for economic development in middle-income countries. In recent years, the "middle-income trap" has received increasing attention among economists. Some middle-income economies have not achieved the transition into high-income status for long years and are allegedly trapped in middle-income status. While most authors give technical advice to overcome this trap, the authors here introduce a political economy perspective to the discussion. They argue that high inequality in the access to economic resources and political power will increase the likelihood of entering a middle-income trap, since under these conditions the position of narrow elites is incompatible with the institutional changes and policies needed to overcome middle-income status. They use a comparative perspective in order to illustrate how the high concentration of economic power and ties of the business elite with political regimes has influenced policy choices.

The second part, which is more empirical and offers evidences of inequality and policy suggestions, starts with Chapter 5 which explores whether "the efficiency thesis" concerning the relation between welfare states and globalization is functional for economic growth or, alternatively, whether "the compensation thesis" produces better results in terms of economic growth. The current economic crisis, in particular, was a test for many advanced economies to determine whether the socio-economic model that those countries built in the previous decades was able to cope with the challenges of globalization. The hypothesis here is that investing in welfare dimension is not a drain on competitiveness or a barrier to economic efficiency. The efficiency thesis, according to which globalization needs to be accompanied by the retrenchment of welfare states in order for firms to be competitive, does not hold. The tests are conducted in a sample of 42 countries made up of OECD and EU members. On the contrary, the econometric exercises, and the empirical analysis, indicate that the "compensation thesis" (i.e., regulated globalization and an expanded welfare state) not only reduces inequality; it is also functional to produce higher economic performance.

In Chapter 6 Perugini and Pompei show that while earnings inequality between education and skill cohorts in Europe has been largely studied, little effort has been devoted so far to analyse the size of within groups disparities and their drivers. However, especially under certain structural and institutional conditions which may favour incomes polarization and the persistence into low-pay traps, this dimension of inequality may be relevant. In this paper the authors employ EU-Silc microdata for 19 EU member countries in 2007 and 2011 to provide evidence on hourly wage disparities within the groups of high, medium and low educated workers. Using quantile regression approaches, the authors look at individual and institutional determinants of earnings inequality within each cohort and across the wage distribution. Then, by focusing on the employment status (temporary/permanent) of workers, they find that remarkable differences exist in the role played by employment protection legislation for temporary and regular workers in shaping wage levels, depending on the group of countries, education groups and year considered.

In Chapter 7 Dannreuther argues that the EU's Lisbon Agenda heralded a new approach to EU policy cooperation. Based on the principles of social inclusion, environmental sustainability and global competitiveness the use of benchmarks to promote social and economic reform agendas by 2010 has been redeployed for the new 2020 agenda. In doing so the actions of the EU have stimulated debates over the nature of a New Social Question in the EU. The chapter, therefore, explores how traditional arguments for addressing inequality stand up at the supranational level in relation to the structure of the EU and its relationship with its society. With these observations in mind it critically assesses the rights-based approach upon which the Lisbon Agenda is based to justify its interventions and demonstrates that these contribute to rather than remove the tendency to durable inequality in the EU.

In Chapter 8 Wallusch and Woźniak-Jęchorek present the modern, mostly not even recognized, inequalities in terms of regional perspective. They try to elucidate the regional disparities in selected R&D variables and confront them with regional inequalities in GDP and unemployment rate. A long-term economic growth rate per capita depends nearly entirely on the rate of qualitative changes, such as technological and institutional innovations as well as employees' skills. In well-developed countries these changes result primarily from the innovativeness of the entire world sector of R&D and the national level of education. In less developed countries, their own innovative activity is marginal and technological changes in economy depend nearly entirely on the absorption of foreign innovations. However, with the GDP per capita at the level of 50–70 per cent of the most developed countries, further fast technological progress of a catching-up country is becoming more difficult, as access to technologies of newer generations is necessary. Nowadays this is the case of CEE states. At this level of development the process of catching-up may be stopped and economists speak about so-called middle-income trap. The chapter will identify and analyse the institutional barriers limiting the regional access to innovations in old and new EU countries.

The last two chapters concern young unemployment. Chapter 9 provides a frame of mind to explain cross-country differences in youth unemployment rates. The key factor is the youth experience gap, namely the gap of work experience of young as compared to adult people, even in a time of ever increasing education attainment. To help young people fill in this gap and ease the school-to-work transition, every country provides its own policy mix, including different degrees and types of labor market flexibility, of educational and training systems, of passive income support schemes and fiscal incentives. Five different country regimes are detected, which tend to overlap with traditional welfare state regimes.

Chapter 10 discusses and analyses the key disadvantages of the young people in the labour market. After a short discussion of the fundamental theoretical issues raised in the literature and a brief presentation of the results of the main empirical studies, the central part of the chapter is dedicated to a comparative analysis of different youth labour market performance indicators in the EU-28 countries. In particular, in addition to the youth unemployment rates, the following indicators are analysed, also distinguishing by gender and sometimes considering more than one age class (or comparing young to adult or to total population):

youth to total unemployment ratios, long-term unemployment rates, employment rates, NEET rates, part-time and temporary employment, hourly earnings. The disadvantage of young people emerged as a persistent phenomenon in many countries with remarkable differences between the European countries. In addition, the impact of the financial crises, the Great Recession and the long crisis in several countries of the Eurozone have been particularly damaging for young people, leading to a very high risk of a "lost generation" in several countries. Thus, a growing intergenerational inequality rapidly emerged with a diffuse worsening of the relative position of the young people in the labour market, in terms of quantity and quality of job opportunities and as regards life-cycle income.

From an empirical perspective, the book, in particular in the second part shows evidence of varieties of inequality and it advances policy suggestions which aim to improve opportunities, welfare states, political rights, civil liberties, and education quality for all. In this context the welfare state does not appear to be a drain on economic performance and competitiveness or as a barrier to economic efficiency. The most generous of welfare capitalism states are also the most efficient and successful economies. The current economic crisis, in particular, was a test for many advanced economies to determine whether the socio-economic model that those countries built in the previous decades was able to cope with the challenges of globalisation. Empirical evidences suggest that investing in welfare dimensions is not a drain on competitiveness or a barrier to economic efficiency. The best economic performance is found in the countries where both employment and social opportunities, and civil rights and political freedom are greatly developed.

References

Ahluwalia, M. S. (1976). "Inequality, poverty and development," *Journal of Development Economics*, 3(4), 307–342.

Alesina, A. and Perotti, R. (1996). "Income Distribution, Political Instability and Investment," *European Economic Review* 40, 1203–1228.

Atkinson, A. (1999). *Is Rising Inequality Inevitable? A Critique of the Transatlantic Consensus.* WIDER Annual Lectures No. 3, Helsinki.

Birdsall, N. and Sabot, R. (1994). "Inequality as a constraint on growth in Latin America", *Development Policy, Newsletter on Policy Research,* Inter-American Development Bank.

Chenery H.B., and Syrquin M. (1975) *Patterns of Development, 1950–1960.* Oxford: Oxford University Press.

Easterly, W. (2001). "The middle class consensus and economic development," *Journal of Economic Growth* 6, 317–335.

Kuznets, S. (1955). "Economic growth and income inequality," *American Economic Review* 45, 1–28.

Milanovic, B. (1994). *Determinants of cross-country income inequality: an augmented Kuznets hypothesis*, Policy Research Working Paper Series 1246.

Piketty, T. (2014). *Capital in the Twenty-First Century.* Cambridge, MA: Belknap Press.

Rawls, J. (1971). *A Theory of Justice.* Cambridge, MA: Harvard University Press.

Sen, A. (1973). *On Economic Inequality.* Oxford:, Clarendon Press.

Sokoloff, K. and Engerman, S. (2000). "History lessons: institutions, factor endowments, and paths of development in the New World," *Journal of Economic Perspectives* 14, 217–232.

Tridico, P. (2010). "Growth, inequality and poverty in emerging and transition economies," *Review of Transition Studies*, 16(4), 979–1001.

Voitchovsky, S. (2005). "Does the profile of income inequality matter for economic growth? Distinguishing between the effects of inequality in different parts of the income distribution," *Journal of Economic Growth*, 10, 273–296.

Part I
Definitions and approaches

1 Not just slicing the pie

The need for a broader approach to economic inequality

Pasquale De Muro

Introduction

In 1958, in the first edition of *The Affluent Society* , John K. Galbraith wrote that "few things are more evident in modern social history than the decline of interest in inequality as an economic issue" (p. 72). The current attitude is quite different, and in fact Milanović (2007), one of the contemporary leading scholars of income inequality, wrote that "world inequality is a topic whose time has come" (p. 3).

At first, because of the effects of late globalization and the post-Fordist accumulation regime, then because of the social impact of the Great Recession, the issue of inequality has recently regained attention in the economic and political debate. The dispute is particularly lively in the USA,[1] where even President Obama and New York's Mayor De Blasio have addressed the issue in some of their public speeches, while Europe – once very concerned about social justice – is now mostly focused on macroeconomic imbalances rather than on its polarizing living standards.

Although we must welcome and support this renewed interest – that reconnects contemporary "economics" to classical "political economy" – we should, however, also notice that unfortunately the debate is still mostly focused on income and/or wealth distribution, i.e. "how the pie is sliced" (Rycroft, 2013), which is a very important but rather narrow view of economic inequality. Even if in the last decades some scholars have introduced and developed more comprehensive and multidimensional approaches to economic inequality (Maasoumi, 1986, 1999; Sen, 1992; Tsui, 1995, 1999 ; Weymark, 2006; Decanq et al., 2009; Decancq and Lugo, 2012; Aaberge and Brandolini, 2015), most of the past and current debate as well as of theoretical and empirical studies produced by economists concern personal income distribution or factor (functional) income distribution. This is more evident in the studies of the evolution and characteristics of contemporary capitalism (Piketty, 2013) and globalization (Cornia, 2003; Maskin, 2014).

A common justification for the focus on income and wealth distribution is that it is considered the "mother" of most other forms of inequality or the "fundamental inequality of capitalism" (Piketty, 2013). Namely, (1) income distribution is generally deemed a paramount sign and indicator of overall inequality, (2) other inequalities are considered a reflection of income distribution, i.e. income may be used as proxy of other variables, and (3) a better income distribution is regarded as a necessary and often sufficient condition for reducing many other inequalities. In those monetary approaches,[2] income or wealth (re) distribution is largely identified with *the* social justice issue.

Following a pioneering but not well-known article of Sen (1997),[3] this work aims at showing that, notwithstanding their importance and role, the exclusive focus on income and wealth has some relevant drawbacks, and it suggests that a broader approach is needed. Section 2 of the paper concerns some relevant semantic problems. In section 3, the limitations of the conventional monetary approach are presented, while section 4 illustrates the complexity of inequality, across multiple dimensions and scales. In the last section, there will be some general conclusions.

Unequal meanings

Before proceeding to our analysis, it is useful to make some preliminary clarifications on the terminology that will be used, in order to avoid possible misunderstandings. The first clarification concerns the term "multidimensional", that has been cited above and is widely used in the recent studies on poverty and inequality measurement. In the vast literature on inequality, there is of course already some attention about the many dimensions of inequality. However, the term "multidimensional" sometimes is used with different, inconsistent meanings. For instance, Sawyer (1989) wrote that "there are many dimensions to inequality, and this would include inequality between and within social classes, between regions and countries" (p. 17). Likewise, also "race",[4] gender and sexuality are often considered as dimensions of inequality (Ferguson, 2016), especially by non-economists. On the other side, Stewart (2002), while introducing the concept of "horizontal inequalities", emphasized that they are «multidimensional—with political, economic and social elements» (p. 2).

What Sawyer and other scholars mean is that there are many *levels, scales* (regions, countries, …) or *groups*, *units* (class, gender, …) to income inequality. However in that conventional approach there is only one *metric*: the monetary metric based on income or resources.

In this work, the term "dimension" will be used with a different meaning: dimension refers to the metric (or space) used for the inequality assessment. Therefore, if we analyse income inequality across regions or across classes, we are using different *levels* – e.g. regions and classes – but the same dimension – income. If we assess education or health inequality across regions or across classes, those will be different dimensions of inequality, as the metrics are education or health – rather than income – measured across different levels or groups. If, for example, we use jointly education, health and income across one or more units, that will be a multidimensional approach. In this sense, multidimensional inequality refers to the fact that inequality is measured and assessed using different metrics, not just different scales. When different units are used, such as individuals and countries, in this work it will be called *multiscale* inequality. An example of the latter can be found in the debate about the effects of globalization: scholars compare the trend of *income* inequality between countries (using the average or median national income), within countries (usually between individuals or households), and between all individuals in the world. Regarding inequality between countries, Milanović (2007) defines it as "Concept 1" of inequality, or unweighted *international inequality*, if each country is not weighted according to its population size, while he defines it as "Concept 2" of inequality, or weighted *international inequality* if we weight each country. Accordingly, he defines "Concept 3" of inequality the distribution of income across all individuals in the world. As we can see, Milanović's concepts of inequality are multiscale, but not multidimensional. The same limitation characterizes the debate about the effects of globalization on inequality at any scale.

Furthermore, we may assess multidimensional and multiscale inequality at the same time. For instance, in the "Inequality-adjusted Human Development Indicator" (IHDI) included in the *Human Development Report* (HDR) of UNDP since 2010, we have three dimensions (income, education, health) and two scales: between countries (though UNDP do not present a measure of intercountry inequality) and between individuals within countries.[5]

Another common misunderstanding concerns the supposed equivalence between income (or wealth) inequality and "economic" inequality. Some authors that study income or wealth distribution, instead of using the general term "inequality", prefer to use the expression "economic inequality", which seems more precise and informs the reader about the fact that the focus will be on income or wealth. Therefore, economists who are aware of the many dimensions of inequality, consider income and wealth distribution as "the economic dimension of inequality" (Atkinson, 2015, p. 14). On the contrary, according to Sen the distinction between income inequality and economic inequality is important, because of "the presence of causal influences on individual well-being and freedom that are economic in nature but that are not captured by the simple statistics of incomes and commodity holdings" (Sen 1997, p. 398). Accordingly, in the following section we will not use "economic" and "income" inequality as synonyms.

A narrow focus

There is no need to prove that the economic and political debate on inequality is almost entirely focused on income and wealth distribution. There is an extensive scientific and grey literature on inequality and in those writings, with very few exceptions, inequality means unequal income distribution. A leading example is the several excellent works on inequality by Atkinson, the "godfather" (Chu, 2015) of these studies. Even in his latest book on the subject, after discussing "what do we mean by inequality", Atkinson concludes that "income is only one dimension, and differences in income should be interpreted in the light of differing circumstances and of the underlying opportunities. But it remains the case that achieved economic resources are a major source of injustice. That is my reason for concentrating here on the economic dimension of inequality" (Atkinson, 2015, p. 14), which for him it is measured by income and wealth. The problem is that for many economists "achieved economic resources" are *the* major source of injustice.

There are a number of interrelated reasons why the narrow focus on income and wealth is inadequate to the analysis of economic inequality, especially in a capitalist world-economy. Some of these reasons have been presented by Sen in his works, others have Marxian roots.

First, the focus on income and wealth leads to neglect or to leave in the background non-income economic and social inequalities that cause other not less severe and intolerable social injustices, which interact and couple with income inequality. Although, according to the conventional wisdom "achieved economic resources are a major source of injustice", gender or ethnic discriminations in the labor market, for example, may be even a greater source of injustice, which may not be alleviated or compensated by better income distribution. For instance, the current participation of women to labor market (i.e. the "activity rate") in Italy is around 54 per cent compared to 74 per cent for men: assuming that in general this is not a choice by women, that dimension of inequality is not less severe or unjust than the existing gender income inequality in Italy, neither can be measured or evaluated just looking at income and wealth distribution by gender. As a matter of fact, the exclusion from labour market is not just a deprivation of income and livelihood but also a source of many non-material severe deprivations and troubles that have been well documented by labour scholars. Another illuminating example is "racial" health inequality in the USA: "Although health outcomes have been tied to income and social economic status, there are black-white differences in life expectancy of at least 3 years at every level of income" (Devi, 2012, p. 1043). Is "living less" not a major source of injustice?

In our examples we cannot assume or conclude –as generally is done in the economic and political debate – that income inequality has a policy priority over employment or health inequality, neither we can assume that the reduction of the former may automatically lower the latter. Also, we cannot think that employment and health inequality are not constituents of *economic* inequality.

Some economists focus on income inequality because they think that non-income inequality is the field of other social scientists, but unfortunately even many sociologists, political scientists and legal scholars largely identify inequality with income and wealth distribution (Handler and Hasenfeld, 2007; Ferguson, 2016).

Second, even if we are interested in inequality of mere material living conditions, the focus on income, assets, livelihood or any economic resource is inadequate. Many assume – often implicitly or without robust justifications – that personal or household income (or consumption) alone is the best or a good measure of the standard of living.[6] While the level of personal or household income is certainly key information for understanding the living standards, it is not the right focus. As Sen has argued, when evaluating the standard of living "the focus has to be on what life we lead and what we can or cannot do, can or cannot be" (Sen and Hawthorn, 1987, p. 16), because "the standard of living is not a standard of opulence [i.e. real income], even though it is inter alia influenced by opulence. It must be directly a matter of the life one leads rather than of the resources and means one has to lead a life" (Sen and Hawthorn, 1987, p. 16).

Third, we should also consider human diversity and social contexts. People have different abilities and possibilities to convert their income into well-being and freedom, because "what use we can respectively make of a given bundle of commodities, or more generally of a given level of income, depends crucially on a number of contingent circumstances, both personal and social" (Sen, 1999, p. 70),[7] but also institutional and environmental. Because of these different conversion factors and rates, persons or groups who have the same amount of real income or purchasing power – and, therefore, an equivalent bundle of goods and services – not necessarily enjoy the same standard of living, well-being, quality of life, and freedoms. Consequently, generally speaking, income (in)equality do not correspond correctly to well-being (in)equality, as different people or groups may need different levels of income to reach the same quality of life. The latter point was already clearly made by Marx in his *Critique of the Gotha Programme* (Marx, 1970 [1875], Part I, Section 3).

Fourth, the focus on income or wealth confines economic analysis to the *space of commodities* – and to the metric of commodities – contributing to reproduce the scourge of "commodity fetishism" and its role in capitalism as well as in mainstream economics. Commodity fetishism is a concept first introduced by Marx, who dedicated to it Section 4 (*The Fetishism of the Commodity and its Secret*) of Chapter 1 of the first Volume of *The Capital*.

There is no room here to illustrate altogether the subtle "riddle of the commodity fetish" (Marx, 1976 [1867], p. 187), therefore, we will borrow the brief but effective account given by Roncaglia (2005):

> … the social relations of production – cooperation between workers active in different economic sectors and different productive units – are obscured by the fact that what is exchanged is not the labour time of one for the labour time of another, but different commodities. The market, while constituting the common ground for the necessary connection between separate workers, operates in such a way that commodities become fetishes, the ultimate end of production and exchange activity, and necessary condition (both as means of production and as means of subsistence) for the survival and reproduction

of individuals, as indeed of the economic system as a whole. [...] In a society based on the division of labour, each worker contributes to the social product and hence to the common well-being with his or her activity. However, this social collaboration is obscured, and so diverted from its true end, by commodity fetishism, since it appears that the ultimate end of every economic agent is ownership of exchange values. (p. 251)

Although the focus of capitalism is everlasting accumulation of capital and, therefore, of wealth, this does not mean that our evaluations on fairness and justice should be confined to the same logic of capital, namely the distribution of wealth or of the flow of wealth, i.e. income. One of the greatest successes of capitalism is precisely of being able to seduce people into thinking that "ownership of exchange value" is the ultimate end. Consequently, commodities became fetishes – idols and objects of desire beyond their use values – as well as their monetary form, that is income. If we assess the fairness of a distribution only on the basis of how income is distributed, we implicitly assume an idea of justice as fair distribution of commodities. Thus, we forgot about the true ultimate ends.[8]

Fifth, the focus on income leads inevitably to a policy debate on inequality that is concentrated on conventional and short-sighted monetary income redistribution, such as basic or minimum income, welfare benefits, subsidies, cash transfers. Mere monetary redistribution may help to alleviate the effects of economic inequality but not to eradicate its roots. The same applies to poverty.

Sixth, though a relatively high income inequality hinders the reduction of inequality in many other dimensions, a lower income inequality is not a sufficient –and sometimes even not a necessary– condition for the latter.

In conclusion, there are several good reasons why inequality of living standards, well-being, opportunities and freedoms cannot be adequately represented in terms of income or wealth distribution and it should, therefore, be analysed and tackled both in a multidimensional and multiscale perspective.

The countless faces of inequality

Table 1.1 is intended to show the joint multidimensional and multiscale nature of inequality and the resulting analytical complexity. Even if we consider just a single dimension (income) and a single scale (individuals), Sen in 1973 observed that inequality "it is an exceedingly complex notion which makes statements on inequality highly problematic" (Sen and Foster, 1997, Preface to the First Edition, p. vii). The complexity to which he was referring concerns the analytical difficulties in "comparing alternative income distributions among a large number of people" (Sen and Foster, 1997, p. 3).

The complexity that emerges from Table 1.1 does not derive from the difficulties in *comparing* alternative income distributions, but from the fact that in principle we have a large number of possible joint distributions (Atkinson and Bourguignon, 1982), with high levels of correlation. The *comparative* complexity is multiplied by the *multidimensional-multiscale* complexity.

The table is merely illustrative and does not purport to be exhaustive or complete. It only serves as a reference for our discussion. Therefore, the size of the table, i.e. the number of rows and columns, is only an exemplification and in principle may be much larger.

The rows of the table represent units, groups, levels, scales through which analyse inequality and thus they are possible answers to the question "Equality Among Whom?". Except for the first (individuals), in each row inequality can be analysed both between and within different

Table 1.1 The many faces of inequality

Levels/groups	Dimensions						
	A. Income/ consumption	B. Wealth	C. Primary goods/resources /assets	D. Standard of living / well-being (health, education ...)	E. Rights	F. Opportunities /freedoms	G. Happiness/ satisfaction/ SWB
1. Persons	I_{1A}	I_{1B}	I_{1C}	I_{1D}	I_{1E}	I_{1F}	I_{1G}
2. Demographic groups (sex, age, ...)	I_{2A}	I_{2B}	I_{2C}	I_{2D}	I_{2E}	I_{2F}	I_{2G}
3. Households	I_{3A}	I_{3B}	I_{3C}	I_{3D}	I_{3E}	I_{3F}	I_{3G}
4. Ethnic/cultural groups	I_{4A}	I_{4B}	I_{4C}	I_{4D}	I_{4E}	I_{4F}	I_{4G}
5. Socioeconomic/ occupational groups	I_{5A}	I_{5B}	I_{5C}	I_{5D}	I_{5E}	I_{5F}	I_{5G}
6. "Factors"/classes	I_{6A}	I_{6B}	I_{6C}	I_{6D}	I_{6E}	I_{6F}	I_{6G}
7. Sectors	I_{7A}	I_{7B}	I_{7C}	I_{7D}	I_{7E}	I_{7F}	I_{7G}
8. Local communities/ cities	I_{8A}	I_{8B}	I_{8C}	I_{8D}	I_{8E}	I_{8F}	I_{8G}
9. Regions	I_{9A}	I_{9B}	I_{9C}	I_{9D}	I_{9E}	I_{9F}	I_{9G}
10. Countries	I_{10A}	I_{10B}	I_{10C}	I_{10D}	I_{10E}	I_{10F}	I_{10G}

units or scales (e.g. between classes or within classes). On the other hand, the columns of the table represent dimensions (or spaces) of inequality and they are possible answers to the question "Equality of What?" (Sen, 1980). Consequently, each column is characterized by a different metric of inequality. In other terms, each column represents a different informational base (Sen, 1999, ch. 3), i.e. the information that we consider decisive for our evaluative exercise.

Also, not only we may have many dimensions, but also they may be nested: for instance, the columns C (*Primary goods*), E (*Rights*) and F (*Opportunities*) are inherently plural, namely they contain a number of sub-dimensions. This nested multidimensionality increases the degree of complexity of inequality.

The rows, as well as the columns, of the table are not mutually exclusive and they may partially overlap. This is the case, for example, of rows 4 (*Ethnic groups*), 5 (*Socioeconomic groups*), 6 (*Classes*): when there is an ethnic division of labour the distinctions between those three rows blur. This is also the case of columns D (*Well-being*) and G (*Happiness/ Satisfaction*) whenever we adopt a purely subjective perspective on well-being. Furthermore, as for columns, rows may be nested too: for example, when analysing global or national inequality we may combine any of the first nine rows of the table. Again, complexity expands.

Concerning the columns, the following observations can be made:

1   The first two columns (*A. Income* and *B. Wealth*) correspond to the conventional monetary dimensions usually considered in the socioeconomic analyses and the political arena. Most of the research and debate is concentrated on those dimensions, whether we examine individuals, classes, countries or gender and "race".

2   The difference between the first two columns and the third one (*C. Resources*) is that the latter is a non-monetary dimension. In fact, it refers to commodities, resources and assets in physical terms: for example, many analysis of inequality, especially in developing countries, concern the distribution of land, which is considered a strategic asset for reducing poverty, increasing employment, improving income distribution and promoting agricultural growth and economic development.

3   The first three columns correspond to the narrow economistic approach to inequality, as they reflect an idea of inequality as problem of "how the pie is sliced", where the pie is either income, wealth or resources. The next four columns (*D, E, F, G*), on the contrary, do not presuppose any pie to slice and, therefore, do not tally with the issues of distribution or re-distribution. The conceptual difference between the first three columns and the others has relevant policy implications.

4   Column *D* might be thought as a duplicate or easily confused with the first three columns. This is the case if we adopt, again, the conventional view that identifies or associate the standard of living and the well-being with income or resources. Here, on the contrary, as mentioned in §3, we assume a perspective in which the standard of living and the well-being are represented by a vector of "functionings" (Sen, 1985).[9] In this approach the metric of the standard of living and the well-being is neither monetary or resource-based. Therefore, column *D* is a distinct dimension, which may have overlaps only with column *G*, to the extent we consider the functioning "being happy" and similar ones, and with column *F*, if we extend our focus from "well-being achievement" (i.e. the vector of functionings) to "well-being freedom" (i.e. the freedom to achieve well-being, which Sen also calls "capability set") (Sen, 1993). Another consequence of adopting this approach is that column D contains many important sub-dimensions, such as education, health, employment, nutrition, housing and others, that are the subject of many fundamental studies on non-monetary inequality.

5   Column *F* refers broadly to any kind of freedoms, and thus may accommodate different approaches (liberal, libertarian, capability, …) and concepts (positive freedoms, negative freedoms, opportunities, …). Therefore, depending on the preferred approach, it may more or less overlap with column *E*. However, while the latter column refers to formal liberties that are legally recognized or to pre-legal moral claims – such as human rights – column *F* refer to broader substantive freedoms and actual opportunities. Consequently, column F may also represent human "capability" (Deneulin and Shahani, 2009).

By crossing rows and columns of the table, we get cells with various types of inequality. As the possible combinations are numerous –a multiple of 70 in our example – here we cannot review them all, also because it is beyond the scope of this work. We will just briefly mention a few types of inequality –the most analysed and well-known – that emerge from the table.

Cell I_{1A} represents "personal income distribution", the most discussed and studied type of inequality, together with cell I_{3A} "household income distribution". In classical political economy as well as in macroeconomic and multisectoral analyses "functional (or factorial) income distribution" (cell I_{6A}) and "intersectoral income distribution" (cell I_{7A}) are more often considered. Regional, territorial and urban studies are interested in income disparity between regions (cell I_{9A}) or cities (cell I_{8A}). In debates about international development and globalization, "international income inequality" (cell I_{10A}) is usually measured. When capitalism is at stake, some authors, like Piketty, prefer to study "personal or household wealth distribution", cells I_{1B} and I_{3B} respectively. Gender studies are often focused on gender inequality in income (cell I_{2A}), in health, education and employment (cell I_{2D}), or in opportunities (cell I_{2F}). Similarly, research or "racial" inequalities look at the above mentioned dimensions (cells I_{4A}, I_{4D}, I_{4F}). Scholars who use the capability approach are mostly interested in inequalities in functionings (cell I_{1D}) and in opportunity freedom (cell I_{1F}).[10] Finally, the neo-utilitarian approaches study inequality in happiness or satisfaction between individuals (I_{1G}), gender and age (I_{2G}) or socioeconomic characteristics (I_{5G}).

The table is useful also for a brief reflection on the multidimensional approaches to inequality. Moving from income to many dimensions presents a number of methodological problems, which concern, on the one side, the construction and use of appropriate multidimensional indices, and, on the other side, the choice of the dimensions, i.e. of the informational base (De Muro, 2014). The former issue has received much attention in the literature and nowadays a number of multidimensional indices built on an axiomatic basis are available and applied (Aaberge and Brandolini 2015). On the contrary, on the latter issue much less work has been developed. As a matter of fact, multidimensional approaches to inequality often use an informational base that is theoretically weak. For example, this is the case of indices that combine resources – as income or assets – with well-being achievements. Those purely empirical and data driven combinations, based on conventional wisdom, cannot but produce inconsistent multidimensional measures. This is a problem that can be found also in multidimensional measures of poverty and of well-being.

Concluding remarks

The distribution of income and wealth is one of the most important outcomes of the working of any economic system and, therefore, deserve great attention, especially in a capitalist world-economy. The fairness of such a distribution is a crucial issue of social justice and also has important institutional and economic consequences.

The central argument of this work is that, despite the importance of "how the pie is sliced", there are a number of good reasons why we should not consider economic inequality as limited to income and wealth distribution. Social justice goes well beyond the command over bundles of commodities. Economic inequality has many dimensions that cannot be represented, measured and analysed by using only the conventional monetary variables.

Although multidimensional inequality presents a greater challenge, both from a methodological and theoretical point of view, it is a more adequate approach to the complexity of economic inequality and social justice. Finally, the multidimensional approach also has a relevant advantage in terms of economic policy because, by highlighting the interconnections between various inequality dimensions, it helps to overcome the narrow limits of mere redistributive policies.

Notes

1 The return of interest for national inequality in the USA dates back to before the Great Recession (The Economist, 2006).
2 Approaches to inequality that use a monetary metric, such as income or wealth, for assessing and/or measuring inequality here will be labeled "monetary approaches".
3 Sen argued for a broader approach to inequality already in his *Tanner Lecture* of 1979 (Sen, 1980) and in his book on inequality (Sen, 1992), but it is in the article of 1997 that he discussed the meaning of "economic inequality".
4 The term "races" referred to human beings makes no sense, because it has not any scientific validity: as paleoanthropologists and other scientists know, since more than 100,000 years ago there is only one human race, *homo sapiens*. Consequently, the common expressions "racial inequality" or "race discrimination" are incorrect and misleading, as well as the label "race" used in the statistics produced by the US Census Bureau. When we refer to inequality and discriminations based on the colors of the skin or the geographical origins, we should not use the word "race" but other more adequate terms. Unfortunately, almost all scholars, especially in the USA, continue to use this word, therefore, here the term "race" is used only for the sake of clarity.
5 The IHDI is presented in the "Technical Notes" of the HDR (UNDP, 2014) and in the web site http://hdr.undp.org/en/statistics/ihdi/
6 A paradigmatic example of this conventional view is the influential and best-selling textbook by Samuelson and Nordhaus. In particular, see chapter 25 "Income and Living Standards" of the 12th edition (1985). On the contrary, Lewis (1955) tried to give a justification for the focus on the availability of "more goods and services": "it gives man greater control over its environment, and thereby increases his freedom" (p. 421).
7 Sen (1999, pp. 70–72) identifies at least five sources of variation between our income and what we get out of it: personal heterogeneities, environmental diversities, variations in social climate, differences in relational perspectives, distribution within the family.
8 Notwithstanding the issue was raised by Marx, who blamed "the fetishism of the political economists" (1976[1890], p. 176), commodity fetishism does not misled only mainstream –or "vulgar"– economists but also many heterodox and radical economists.
9 For the sake of brevity, here we do not introduce the distinction between standard of living and well-being, which is discussed by Sen (Sen & Hawthorn, 1987, pp. 26–29).
10 For an extensive presentation and discussion on (in)equality of capabilities, besides the cited works of Sen, see Kaufman (2006).

References

Aaberge, R. and Brandolini, A., 2015. Multidimensional poverty and inequality. In: Atkinson, J. and Bourguignon, F., eds. *Handbook of Income Distribution*. Amsterdam: Elsevier B.V., 141–216.
Atkinson, A. B. 2015. *Inequality: what can be done?*, Cambridge, MA: Harvard University Press.

Atkinson, A. B. & Bourguignon, F. 1982. The comparison of multi-dimensioned distributions of economic status. *Review of Economic Studies,* XLIX, 183–201

Chu, B. 2015. Sir Anthony Atkinson and the curious optimism of the godfather of inequality *The Independent* [Online]. Available: www.independent.co.uk [Accessed 29 May 2015].

Cornia, G. A. 2003. Globalization and the distribution of income between and within countries. In: Chang, H.-J. (ed.) *Rethinking development economics.* London: Anthem Press.

De Muro, P. 2014. Reconceptualizing well-being and poverty. Paper presented at the EAEPE Annual Conference, Cyprus, November 6–8

Decancq, K. and Lugo, M.A. 2012. Inequality of wellbeing: A multidimensional approach. *Economica,* 79 (316), 721–746.

Decancq, K., Decoster, A. & Schokkaert, E. 2009. The evolution of world inequality in well-being. *World Development,* 37(1), pp 11–25.

Deneulin, S. & Shahani, L. (eds) 2009. *An introduction to the human development and capability approach : freedom and agency,* London: Earthscan.

Devi, S. 2012. Getting to the root of America's racial health inequalities. *The Lancet,* 380 (9847), 1043–1044.

Ferguson, S. J. 2016. *Race, gender, sexuality, and social class: dimensions of inequality and identity,* Thousand Oaks, CA.: SAGE Publications, Inc.

Galbraith, J. K. 1958. *The affluent society,* Boston, MA: Houghton Mifflin.

Handler, J. F. & Hasenfeld, Y. 2007. *Blame welfare, ignore poverty and inequality,* New York: Cambridge University Press.

Kaufman, A. 2006. *Capabilities equality: basic issues and problems,* London: Routledge.

Lewis, W. A. 1955. *The theory of economic growth,* London: George Allen & Unwin.

Maasoumi, E. 1999. Multidimensioned approaches to welfare analysis. In: Silber, J. (ed.) *Handbook of income inequality measurement.* London: Kluwer Academic.

Marx, K. 1970 [1875]. Critique of the Gotha Programme. *Marx/Engels Selected Works, Volume Three.* Moscow: Progress Publishers.

Marx, K. 1976 [1867]. *Capital: a critique of political economy,* Harmondsworth: Penguin Books in association with New Left Review.

Maskin, E. 2014. Why haven't global markets reduced inequality in developing economies? Annual Bank Conference on Development Economics 2014: The Role of Theory in Development Economics. Washington, DC: World Bank.

Milanović, B. 2007. *Worlds apart : measuring international and global inequality,* Princeton, NJ: Princeton University Press.

Piketty, T. 2013. *Le capital au XXIe siècle,* Paris: Éditions du Seuil.

Roncaglia, A. 2005. *The wealth of ideas: a history of economic thought,* Cambridge: Cambridge University Press.

Rycroft, R. S. 2013. *The economics of inequality, poverty, and discrimination in the 21st century,* Santa Barbara, CA: Praeger.

Sawyer, M. C. 1989. *The challenge of radical political economy : an introduction to the alternatives to neo-classical economics,* London: Harvester Wheatsheaf.

Sen, A. K. 1980. Equality of what?. In: McMurrin S (ed.) *Tanner Lectures on Human Values,* Volume 1. Cambridge: Cambridge University Press

Sen, A. K. 1985. *Commodities and capabilities,* Amsterdam: North-Holland.

Sen, A. K. 1992. *Inequality reexamined,* New York: Russell Sage Foundation.

Sen, A., 1993. Capability and well-being. In: M. Nussbaum and A. Sen, eds. *The Quality of Life.* Oxford: Clarendon Press, 30–53.

Sen, A. K. 1999. *Development as freedom,* New York: Knopf.

Sen, A. K, 1997. From income inequality to economic inequality. *Southern Economic Journal,* 64(2), 348–401

Sen, A. K. & Foster, J. E. 1997. *On economic inequality,* Oxford: Clarendon Press.

Sen, A. K. & Hawthorn, G. 1987. *The standard of living,* Cambridge: Cambridge University Press.

Stewart, F. 2002. Horizontal inequalities: a neglected dimension of development. WIDER Annual Lecture. Helsinki: UNU-WIDER.

The Economist. 2006. *Special report inequality in America*. London: The Economist Newspaper Limited.

Tsui, K. Y., 1995. Multidimensional generalizations of the relative and absolute inequality indices: The Atkinson–Kolm–Sen approach. *Journal of Economic Theory*, 67 (1), 251–265.

Tsui, K. Y. 1999. Multidimensional inequality and multidimensional generalized entropy measure: an axiomatic derivation. *Social Choice and Welfare,* 16(1)**,** 145–157.

UNDP. 2014. *Human Development Report 2014*, New York: United Nations Development Programme

Weymark, J. A. 2006. The normative approach to the measurement of multidimensional inequality. In: Farina, F. & Savaglio, E. (eds) *Inequality and economic integration.* New York: Routledge.

2 Income inequality

What causes it and how to curb it

Sebastiano Fadda

Introduction: basic definitions

As anybody can see, the answer to the first question in the title is functional to the second. Knowledge of the causes of inequality is required in order to choose appropriate measures to reduce it. But the question of whether it is proper or not to take measures against income inequality is to a certain extent influenced by what is thought to be at the root of inequality. The aim of this chapter is actually to suggest measures to curb income inequality, and this implies the idea that inequality is for some reason "bad" and not the natural consequence of a good working of a competitive economic system. But precisely this view has to be put under question in the first place. Nevertheless, even if inequality was thought as simply mirroring the correct working of a competitive system, it would still be possible to encourage measures to restrain it on the grounds of ethical or social reasons.

In order to consider all the above aspects it is first necessary to define clearly what is meant by "income inequality". This concept has to do with the distribution of income, and, therefore, has to be considered under two aspects: functional distribution and personal distribution. The first is related to the shares of GDP which go to different factors of production and can be represented respectively by the ratio of labour income (wages, salaries and other work-related compensations) to total income and by the ratio of capital income (interests, dividends and other returns on capital) to total income. The second aspect is the dispersion of annual income across households and it is mostly indicated by the Gini coefficient.

Accordingly, considering capital income as the residual of labour income, the capital share, can be defined as

$$\frac{\text{GDP} - (\text{employee compensation})}{\text{GDP}}$$

This definition still embodies some ambiguities. For instance, it does not consider the income of the self-employed, underestimating in this way the labour share. To adjust for this, Gollin (2002) suggests to include "the operating surplus of private unincorporated enterprises (OSPUE)" in the computation of labour share. Some doubts also exist about where to locate the fiscal wedge. Surely it is neither profit, nor rent: it should be labour income although workers do not perceive it as such. On the contrary, workers perceive as income the interest paid on public debt. Rent from owner-occupied houses, social transfers and government benefits, pension funds, the aggregation of profits and rents (Atkinson, 2003), and also the aggregation of physical capital and natural capital (Gollin, 2008) all pose similar problems.

Leaving apart these complications (which are beyond the scope of this chapter) the share of labour in a simplified model can be defined as:

$$\frac{\text{Total labout cost}}{\text{GDP}},$$

which may also be expressed as:

$$\frac{N_d \cdot w}{Y \cdot p}$$

or, if Gollin's suggestion is followed,

$$\frac{N_d \cdot w + ospue}{Y \cdot p}$$

Where:

N_d is the number of employees,

w the nominal wage,

ospue is the proxy of the number of self-employed multiplied by their unit income,

Y is the physical output,

p the price level.

Alternatively, whatever the measures used for the aggregates, supposing that the average compensation for selfemployed and similar is the same as for employees, the share of labour can be viewed as:

$$\frac{W \cdot N / L}{Y}$$

Where:

W is total wage compensation,

N is total employment,

L is total employees and

Y is total value added.

Therefore

$$\frac{W}{Y} \cdot \frac{N}{L}$$

And so

$$\frac{W / L}{Y / N}$$

is the share of labour

The ratio of capital income to labour income, on the other hand, can generally be described as:

$$\Pi / W = K / L \cdot \pi / w$$

Therefore, changes in labour and capital share depend on the relative behaviour of the two ratios: capital/labour ratio and rate of profit/rate of wage ratio, and on all the factors that impact on them, technical progress included.

Income inequality is the extent to which the distribution of income among individuals or households within an economy deviates from a perfectly equal distribution. Obviously there are connections between factor shares and income inequality. A first connection is a structural one: since labour income is generally more evenly distributed than capital income, a change in factor shares entails *per se* a change in personal income distribution, in the sense that a decline in labour share is associated, given the previous assumption, automatically to a more uneven distribution of personal income. This effect is, obviously, stronger the higher the difference between the dispersion of income distribution, say the Gini coefficients, within each of the two categories. In addition, empirical evidence can be found that functional distribution of income is an essential and statistically significant determinant of the personal distribution (Daudey and Garcia-Penalosa, 2007).

As is well known, different measures of income inequality show different properties and may give different estimates of the change in inequality over time. The Gini coefficient does not allow to detect where exactly the changes in income distribution may occur, while the percentile ratios restrict the information to the percentiles selected. We don't enter here the discussion about the statistical aspects of these and other measures of inequality.

First question: why care about income distribution?

In order to proceed there is a preliminary question which has to be explored; that is whether it makes sense at all to care about income distribution. There are two main reasons why it doesn't seem to make sense. The first one is the belief that inequality is in any case beneficial to growth. We can still read (Chegg Study on internet) statements like this: "As income shares become more equal, the incentive for individuals to accumulate skills, work hard and take risks may become smaller, thus shrinking the size of the economy". So, any attempt to promote equity by interfering with market forces would be detrimental to growth (Welch, 1999) and, therefore, in the end, would cause everybody to be worse off. In general terms, insomuch as the functional distribution is a reflection of the marginal productivity of factors, it represents the optimal resources allocation; any other distribution would be inefficient. The alleged trade-off between equity and growth, therefore, should be always resolved in favour of growth.

The second reason is connected to the idea that an intrinsic law in the working of the economy operates in order to keep constant, in the long run, the factor shares of income. This vision goes back to the well-known "Bowley's law", derived from empirical observation, but it is also part of theoretical models of growth, from Solow to Kaldor, who included the constancy of factor shares among his "stylized facts".

Through his technical progress function, Kaldor sees the economy as converging towards a balanced path of growth in which $\Delta y/y = \Delta k/k$ (being $k = K/L$ and $y = Y/L$), therefore, a growing capital-labour ratio at the same rate as the output-labour ratio would imply a constant $\Delta Y/\Delta K$: that is neutral technical progress with a constant profit rate and constant factor shares of income. The similar growth of income and factors productivity in the presence of a growing population and full employment may be explained by compensating trends in productivity per hours worked and number of hours worked per man. Kaldor (contrary to recent data) found empirical support for this model.

The same vision of stable factor shares belongs to the neoclassical world, where distribution is obviously and always "fair" since it is "technically" determined by the marginal productivity of factors, and any attempt to violate this natural law should be rejected. In the Cobb–Douglas production function the factor shares are simply the exponents of K and L and the stability of factor shares is explained by the unit elasticity of capital-labour substitution, regardless of movements in the capital/labour ratio. But if the unit elasticity assumption is removed, the factor shares need not to be constant any more. Precisely: if the increase in the capital labour ratio is associated with a more than proportional fall in the ratio between rate of profit and rate of wage then the wage share would rise. The opposite would happen in case of increase in the capital labour ratio associated with a less than proportional fall in the ratio between profit rate and wage rate. It is worth noticing, though, that according to Blanchard (2000) only between 10 per cent and 40 per cent of the wage share decline could be explained using this neoclassical model.

Kalecki seems to accept the stability of factor shares in his basic model but actually he introduces two factors that can alter the shares: the degree of monopoly, as it influences the mark-up, and the relative power of social parts (Sylos Labini 1984). The degree of monopoly plays its role according to the following formula:

The value of production

$$Y = W + O + P + M \cdot Y$$

where:
   W = total wages;
   O = total overheads;
   P = total profits;
   M = cost of materials.
Therefore:

$$O + P = Y - (W + M)$$

calling k the ratio $Y / W + M$ we have:

$$O + P = (kW + + kM) - (W + M)$$

which gives:

$$O + P = (k - 1)(W + M)$$

where the ratio k is determined (through his theory of prices) by the degree of monopoly.

The share of wages in the value added can so be written as:

$$W / W + (k - 1)(W + M) \ .$$

And if we denote the ratio of the cost of materials to the wage bill by j, the above share can be written as:

$$1 / 1 + (k - 1)(j + 1)$$

This allows Kalecky to conclude that "the relative share of wages in the value added is determined by the degree of monopoly and by the ratio of the materials bill to the wage bill" (Kalecky, 1965).

He also explicitly states that although "the share of wages does not seem to show marked cyclical fluctuations", "no a priori statement is possible as to the long run trend of the relative shares of wages in income" (ibid.)

As for the classical economists, no specific indications about the evolution of labour shares are made. Ricardo, who thought of distribution as the principal problem of the economy, complicated the frame by introducing the role of land rent, which progressively would squeeze profits, while wages were considered set at the subsistence level. Marx was more interested in the movement of the rate of profit, rather than the share of profits, and expected it to fall in the long run due the growth of the "organic composition of capital", although he was aware of counteracting forces which could delay this result. The role of relative powers in the class struggle was emphasized in determining the rate of surplus value on which the rate of profit mainly would depend. We should also mention here the well-known inverted U "Kuznets curve", which being, as stated by himself, "perhaps 5% empirical information and 95% speculation, some of it possibly tainted by wishful thinking", and being based on a few data of only three countries, has not been recognised as generally valid, and his supposed re-equilibrating factors (such as the "dynamism of a growing and free society") have not been seen to operate.

A further argument is sometimes raised against "worrying too much" about income inequality: the fact that the absolute level of income of the poor should be more important than the disparity in income distribution. It is argued on the one hand that if income and standard of living of the lower layer of population are high enough, it would not make much sense to worry about inequality, and on the other hand that if the absolute level of the poorer is miserable, precisely that and not inequality is the problem. This objection does not hold, though, because the two problems do not cancel each other, and there is not trade-off between egalitarian distribution and income level of the poorest (or even middle) class of the population. Moreover, some empirical research reveals perverse effects of perception of inequality on people's behaviour (Carlsson, 2005). Some studies have also found that the impact of inequality is not in general positive on the standard of living of medium- and low-income people and that increases in the top share of income (whether of the top 10 per cent or top 1 per cent) lead to declines in the actual incomes (and earnings) of low- and middle-income households (Thompson and Leight 2011).

Reasons to be concerned about income inequality

The statement that labour shares are constant over time is not only theoretically weak, as it has been said, but is also contrary to empirical evidence. Figures 2.1 and 2.2 are enough to show an overall declining share of labour during the last 30–40 years.

On the side of personal distribution, there is also wide empirical evidence of the general increase in the Gini coefficient in the last decades (Figure 2.3).

Then, there is the appalling difference among top-level salaries and ordinary wages. It is not an irrelevant fact that while in the 1970s and 1980s the salary of staff in the 350 largest companies in the US were 20–30 times the wage of an ordinary worker, around 2010 the difference jumped to 200–400 times, and in the UK above 300 times (Mishel and Sabadish, 2012). Moreover, in general,

> In most OECD countries, the gap between rich and poor is at its highest level for 30 years. Today, the richest 10 per cent of the population in the OECD area earn 9.5 times the income of the poorest 10 per cent; in the 1980s this ratio stood at 7:1 and has been rising continuously ever since.
>
> (Cingano, 2014)

The reasons to care about the undoubtable worsening of wage share and income inequality are grounded on the one side in fairness issues, and on the other side in the impact on economic performance itself.

Fairness is obviously connected with a system of value judgements, but in general terms excessive inequality (we always speak of excessive and growing inequality) is becoming more and more socially rejected, and fairness in income distribution, conceived as a low

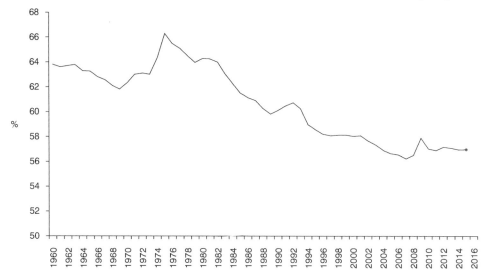

Figure 2.1 Labour share on GDP in G7 economies (weighted), 1960–2016

Source: Ameco database 2015

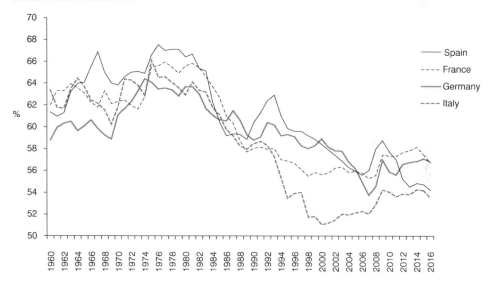

Figure 2.2 Adjusted wage shares, continental European countries 1960–2016

Source: Ameco database 2015

level of inequality, is more and more being considered as a positive requirement of modern and democratic societies. Apart from an "abstract" principle of justice, this is also due to some negative consequences that income inequality as such is bound to produce in society.

One of these is the reduction of social mobility. There is wide empirical evidence that high levels of income inequality as measured by Gini coefficients are associated with high levels of intergenerational elasticity (which is the coefficient obtained by regressing children's income in adulthood on their parental income; a coefficient of 1 would mean that all the income difference between parents would be passed on to children). This is shown in the Figures 2.4 and 2.5.

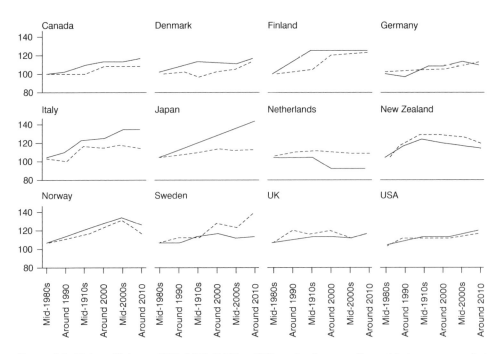

Figure 2.3 Gini coefficients, 1980–2010 (1980 = 100) market income, disposable income = market
income minus taxes and transfers

Source: OECD data elaborated by Smeeding, Morelli, Thompson (2013)

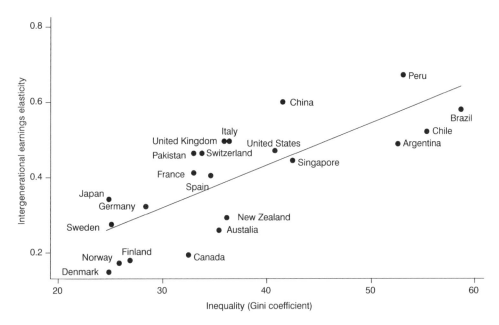

Figure 2.4 Income and intergenerational earnings inequalities

Source: Corak, 2013

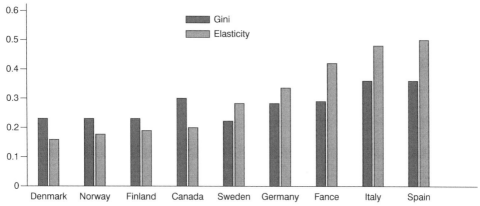

Figure 2.5 Incomes inequality and intergenerational income mobility

Source: Esping-Andersen, 2009

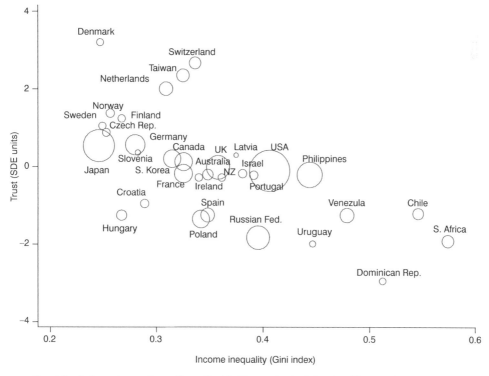

Correlation between income inequality and trust in 33 countries (r=0.51, after differences in per capita income are held constant) SD = standard deviation units. Circles illustrate weighting by country population

Figure 2.6 Correlation between trust and income inequality

Source: *American Journal of Public Health*

Another unpleasant consequence is the lowering of social cohesion, and particularly of trust relationships, which is of vital importance for the good and smooth working of markets and of social interactions as a whole. The sense of unfairness which is connected with large inequality creates distrust and lack of cooperative attitude among people. Furthermore, since

Table 2.1 Relationship between (net) income inequality in reach countries and some social problems

Social variable	Correlation coefficient
Social immobility	0.93
Teenage births	0.73
Imprisonment	0.67
Trust	−0.66
Mental illness	0.59
Obesity	0.57
Homicides	0.47
Educational performance	−0.45
Life expectancy	−0.44
Infant mortality	0.42
Overall index	0.87

Source: Wilkinsons and Pickett (2009)

unleashed inequality is perceived as a violation of the principles of appropriate rewards and reconnaissance of merits and skills, it appears to be a consequence of "predatory behaviour" (Fitoussi, 2011) and it may also discourage young people from engaging in skill acquisition and in accumulation of human capital (Figure 2.6)

Finally, income inequality has been proved to be positively correlated with all sort of bad social indicators, such as crime, violence, drug abuse and so on. Also health and life expectancy are correlated with income inequality (Wilkinson and Pickett, 2009) (Table 2.1).

Clearly, most of these problems could be more plausibly explained by the absolute level of individual income, rather than by inequality, although in general it is inequality that pushes individual incomes below a problematic threshold, so establishing a link between the two. Inequality "per se", when not accompanied by a critical absolute income level, seems to act negatively on social indicators through the creation of "status anxiety", "because it places people in a hierarchy that increases status competition and causes stress, which leads to poor health and other negative outcomes" (Rowlingson, 2011).

Having considered all this, it may still be objected that the fairness argument is not decisive in order to make a choice towards taking action to reduce inequality.

It could well be that equity was detrimental to economic performance or more specifically to the rate of GDP growth, as one could deduct if less inequality were empirically associated with lower economic performance or lower growth. In that case it might as well be preferable to sacrifice some equity in order to achieve more growth. A trade off would appear and the choice would become dependent on the preference function of society. But, as is well known, it's impossible to aggregate individual preferences into a social welfare function. Nevertheless, it may be that transferring some money from a rich person to a poor person results in an aggregate wellbeing gain because the benefit to the poor individual exceeds the loss to the rich person (Sacks et al., 2012). Since the goal of economic policy is to maximize happiness (or "utility"), societies may thus be able to increase the "aggregate" welfare or wellbeing through policy changes which increase equality. This view is consistent with the principle of decreasing marginal utility of income and in line with what Pigou wrote:

The old "law of diminishing utility" thus leads securely to the proposition: any cause which increases the absolute share of real income in the hands of the poor, provided that it does not lead to a contraction in the size of the national dividend from any point of view, will, in general, increase economic welfare.

(Pigou, 1920)

As a matter of fact, the alleged trade-off between equity and growth does not seem to exist. It is not possible here to comment on all the existing literature on this issue, but it is possible to say that in general the empirical evidence shows that "there is a strong negative relation between the level of net inequality and growth of income per capita in the sequent period; the statistical evidence generally supports the view that inequality impedes growth, at least over the medium term, and have found that inequality is associated with slower and less durable growth. The few exceptions (Forbes, 2000; and Banerjee and Duflo, 2003) tend to pick up ambiguous short-run correlations" (Ostry et al., 2014). On the same line: "Drawing on harmonised data covering the OECD countries over the past 30 years, the econometric analysis suggests that income inequality has a negative and statistically significant impact on subsequent growth" (Cingano 2014). This is shown in the figures below.

As far as developing countries are concerned it seems that "longer growth spells are robustly associated with more equality in the income distribution" (Berg, 2011). As for the relation between redistribution policies and growth, some qualifications have to be introduced, which we shall discuss later.

Figure 2.7 shows the relationship between disposable Gini of 2008 and per capita real GDP in the next five years.

The factors to which such relation can be attributed are now to be pointed out.

A first factor is the shrinking of effective demand, with direct consequences on this fundamental driver of growth, Due to different (and decreasing) marginal propensity to consume, a growing concentration of income implies a declining consumer demand. This decline could lead to underconsumption crisis (of Marxian flavour), which if not treated with appropriate economic policies would not only undermine growth but possibly start a recession.

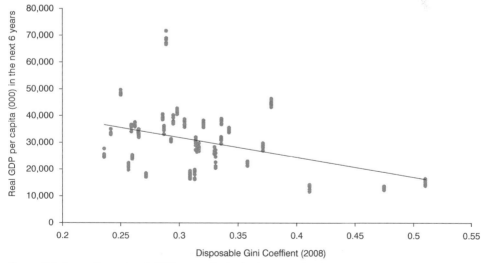

Figure 2.7 Inequality and real GDP per capita in OECD countries (2008–2014)
Source: OECD statistics

A second factor of impairment to growth is due to the financial instability created by inadequate aggregate consumer demand: the need to sustain aggregate demand may lead to allow excessive increase of private indebtness. Actually this is what has happened between 2000 and 2008 particularly in the USA, UK, Ireland. Greece, Portugal and Spain.

A third factor is the accumulation of enormous wealth in the hands of a restricted number of people. This accumulation takes place through a combined dynamic of uneven distribution of income and expansion of the financial sector, implying in this way a significant change in factor share due to growth of financial rents. As a consequence, and with the help of lacking financial markets regulation, financial excess becomes possible and likely, and with it the fading of growth and the developing of financial instability (Stiglitz, 2012; Galbraith, 2012). Milanovic (2009). Lansley (2009) explicitly attributes a central role to widening inequality in the build-up of the financial crisis, credit crunch and subsequent recession.

Besides, the richest may come to get enough power as to gain full control of the policy makers. In this way they can prevent the adoption of policies capable of reducing inequality, and possibly they will be also able to effectively support policies capable of increasing income and wealth concentration.

A fourth factor can be detected in the fact that income inequality undermines progress in health and education. Bad health conditions, low living standards and poor education among the population lead to hold up growth (Galor and Moav, 2004).

Although the relation between human capital and growth, or per capita income, is far from univocal, mostly due to ambiguities in human capital measurement, it is generally recognized, though, that higher levels (and better quality) of education improve the pro-growth attitudes of economic agents and increase the absorption capacity of innovations. Since excessive income inequality negatively affects human capital accumulation it also negatively affects growth.

Finally, "a contrario", a low level of inequality is thought to enhance social cohesion, and this in turn is able to provide an institutional set up capable of solving conflicts and better reacting to external shocks (Rodrik, 1999). The lack of social consensus, which is favoured by inequality, is bound to seriously dampen social and political stability, the efficient working of the market and the process of growth.

Causes of income inequality

Since, beside being considered unfair, excessive income inequality is also detrimental to growth, there are enough reasons to believe that action should be taken to reduce it. There are essentially two ways to reduce inequality: one is to adopt redistribution measures once it has happened, the other is to adopt measures and strategies to prevent it from happening. In order to be able to act on this second line it is necessary to consider the causes which are at the root of the process of growing unequal distribution.

As we hinted at the beginning, there is a link between personal income distribution and functional income distribution. In fact "household market income" is made up of individual and household labour earnings, plus capital income. Therefore, all factors that impact on any of these components (including changes in functional distribution) also affect the "household market income", on the unequal distribution of which the level of unemployment obviously plays a great role, given that unemployed people have no labour earnings. The unequal distribution of such "market income", when considered excessive, can subsequently be the object of policy measures aimed at "correcting" it. The result of these measures is the "household disposable income", which is household market income after taxes and transfers. Furthermore, when "in kind" transfers of the welfare system are taken into account, a sort of household "effective" disposable income will be arrived at.

Considering all that, it can be agreed that the deepest root of the general growth of income inequality that has taken place in the last decades is surely to be found in the change of political climate towards neo liberalism (Dumenil, 2001). Political and institutional evolution has been deeply influenced by this ideological orientation so that the entire working of the economic system has taken a shape coherent with the growth of inequality.

An expression of this attitude is given by labour market policy. Here the insistence on "flexibilization" together with "wage devaluation" in order to win competition has led to a strong segmentation of labour markets with high wage dispersion and a fall in their general level. The orthodox model assumed that the consequent fall in aggregate demand would be compensated by an increase in exports due to higher competitiveness; something that, of course, cannot stand if all countries are taken together as a whole. These policies have been completely unsuccessful with regard to overcoming the recent crisis, nevertheless, they have led to increasing dispersion of labour earnings and growing income inequality.

A second expression of the offensive of neoliberalism has been the adoption of recessive macroeconomic policy. The obsessive concentration on fiscal consolidation, the pro-cyclical automatic mechanism of balanced public budget adopted by the European Union, the set of recessive economic policies imposed by international financial institutions (particularly the IMF) in change for financial assistance to countries with difficulties has led to an increase in unemployment and, therefore, to growing income inequality.

As a consequence of growing unemployment, of the so called "flexibilization" of the labour market and of deliberate steps to reduce trade unions' power and role, the neo-liberalism attitude has led to a decline of unionization. But both union density and union coverage appear to be negatively correlated with income inequality, as can be seen in Figures 2.8 and 2.9.

In addition, the space of collective bargaining has diminished everywhere. An increasing trend towards decentralization of collective bargaining to firm level on the one hand, and to

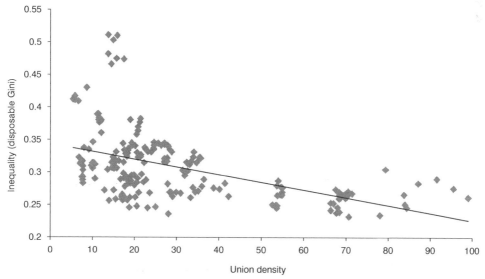

Figure 2.8 Inequality and unionization in OECD countries (2004–2012)

Source: Own elaboration on OECD database (download May 2015)

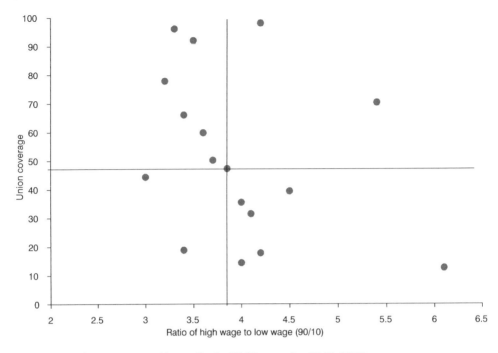

Figure 2.9 Union coverage and inequality in OECD countries (2007–2011)

Source: Own elaboration on OECD. stat – ILOSTATdata

individual agreements on the other hand, has weakened the resistance against wage fall and has enhanced the inequality in labour earnings.

A fourth cause of the rise of income inequality is the progressive rise of financialization since the '80s. One relevant aspect of this rise is the size of the financial capital involved and the other is the absence of appropriate regulation of financial markets. The unleashed diffusion of derivatives, the large proportion of OTC transactions, the mixture of commercial and investment banks have enhanced the possibility of gains for those at the top to such an extent to allow wide and excessive speculative behaviour. In addition, the financial sector has been so empowered to gain control over the policymakers and the institutions that policy action to change the status quo is rendered highly unlikely, if not impossible. (Epstein, 2005; Glyn, 2006; Palley, 2008). Another unpleasant consequence concerns the real sector: the possibility that investment in financial assets (which offer higher returns) becomes substitute for investment in physical capital, dampening the growth of productive capacity and depressing the level of economic activity (Stockhammer, 2004). It is also possible that the increasing transfer of firms ownership to financial institutions exerts on them a stronger pressure for higher returns, which means a pressure for increasing profits at the expense of wages, consequently boosting the inequality of income distribution.

A further cause of inequality is abundantly mentioned in the literature: globalization. Globalization actually boils down to the fact that goods can be produced everywhere and sold everywhere, with no restrictions to their mobility and with diminishing transport costs. This situation is able to produce a series of consequences that affect income distribution. Contrary to the ambiguous advantages alleged by traditional mainstream trade theory fundamentally based on the Samuel theorem, the empirical evidence shows that globalization has definitely contributed to the decline of the wage share, as also the IMF has come to admit: "globalization is one of several factors that have acted to reduce the share of income accruing to labor in advanced economies" (IMF, 2007, 161). There is no evidence at all that the opposite might have happened in developing economies. There are presumably three main ways through which a pressure to reduce wages is exerted by globalization. The first is the attempt of firms to become more competitive through wage cost reduction, the second is the offshoring of production to where total unit costs (not only labour) are lower, which undermines the levels of employment in advanced countries and so acts against wage rise. The third is the simple threat of relocating production, which can be used as a sort of "discipline device" to cut down the bargaining power of trade unions and workers in general (Rodrik, 1997). Such a threat is also used to induce workers to accept not only lower wages but also worse working conditions, and governments to change labour market regulation towards lower labour standards and lower employment protection.

A sixth causal factor of inequality has to be pointed out, and that is technological change. Although deducting the evolution of "capital intensity" of production from a neoclassical production function is somehow less than correct, empirical evidence shows an association between the evolution of productive technology and the evolution of income inequality. The European Commission, in a report of the 2007, states that "the estimation results clearly indicate that technological progress made the largest contribution to the fall in the aggregate labour income share". The possible explanations for its influence on unequal income distribution go from the one saying that skill biased technical progress increases the marginal productivity of high skilled workers relative to low skilled, so determining a widening of the different compensations to another one saying that, being technologically advanced capital goods substitutes for unskilled labour, the demand for this kind of labour tends to fall compared to demand for skilled workers and consequently the wage gap tends to increase. Summers' suggestion may be included in this broad category. His modified production function $Y = F(\beta K, L + \lambda(1-\beta)K)$ assumes that one unit of capital designed to substitute for labour is equivalent to λ units of labour; one share of the capital stock being used in a customary way and the other to substitute for labour. "When capital is reallocated to substituting for labour, the stock of effective labour rises and the stock of conventional capital falls, and so wage rates fall" (Summers, 2013, 4).

A last causal factor to be mentioned is the growth of bargaining power of firms. This power enables them on one side to compress the level of nominal wages and on the other side to increase the mark-up and raise the level of prices. The intensity of this process is determined by the degree of monopoly, as Kalecki pointed out. The consequent increase in profits is then enjoyed by the executives of the monopolistic firms, through decisions about their salaries and benefits taken at the level of the board of administrators. No restrictions whatsoever are met in taking these decisions, so the enormous and growing gap between top-level salaries and ordinary-level wages cannot be ascribed to increasing productivity or other imaginary forces of a perfect competitive market, but only to what has been called the "predatory behaviour" of the executives, made possible precisely by the enormous power obtained by the high degree of monopoly in the market.

Policy suggestions to counter the rise of inequality

Once established that (excessive) income inequality is detrimental not only to fairness but also to growth, the problem arises of how to curb it, or how to avert it. Care should be taken of the risk that measures adopted to counteract inequality might be detrimental to fairness and growth more than inequality itself (Okun, 1975; Barro, 1990). If it were so, the damage of inequality would be double: not only would it be pernicious in the first place, but also because it would call forth counteracting measures, which would possibly add together in harming the proper working of the economic system.

The ways to counteract income inequality are substantially of two kinds. The first is to let the market forces act freely and produce whatever inequality they can, and only afterwards intervene to correct it with redistributions measures; the second is to take measures to prevent excessive inequality from happening in the first place. While the first way is exposed to the risk of adopting a medicine that may turn out to be worse than the illness and, therefore, requires careful attention to select the right measures, the first can be accused of interfering with the free-market mechanism.

On the basis that reducing market inequality (that is inequality before redistribution through taxation and transfers) would also reduce the magnitude of measures needed for redistribution, the first way should be preferred. It also should be preferred because the so-called "interference" with the free-market mechanism is in fact directed precisely to avoid distortions in the market, since most causes of inequality are linked with market failures, monopolistic power or absence of appropriate regulation. This first category of measures should then be given priority and will be considered in the following section.

Measures to prevent the rise of "market" inequality

The measures that can be suggested in this direction must be strictly related to the causes of inequality of income that have been mentioned above.

In this regard, the first market failure to take account of is monopolistic concentration. Fighting monopolistic concentration is not an easy goal, but concrete steps should be taken at national and international level to safeguard free competition and provide in this way less opportunity for mark-up increases. Being the level of mark-up, as it has been mentioned (Kalecki, 1965), a factor that affects the functional income distribution, its restraint would also help to lessen the growing of income inequality. Since the concentration of market power in the big corporations has been facilitated worldwide by the process of globalization, the strength of antitrust institutions should be improved at the international level (for instance within the European Union) as well as at the national level. As for natural monopolies, great attention has to be drawn on the need to reinforce the regulatory system, particularly in the field of utilities.

Turning to financialization, which has been one of the most influencing factors of the unequal income distribution, a whole range of institutional regulatory innovations appears to be necessary. The lack of appropriate global financial governance has left unrestricted freedom not only relative to propagation but also relative to the unlimited invention of financial products. National states do not seem to be able to cope with this enormous geographical mobility of incredible masses of financial capital; international institutions seem to be reluctant to take significant action. The set up in the European Union of the Systemic Risk Board and the three connected agencies does not seem so effective in regulating the financial markets, probably because of their composition and because of the limited powers with which they have been endowed. Stronger action must be taken, such as separating commercial banks from investment banks, restricting the operation activity in unregulated markets (OTC transactions), redefining the role of the rating agencies.

A third step towards improving equality in market income distribution should be the adoption of policies to rise rate and quality of employment (more and better jobs, as the Lisbóna Strategy puts it). This implies two lines: first, abandon recessionary policies and turn to expansionary macroeconomic and real (industrial, agricultural, development) policies; second, improve the quality of human capital by increasing investments in education and improving its quality.

A fourth step should lead to a deep restructuring of collective bargaining and labor market regulation. Undoubtedly the growth of unemployment due to recession weakens the bargaining power of workers as far as wage settlement is concerned. Nonetheless, institutional factors play a relevant role in industrial relations: pushing the decentralization of bargaining too far may offer some relief to single enterprises but also implies less power left to workers organizations and also less attention paid to macroeconomic aspects of wage settlements (such as aggregate demand, growth, inflation, international competition). The same is bound to happen when the labour market is fragmented (often in the name of flexibility) in an excessive variety of labour contracts. A stronger association between productivity and labour compensation dynamics should be pursued, in order not to let profits to enjoy bigger and bigger shares of growing productivity. In parallel, the growth of productivity should be stimulated, avoiding to provide a negative incentive towards innovation by the use of low-paid–low-skilled work. To the same end, in order not to permit that slow innovating firms be allowed to compensate their delay in productivity with lower wages, a kind of planned rate of productivity increase could be adopted as a reference for wage increase (Fadda, 2013; Tridico, 2014).

Parallel to these labour market measures, a general stronger involvement of trade unions in a kind of interactive, network, governance has to be recommended. The graphs previously shown reveal an inverse relationship between union coverage and income inequality. A social partnership capable to stimulate a responsible interaction and a cooperative participation of trade unions (as it is in the German case) would also improve the economic performance as a whole. Of course this cannot be only the result of institutional structures created by institutional designers, nor a simple rejection of the present neo-liberal trend; it requires an improved maturity in trade unions which should enable them to be reliable in their role of contributing to solve social conflicts, increase trust in society and enlarge social consensus.

Counteracting the negative effects of globalization with regard to income inequality requires a set of general economic policy measures which run from international trade regulation to bilateral agreements between nation states. Looking more closely at the aspects mentioned above, and particularly at the actual or threatened relocation of production, two lines of action can be suggested. The first has to do with production costs. It would be wise, instead of reducing wages, to act on the one side to lower the share of labour costs within total costs by increasing labour productivity through innovation, and on the other side to lower other production costs, such as energy, tariffs, transports, services to firms, raw materials and so on. The second line is to obtain an adequate level of international harmonization and cooperation among national trade unions. This would help to avoid social dumping and to prevent a downward wage and labour standard competition among workers in different States in order to subtract to each other the location of firms. It surely sounds strange that trade unions, which were created precisely in order to avoid such competition between individual workers, let it operate among workers of different nations through the absence of international coordination of workers organizations.

Finally, there is the need to refrain the "predatory" behaviour of the richest which has been mentioned above as a cause of rising income inequality. This predatory behaviour finds expression in two ways: the extraction of rents in different fields (monopolistic quasi-rents, financial rents, urban rents, political and public sector rents, rent seeking behaviour in the Public Administration and so on) and the self-decisions about compensations and fringe benefits taken within the boards of executives. There are mainly two ways of counteracting this trend (apart from a general change of cultural attitudes relative to the maximum acceptable gap between the best paid and the less paid). The first is to set a ceiling by law to salaries and all the executive benefits. Whether this is possible also for the private sector rather than only for the public sector is an open question, and it is anyway subject to political choice (for instance, it has been recently rejected in Switzerland through a referendum). Nevertheless, corporate governance laws could provide more limits to the arbitrary and unrestricted power of top managers in deciding their compensations. The second way could be to include in the board of executives some worker representatives. Although they cannot obviously alter the majority in the board, their presence can help rendering the issues more known and expose in this way the aspects of fairness that are involved to all workers and to the public opinion.

Redistribution measures

The set of the above suggested measures intended to inhibit the growing of market income inequality is surely a wide one, and requires an intense and coordinated policy action. They should be given priority both because they are able to improve the performance of the economy and because if successful they would reduce the need and the magnitude of policies for redistributing market income.

But, once all these measures are successfully implemented, there will always be a residual inequality, which might be called physiological, not due to distortions of the market or to power relationships, but reflecting different skills, different efforts, different productivities and different responsibilities. Whether this residual inequality should be considered excessive or not depends on the value that society attributes to all these elements.

Value judgments are, therefore, determinant in establishing the "acceptable" level of inequality. If this residual inequality is considered socially unfair it may also call for adjustment through redistribution by taxation and transfers, and this would add up to the demand for redistribution deriving from the inequality due to the failure, or the absence, of measures to prevent it. It is obvious that the higher the "market" inequality, the stronger will be the demand for redistribution. In fact, the empirical evidence shows that redistribution measures are generally wider and stronger precisely where market inequality is higher (see appendix).

A first possible consequence of neglecting policies to inhibit the growth of market inequality and relying only on subsequent redistribution measures is that people who have benefited from inequality may have accumulated so much wealth and so much power as to be able to buy votes or to adopt other corruption practices to resist against such measures being decided or being actually implemented. This would drive the political and economic system into a dangerous tunnel of inefficiency and decay. Here is another reason why measures to prevent the rise of excessive disparities in income and wealth before tax and transfers should be preferred, and why great care should be subsequently given to the choice of appropriate redistribution measures.

Another possible negative consequence of strong redistribution measures is that they might stimulate some opportunistic behaviour of economic agents (individuals and firms) relative to both transfers and in-kind benefits. This behaviour could materialize, for instance, through turning to irregular economy in order to avoid paying tax, or diminishing work effort if taxation is too progressive, or also acting strategically or fraudulently in order to get higher transfers. In addition, there is the risk that badly designed transfers may accrue to people

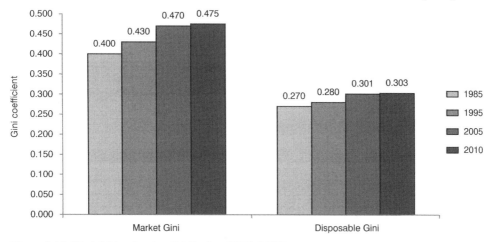

Figure 2.10 Diminishing fiscal redistribution (1985–2005)
Source: Caminada (2012)

who are already better off. In all these cases the redistribution effect would be nullified and the working of the economy would be badly affected. It would be a case of "medicine worse than the illness".

A general question has to be raised at this point as to what is meant by redistribution and how it is measured. Generally by redistribution is meant a change in the Gini coefficients, and the size of the change (that is the difference between the "market" Gini coefficient and the "net" Gini coefficient, or between "market" income inequality and "disposable" income inequality) is taken as its measure. Progressive taxation as well as transfers may have similar effects in this regard, but it should be noticed that the effect of progressive taxation, although it reduces the Gini coefficients, might not produce any actual improvement of the income of the poorer; so, in a sense it is doubtful whether a "substantial" (rather than a merely "statistical") redistributive effect can be attributed to taxation in itself. Only if taxation is used to finance transfers (either monetary or in the kind of welfare services) to low-income people it will imply a significant substantial "redistribution". Otherwise, if used to finance public expenditure as such, it would be only a fair way of sharing the burden of government expenditure. Excessive personal disposable incomes would in fact be cut, but the low income people would not benefit from it. This is, of course, a simple consequence of the fact that the Gini coefficient can be reduced by the same amount either by lowering incomes at the top or by increasing incomes at the bottom. In statistical terms it is the same, but if we have to give to the word "redistribution" a full meaning, it makes a difference. The terms "redistribution" and reduction of the Gini coefficient cannot be considered, in this respect, as synonymous. This clarification is of paramount importance also in view of the impact of income inequality on growth; in fact it has been found that "what matters most is the gap between low income households and the rest of the population. In contrast, no evidence is found that those with high incomes pulling away from the rest of the population harms growth" (Cingano, 2014).

Figure 2.10 describes the effect of fiscal redistribution in the OECD countries in Gini terms. As can be seen, fiscal redistribution has not been able to offset the increasing trend in inequality over time, which has been retained also in terms of net income. But actually disposable income inequality has become substantially lower than market inequality.

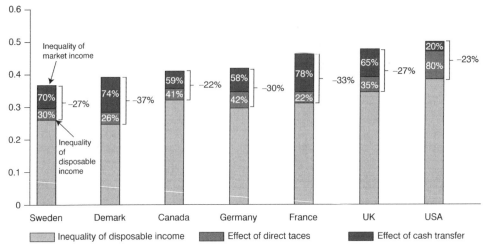

Figure 2.11 Respective distributive effects of direct taxes and cash transfers (2011)
Source: OECD 2014, preliminary data

The relative impact of the two components of fiscal measures (direct taxes and cash transfers) is different in different countries, as shown in the Figure 2.11.

Obviously, different systems of taxation can have different impact on inequality in disposable income. The more progressive is taxation, the higher will be the Gini coefficient reduction: therefore the idea of increasing the weight of indirect taxation (which is regressive) relative to direct income taxation is opposite to the target of decreasing inequality. "In an analysis of 12 European Union economies, the effective indirect tax rate, calculated as the share of consumption taxes in total household income, is on average three times higher for the bottom income decile than for the top decile. While both value added tax and excise duties are regressive in all economies, excise taxes are especially regressive, their share in total income being four time higher in the bottom income decile than in the top decile" (Bastagli et al., 2012). This regressive effect could be avoided if a progressive tax on consumption were designed. The idea is not bad in principle, but it is technically complicated to be put into practice. It has been suggested (Frank 2012) that what ought to be taxed with increasing marginal rate is the difference among the annual reported income and the annual reported saving, allowing for a standard deduction linked to the size of the family. Risks of recessionary effects could be averted by proper gradualism in its introduction and by converting savings into public or private investment. Moreover this would be a more manageable and more effective fiscal instrument for anti-cyclical policy.

In any case, rising tax rates with increasing income (although not too rapidly in order not to discourage work effort), fighting tax avoidance, cancelling tax havens should be at the basis of policies towards more equity in the distribution of disposable income.

Action towards reducing disposable income inequality has to be pursued also by means of transfers and provision of welfare services. In this way not only a "statistical" decline of Gini coefficients, but also an actual benefit to low income people would be obtained.

The relative impact of the two kinds of measures can be seen in Figure 2.12.

A warning has to be made about these data. They are simple estimates of the likely effects. They could be called "blackboard effects", since they describe the "statutory incidence" of policies, rather than their actual incidence, not enough data being available for that. As it has

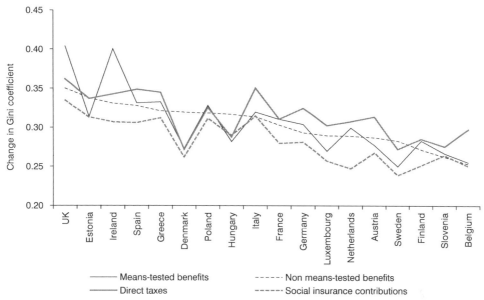

Figure 2.12 Redistributive impact of income taxes and transfers in the EU for early 2000

Source: Bastagli et al. 2012

Note: Lines show the increase in the Gini coefficient of disposable income due to the removal of each tax or transfer as existing in 2000–2005 in different countries

been mentioned above, opportunistic behaviour of agents and bad policy design could result in a negative impact on redistribution but also on the level of activity of the entire economy and the path of growth.

On the other hand if transfers and in-kind benefits are devoted to improve the access to, and the quality of, educational services, or to improve the access to and the quality of health services, or to cope with the housing problems they are beneficial to social cohesion and to growth. Therefore, the above warning, more than about the interpretation of these data, should be about stressing the need for great care in designing the structure and the intensity of fiscal policy.

If wealth inequality is considered in addition to income inequality, the disparity among households is still wider, as can be seen in the figure below. Taxes on wealth are generally lower than income taxes, and so are taxes on property and on inheritance; therefore, both gross and net wealth inequalities are higher than gross and net income inequalities. Although a reinforcement of non income taxation is generally advocated, some doubts can be raised on ethical grounds. If the accumulation of wealth is considered as a result of decisions to save it may look unfair to tax the savings out of disposable incomes which have been already taxed. On the other hand if the amounts of savings are seen as dependent on the levels of income, wealth inequality would appear as a projection of income inequality. Being the accumulation of wealth the result of these two components, a balanced approach should be recommended in order not to push wealth and property taxation as far as to act as a punishment for decisions to save. Clearly the higher the income inequality the stronger its impact on the building of wealth inequality. Therefore, the design of wealth and property taxation should take account of the level of disposable income inequality to begin with. Quite different is, of course, the question of inheritance and gift taxation. In this case the

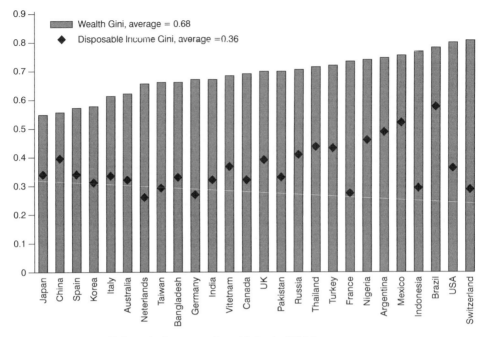

Figure 2.13 Gini coefficients for income and wealth (early 2000s)
Source: Davies 2008

individual who bears the fiscal weight is not the same individual who has created with his earnings the wealth which is being transferred.

The disproportion between income and wealth inequality can be seen in Figure 2.13 This disproportion has even increased in times of fiscal consolidation.

This is mostly due to the way in which the target of fiscal consolidation is being pursued in most European countries. It includes on one side the downsizing of social and welfare services and on the other side a rise in taxation either too little progressive or more often regressive in its indirect component. This is accompanied by a pressure towards lowering wages. A heavier fiscal pressure on low range pensions in some countries also contributes to growth of inequality.

According to the above considerations, it is surely possible to design fiscal and transfer policies in such a way as to effectively reduce the disparities in disposable income and at the same time avoid a negative impact on economic performance. This requires to impressing on fiscal policy the following directions.

In the first place a switch towards more progressive taxation and less regressive indirect taxes. This would not only ensure a greater impact on equalitarian redistribution, but would also be a stimulus to growth, due to the increase in aggregate demand, given the higher marginal propensity to consume of lower income people relative to higher income. In the second place, the basis for the tax revenue should be expanded by means of extension of taxation to wealth and property (in a reasonable and balanced way as suggested above), by means of effectively counteracting tax evasion and by means of effectively preventing the use of fiscal havens. A progressive consumption tax of the kind suggested above could also be considered.

As for transfers and welfare services, expenditure on public housing, public health services and public education services would be beneficial both for reducing inequality and for fostering the growth of the economy. In order to avoid these social services and benefits being appropriated mainly by the rich, the provision of such services on the basis of means-tests has been often advocated. The question is still a controversial one, but two things should be noticed. First, the effectiveness of this approach requires absolute reliability of the tests; in many countries, and particularly in Italy the system would turn towards opposite effects due to the unquestionable unreliability of the official data about personal incomes. Second, if the tax system was really and strongly progressive, a redistributive effect would come out automatically even with universal access to welfare services because, in the end, people would pay differently for the same services according to their incomes being differently taxed according to their levels. Child allowances are a case in point. It is often recommended that these be provided through means testing and kept relatively low on the ground otherwise they would discourage women's participation in the labour market. It could be objected that precisely insufficient financial resources to match the growing expenses for childcare could force mothers to give up their jobs. On the contrary, if they were given financial support they would be able to both stay in the labour market and at the same time pay for care services at market prices. Clearly, concentrating social public expenditure on those goods and services which form a larger share of the consumption basket of lower income households would help avoiding a misallocation of such in-kind transfers.

It should be added that precisely in times of crisis, a higher public expenditure on selected public services would have a positive effect both on income redistribution and growth, and in this way also on fiscal consolidation. Particularly two sectors are mostly relevant in order to get "more and better jobs": the improvement of skills through better education and vocational training, and the reinforcement of employment services to help the matching between demand and supply in the labour market.

> The best performers among the rich countries in terms of economic, employment, social cohesion and equality outcomes have one thing in common: a large welfare state that does several things at the same time, invest in people, stimulating and supporting them to be active, and also adequately protecting them and their children when everything else fails.
>
> (Marx and Verbist 2014)

This conclusion of an empirical study adds to theoretical considerations put forward in the dispute about supposed detrimental effects of welfare state on economic performance (Fadda, 2014).

As a final conclusion it can be said that although acting to prevent excessive gross pre-tax-transfers inequality is preferable, active appropriate redistribution fiscal and welfare policies are also necessary. Unfortunately, both the crisis and the trend impressed in most countries onto fiscal consolidation policies seems to make it difficult to take measures to restrain inequality and to redistribute income. But unless this trend is reversed we are bound to see, in the near future, a growth rather than a decline in income and wealth inequality.

References

Alesina, A. and Rodrik, D. (1994) Distributive politics and economic growth, *Quarterly Journal of Economics*, 1(2): 465–90.

Atkinson, A.B. (2003) Income inequality in OECD countries: data and explanations, *CESifo Economic Studies* 49(4): 479–513.

Barro, R.J. (1990) Government spending in a simple model of endogeneous growth, *Journal of Political Economy*, 98(5): 103–25

Barro, R.J. (2000) Inequality and growth in a panel of countries, *Journal of Economic Growth*, 5(1): 5–32.

Banerjee, A. and Duflo, E. (2003) Inequality and growth: what can the data say, *Journal of Economic Growth*, 8(3): 267–299.

Bastagli, F., Coady. D. and Gupta, S. (2012), *Income Inequality and Fiscal Policy*, IMF Staff Discussion Note 12/08

Berg, A. and Ostry J.D. (2011) *Inequality and Unsustainable Growth: Two Sides of the Same Coin?*, IMF Staff Discussion note, April.

Berg, A., Ostry, J.D. and Zettelmeyer, J. (2012) What makes growth sustained?, *Journal of Development Economics*, 98(2): 149–66.

Blanchard, O. (2000) Lecture 2: Rents, product and labor market regulation, and unemployment, Lionel Robbins Lectures, London School of Economics, London.

Caminada, K., Goudswaard, K. and Wang, C. (2012) *Disentangling Income Inequality and the Redistributive Effect of Taxes and Transfers in 20 LIS Countries Over Time*, Luxembourg Income Study Working Paper 581.

Carlsson ,F., Daravola, D., and Johanson, O. (2005), Are people inequality-averse or just risk-averse?, *Economica*, 72(287): 375–396.

Cingano, F. (2014) *Trends in Income Inequality and its Impact on Economic Growth*, OECD Social, Employment and Migration Working Papers, No. 163.

Corak, M. (2013) *Inequality from Generation to Generation: The United States in Comparison*, in Robert Rycroft (ed.), *The Economics of Inequality, Poverty, and Discrimination in the 21st Century*, London: ABC-CLIO.

Daudey, E. and Garcia-Penalosa C. (2007) The personal and the factor distributions of income in a cross-section of countries, *Journal of Development Studies*, 43(5): 812–829.

Davies, J.B., Sandstrom, S., Shorrocks, A. and Wolff, E.N. (2008) *The World Distribution of Household Wealth*, UNU-WIDER Discussion Paper 2008/03, Helsinki.

Duménil, G. and Lévy, D. (2001) Costs and benefits of neoliberalism: a class analysis, *Review of International Political Economy*, 8(4): 578–607.

Epstein, G. A. and Jayadev, A. (2005) The rise of rentier incomes in OECD countries: financialization, central bank policy and labor solidarity', in: G.A. Epstein (ed.): *Financialization and the World Economy*, Cheltenham: Edward Elgar.

Esping-Andersen, G. (2009), *The Incomplete Revolution*, Cambridge: Polity Press

Fadda, S. (2014), Should we cut the welfare state in order to get out of the crisis?, in: S. Fadda, and P. Tridico (eds), *The Economic Crisis in Social and Institutional Context. Theories, Policies and Exit Strategies*, London: Routledge.

Fadda, S. (2013) Produttività, contrattazione e patto sociale, *Quaderni di Rassegna Sindacale*, 2: 157–177.

Forbes, K. (2000) A reassessment of the relationship between inequality and growth, *American Economic Review*, 90(4): 869–887.

Frank, R.H. (2012) *The Darwin Economy*, Princeton, NJ: Princeton University Press.

Fitoussi, I and Saraceno, P.-F. (2011) 'Inequality, the crisis and after', *Rivista di politica economica*, 1: 9–27.

Galbraith, J.K. (2012) *Inequality and Instability: A Study of the World Economy Just Before the Great Crisis*. Oxford: Oxford University Press.

Glyn, A. (2006) *Capitalism Unleashed: Finance, Globalization, and Welfare*, Oxford: Oxford University Press.

Galor, O. and Moav, O. (2004) From physical to human capital accumulation: inequality and the process of development, *Review of Economic Studies*, 71: 1001–1026.

Gollin, D.(2002) Getting income shares right, *Journal of Political Economy*, 110(2): 458–474.

Gollin,D. (2008), Labour share of income, *New Palgrave Dictionary of Economics*, London: Macmillan

Gustafsson, B. and Johansson, M. (1997) *In Search of a Smoking Gun: What Makes Income Inequality Vary Over Time in Different Countries.* Luxembourg Income Study Working Paper no.172.

IMF (2007) *World Economic Outlook: Spillovers and Cycles in the Global Economy*, April

Kalecki, (1965) *Theory of Economic Dynamics*, London: Unwin University Books.

Kramer, H. (2011) *Decomposition of the Wage Share of Income*, Karlsruhe University.

Lansley, S. (2009) *How Soaring Inequality Contributed to the Crash*, London: Friedrich Ebert Stiftung.

Marx, I. and Verbist, G. (2014) The policy response: boosting employment and social investment. In: W. Salverda et al. (eds), 2014. *Changing Inequalities in Rich Countries: Analytical and Comparative Perspectives.* Oxford: Oxford University Press.

Milanovic, B. (2009) *Income Inequality and Speculative Investment by the Rich and Poor in America Led to the Financial Meltdown. Two Views on the Cause of the Global Crisis – Part I.* Yale Global Online.

Mishel, L. and Sabadish, N. (2012) *Pay and the Top 1%: How Executive Compensation and Financial-Sector Pay Have Fuelled Income Inequality.* Issue Brief: Economic Policy Institute.

Okun, A.M. (1975) *Equality and Efficiency: the Big Trade-Off,* Washington, DC: Brookings Institution Press.

Ostry J., Berg A. and Tsangarides, C. (2014) *Redistribution, Inequality and Growth,* IMF Staff Discussion Note, April.

Palley, T. I. (2008) Financialization: what it is and why it matters, in E. Hein, T. Niechoj, H.-P. Spahn, and A. Truger, A. (eds): *Finance-led Capitalism? Macroeconomic Effects of Changes in the Financial Sector*, Marburg: Metropolis-Verlag.

Pigou, A. (1920) *The Economics of Welfare*, London: Macmillan.

Rajan, R. (2010) *Fault Lines: How Hidden Fractures Still Threaten the World Economy,* Princeton, NJ: Princeton University Press.

Rodrik, D. (1997) *Has Globalization Gone Too Far?* Washington, DC: Institute of International Economics.

Rodrik, D. (1999) Where did all the growth go? external shocks, social conflict, and growth collapses, *Journal of Economic Growth*, 4: 358–412.

Rowlingson, K. (2011) *Does Income Inequality Cause Health and Social Problems?* York: Joseph Rowntree Foundation

Sacks, D., B. Stevenson, and J. Wolfers (2012) *The New Stylized Facts about Income and Subjective Well-Being,* Institute for the Study of Labor. University of Pennsylvania; University of Michigan, Working Paper December 2012

Smeeding T., Morelli, F. and Thompson, J. (2013) Recent trends in income inequality in the developed countries, *Progressive Economy*, 2: 24–33.

Stiglitz, J. (2012) *The Price of Inequality: How Today's Divided Society Endangers Our Future,* New York: W. W. Norton & Company.

Stockhammer, E. (2004) Financialization and the slowdown of accumulation. *Cambridge Journal of Economics*, 28(5): 719–741.

Sylos, Labini (1984) *The Forces of Economic Growth and Decline*, Cambridge, MA: MIT Press.

Summers, L. H. (2013) *Economic Possibilities for Our Children*, NBER Report, no. 4

Thompson J., Leight E. (2011) *Searching for the Supposed Benefits of Higher Inequality: Impacts of Rising Top Shares on the Standard of Living of Low and Middle-Income Families*, University of Massachusetts, Amherst, Working Paper no. 258.

Tridico, P. (2014) *Produttività, contrattazione e salario di risultato. Un confronto tra l'Italia e il resto d'Europa.* ASTRIL Working Paper (www.astril.org).

Welch, F. (1999), In defense of inequality, *American Economic Review,* 89(2): 1–17.

Wilkinson, R. and Pickett K. (2009) *The Spirit Level: Why Greater Equality Makes Societies Stronger,* New York: Bloomsbury Press.

Appendix

Table 2.2 Market and disposable Gini coefficients in OECD countries

Country	Inequality/Redistribution	Mid-1990s	Around 2000	Mid-2000s	Around 2010
Australia	A. Market Gini	0.467	0.476	0.465	0.469
	B. Disposable Gini	0.309	0.317	0.315	0.334
	C. Redistribution = A–B	0.158	0.159	0.151	0.135
Austria	A. Market Gini			0.467	0.483
	B. Disposable Gini			0.261	0.269
	C. Redistribution = A–B			0.206	0.214
Belgium	A. Market Gini			0.490	0.483
	B. Disposable Gini			0.279	0.264
	C. Redistribution = A–B			0.211	0.219
Canada	A. Market Gini	0.430	0.440	0.436	0.447
	B. Disposable Gini	0.289	0.315	0.317	0.319
	C. Redistribution = A–B	0.141	0.125	0.120	0.127
Czech Republic	A. Market Gini	0.442		0.464	0.453
	B. Disposable Gini	0.257		0.261	0.258
	C. Redistribution = A–B	0.185		0.202	0.195
Denma rk	A. Market Gini	0.417	0.416	0.416	0.429
	B. Disposable Gini	0.215	0.227	0.232	0.252
	C. Redistribution = A–B	0.202	0.189	0.184	0.177
Finland	A. Market Gini	0.480	0.476	0.481	0.485
	B. Disposable Gini	0.222	0.255	0.266	0.265
	C. Redistribution = A–B	0.258	0.221	0.215	0.220
France	A. Market Gini	0.473	0.490	0.485	0.505
	B. Disposable Gini	0.277	0.287	0.288	0.303
	C. Redistribution = A–B	0.196	0.203	0.197	0.202
Germany	A. Market Gini	0.459	0.471	0.499	0.492
	B. Disposable Gini	0.266	0.264	0.297	0.286
	C. Redistribution = A–B	0.193	0.207	0.202	0.206
Greece	A. Market Gini			0.478	0.528
	B. Disposable Gini		0.361	0.346	0.338
	C. Redistribution = A–B			0.132	0.191
Israel	A. Market Gini	0.494	0.504	0.513	0.501
	B. Disposable Gini	0.338	0.347	0.378	0.376
	C. Redistribution = A–B	0.156	0.157	0.135	0.125
Italy	A. Market Gini	0.467	0.475	0.512	0.507
	B. Disposable Gini	0.327	0.323	0.331	0.321
	C. Redistribution = A–B	0.140	0.152	0.181	0.186
Japan	A. Market Gini	0.403	0.432	0.462	0.488
	B. Disposable Gini	0.323	0.337	0.329	0.336
	C. Redistribution = A–B	0.079	0.095	0.133	0.153

Country	Inequality/Redistribution	Mid-1990s	Around 2000	Mid-2000s	Around 2010
Luxembourg	A. Market Gini			0.467	0.468
	B. Disposable Gini	0.259	0.261	0.283	0.271
	C. Redistribution = A–B			0.184	0.197
Netherlands	A. Market Gini	0.484	0.424	0.426	0.421
	B. Disposable Gini	0.297	0.292	0.284	0.283
	C. Redistribution = A–B	0.187	0.132	0.142	0.138
New Zea la nd	A. Market Gini	0.488	0.484	0.473	0.454
	B. Disposable Gini	0.335	0.339	0.335	
	C. Redistribution = Λ B	0.153	0.145	0.138	
Norway	A. Market Gini	0.404	0.426	0.447	0.423
	B. Disposable Gini	0.243	0.261	0.276	0.249
	C. Redistribution = A–B	0.161	0.165	0.171	0.174
Sweden	A. Market Gini	0.438	0.446	0.432	0.441
	B. Disposable Gini	0.211	0.243	0.234	0.269
	C. Redistribution = A–B	0.227	0.203	0.198	0.172
United Kingdom	A. Market Gini		0.512	0.503	0.523
	B. Disposable Gini		0.352	0.335	0.341
	C. Redistribution = A–B		0.160	0.169	0.182
United States	A. Market Gini	0.477	0.476	0.486	0.499
	B. Disposable Gini	0.361	0.357	0.380	0.380
	C. Redistribution = A–B	0.116	0.119	0.106	0.119

Sources: Own elaboration on OECD Statistics (download May 2015)

3 Gender, class and the crisis

Valeria Cirillo, Marcella Corsi and Carlo D'Ippoliti

Introduction

In the economic literature, several scholars have addressed the narrative of a two-stage European crisis. In a first stage, the so-called "he-cession", men would have been hit the most by the economic recession induced by the financial crisis. Shortly thereafter, in the "she-austerity" stage, women would have suffered the heaviest burdens of the fiscal retrenchment measures. If that were the case, the policy response to the crisis would be producing an increase in the – already high pre-existing – gender inequality.

In this chapter we analyse the most recent micro-data available at the European level, the European Union Statistics on Income and Living Conditions (EU-SILC), containing information on European men's and women's incomes in 2012. As it turns out, the crisis and the policy response to it have impoverished several European households and increased income inequality in Europe. However, there is no strong evidence to support or reject the abovementioned narrative on the gendered impact of the crisis yet. As a consequence, it may be necessary to wait for further evidence before taking the two-stage narrative for granted, while stronger emphasis on pre-existing structural gender equality may be warranted.

Gender and the crisis

The *gender of the crisis* has been the focus of an intense debate both in the academic literature and the media.

According to a report published by the European Commission (Bettio et al. 2012) it is necessary to distinguish two phases of the European crisis. During a first phase, of financially induced economic crisis, men have suffered higher income reductions and job losses than women. Then, with the implementation of 'austerity' measures (after 2010), a second phase of the crisis started. According to this periodization, since austerity in Europe is characterized by downsizing of the public sector and cuts to social spending in particular, the second phase of the crisis would be now producing a higher impact on women's employment and incomes.

This narrative departs from the observation that, beginning in 2007/2008, the financial difficulties of banks and other monetary and financial intermediaries produced a serious impact on the real economy through deleveraging along with the 'credit crunch'. These phenomena would have disproportionally impacted on men because they have mostly affected men-dominated industries (i.e. finance and construction) and because men were overrepresented among workers in the more cyclically sensitive sectors (such as export-oriented manufacturing). Indeed, already Milkman (1976) noted that in general gender-based

Table 3.1 Trends in European employment: compound annual growth rate (2008–2013, per cent)

	Employees		Temporary employees	
	Women	Men	Women	Men
All economic activities				
EU27	−0.07	−0.85	−1.02	−0.99
EZ17	0.02	−1.11	−1.53	−1.82
GIPSI	−0.96	−2.77	−4.11	−4.56
Public administration				
EU27	−0.62	−0.96	−2.73	−1.23
EZ17	−0.75	−1.14	−3.41	−2.56
GIPSI	−1.07	−1.35	−8.14	−5.66
Education				
EU27	0.68	0.03	−0.17	0.76
EZ17	0.56	−0.67	−0.63	0.31
GIPSI	−0.40	−1.65	−3.85	−2.75
Human health and social work activities				
EU27	1.32	1.38	0.56	1.38
EZ17	1.55	1.51	0.28	1.74
GIPSI	1.01	1.04	−2.16	−0.81
Activities of households as employers				
EU27	0.40	−0.15	−2.97	−2.70
EZ17	0.39	0.58	−3.37	−3.33
GIPSI	1.61	7.67	−4.62	3.03

Source: Eurostat, Labour Force Survey (LFS), 15–64 age cohort.

Note: Sector "Public administration and defence; compulsory social security" (Section O, NACE Rev.2) includes activities of governmental nature carried out by the public administration such as general administration, activities of providing health care and other social services, foreign affairs, defence, public order and compulsory social security activities. "Education" (Section P, NACE Rev.2) includes public and private education at any level or for any profession. "Human health and social work activities" (Section Q, NACE Rev.2) include a wide range of health activities performed by hospitals, medical doctors, dentists or other providers, and a variety of social assistance directly to clients (for elderly, disabled and child-day care). "Activities of Households as Employers; Undifferentiated Goods- and Services-producing Activities of Households for own use" (Section T, NACE Rev.2) includes activities of domestic personnel consumed by the employing household and undifferentiated goods- and services-producing activities of private households for own use.

employment segregation makes women's employment a complement, rather than substitute, for men's. As a consequence, the hypothesis (suggested by economic theories of the sexual division of labour within the household) of women's employment acting as a buffer during crises should be rejected. Cho and Newhouse (2013) attested a similar trend outside Europe, suggesting that the negative impact of gender segregation on men's employment during crises is empirically more relevant than the so-called added worker effect.

However, the most recent available data (arguably not yet updated enough to be deemed as conclusive) suggest a more complicated story. Table 3.1 reports the trends in European employment in the 2008–2013 period for men and women, separately considering the European Union (EU27),[1] the Eurozone (EZ, i.e. the countries that adopt the euro as their currency) and the GIPSI countries (Greece, Ireland, Portugal, Spain and Italy, where the crisis hit hardest). As expected, in all three areas men were hit more than women, and only for temporary employees in the EU27 a slightly higher reduction of women's employment is observed. However, even when considering NACE sectors in which women are more represented (e.g. health and social work activities, and household activities, where women represent 80 per cent and 89 per cent of employees respectively), with few exceptions men's employment fell more than women's. In other words, men's employment seems to have been hit hardest by the crisis, even if marginally, in women-dominated industries too.

The reduction of men's employment has implied a levelling down of gender employment and pay gaps, which came to be labelled as "man-cession" (Sierminska and Takhtamanova 2011, Perry 2010, Wall 2009, Thompson 2009). Indeed, this trend is not specific of the euro crisis. As has been noted, it is often the case that the initial burden of an economic downturn tends to be borne by men workers (McKay et al. 2013). However, according to Signorelli et al. (2012) when considering a longer time span (1980–2005), an analysis of past financial crises highlights a greater impact on women's participation and unemployment rates, especially in high-income countries.[2]

What characterizes the current recession in the EU is that it has been simultaneously dominated in all countries by the implementation of gender blind fiscal consolidation programs aimed at tackling financial speculation on sovereign debts. The crisis years have seen a gender equality perspective deprioritized within the EU policy process – as is clearly evident in the lack of a stipulation for sex-disaggregated data in the targets selected for the "Europe 2020" strategy. Across the whole strategy, the hard fought for attention to gender equality in the 1990s and 2000s has almost disappeared, leaving little trace even in the gender-related themes of poverty and social inclusion (Villa and Smith 2012). Accordingly, Karamessini and Rubery (2014a) warn that the observed short-term decrease in the gender employment gap may turn into long-term harmful implications for gender equality when the implementation of fiscal consolidation plans is completed, and refer to this scenario as "she-austerity".

Austerity policies have the potential to generate greater challenges to women than men due to the associated downsizing of the public sector, because (i) women are relatively more represented and concentrated in terms of public sector employment (Rubery 2013, Karamessini and Rubery 2014a);[3] (ii) gender equality policies are threatened by spending retrenchment; and (iii) women are more affected by the loss of social benefits that form a higher share of their incomes (Bettio et al. 2012).

Some country-level analysis raises preliminary evidence of a possible reversal of the he-cession: Périvier (2014) reports a "seesaw effect" in Spain, the UK and in Denmark, i.e. a worsening of employment in female dominated sectors and an improvement in male dominated ones; according to McKay and colleagues (2013) in the UK between 2011 and 2013 job loss in the public sector increased for women by 61,000 and fell for men by 31,000 while 73 per cent of public sector pay freezes affected women threating an expected widening of an already significant gender pay gap (20 per cent in 2012; WBG 2010). However, in general it seems too early to assess the gendered impacts of austerity, given the still ongoing and differentiated developments in fiscal consolidation plans by EU countries (Karamessini and Rubery 2014b) and above all the lack of updated data on men's and women's incomes.

Class, inequality and the crisis

Since the crisis, political and academic concern over inequality has considerably increased. Economists, sociologists and political scientists have investigated the role of increasing income inequality as a cause of the 2007–2008 crisis (and in some cases of the euro crisis too) as well as the distributional impact of the crisis and of the policy responses to it.

On the one hand, Bazillier and Héricourt (2014) point out that the economic literature is substantially in agreement on the identification of a causal nexus from income inequality to the growth of debit. This is associated to the empirical finding that credit booms are the prime determinant of financial crises, including the 2007–2008 US crisis. Todorova (2009) explicitly links such inequality-induced credit bubbles to gender inequality, defined both as labour market discrimination and sexual division of labour in the household. Post-Keynesian economists have explicitly linked also the euro crisis with the accumulation of macroeconomic imbalances in the real sector. In particular Hein (2012) and Hein (2013) pointed out growing income inequality and the lower share of national income accruing to labour as a cause of increasing balance-of-payments imbalances, which are in turn considered in this literature as the trigger of the sovereign debt crisis after 2009.

On the other hand, the distributional impact of financial crises is less clear-cut. According to Bazillier and Héricourt (2014), the economic literature has so far found an obvious causal link from crises to poverty, while mixed results are found concerning the link from crises to inequality. However, austerity policy has been explicitly linked to a further growth in inequality (e.g. by Green and Lavery 2014), in particular due to the peculiar mix of restrictive fiscal policies (which reduce the size of the public sector and thus the redistribution of income) and expansionary monetary policies (which are likely to produce asset price inflation and thus disproportionally benefit the owners of financial assets).

In the study of inequality, mainstream economics typically focuses on the distribution of individual or household incomes. Statistical offices and research institutions in the EU and the USA are currently working on improving the instruments to collect and analyse data on wealth inequality at the individual or household level too (Atkinson and Brandolini 2008, 2011, OECD 2008, OECD 2011, Jenkins et al. 2013).

By contrast, functional income distribution, i.e. the shares of national income accruing to labour and capital, is relatively understudied in mainstream economics. When economists speak of social classes, they normally refer to loosely defined groups of people who belong to a certain quintile of the income distribution. For example Palley (2013) presents a three class model encompassing "workers", "middle management middle class" and "top management capitalist class". In this model, the author identifies the existence of three classes on the base of three cut points in the income distribution, corresponding to the 1%, 20% and 80% percentiles. In some cases the definition is even looser: for example Summers and Balls (2015) write "the term 'middle class' is used interchangeably throughout this report with 'low and middle income'" (p. 1).

Concerning functional income distribution, a recent body of literature has documented a structural change in factor shares during the second half of the twentieth century, towards higher profit incomes (Schlenker and Schmid 2015, Arpaia et al. 2009, Checchi and Garcia-Penalosa 2010, ILO 2013, van der Hoeven 2014). Some works linked the increasing share of capital incomes to the observed increase in personal or household income inequality (Adler and Schmid 2013, Atkinson 2009, Glyn, 2009). Schlenker and Schmid (2015) study the effect of changing capital income shares upon inequality of gross household income showing how the transmission of a shift in capital income shares into the personal distribution of income depends on the concentration of capital income in an economy.

However, usually these works do not consider the relation between the two concepts at the micro level. For example, Stockhammer (2013) investigates the determinants of a declining wage shares in OECD countries focusing on macroeconomic factors such as financialization, globalisation, welfare state retrenchment and technological change. While macro factors are certainly relevant, a micro analysis is useful too, because the two perspectives convene different information: while personal or household income distribution concerns the relative "position" of the individual (or household) in his or her society, functional distribution refers to people's roles in the production process and, accordingly, the type of income that they receive. A crucial consequence of the macro perspective is that – it is almost needless to remark – the economics literature on functional income distribution (and vast part of that on personal income distribution) adopted a gender blind approach.

In this work, we link the analysis of household and functional income distribution in light of gender inequality, during the European crisis. As explained in the next section, the nature of the data available at the international level imposes strict limitations to any empirical analysis of these topics. Yet, reference to quantitative data available today provides an irreplaceable complement to the gender analyses reviewed above which, in some cases, seem to require certain qualifications.

Data and methodology

Our empirical investigation is based on the "European Union Statistics on Income and Living Conditions" (EU-SILC) database provided by Eurostat. EU-SILC contains data on sources of income at the household level, distinguishing incomes from rent, labour, dividends and profits. We employ the cross-sectional version of the database containing data for the years 2007, 2010 and 2012, containing a representative sample of European households before the crisis and at different stages through it.[4]

A crucial limitation for quantitative analyses that try to include a gender perspective is the lack of adequate data. Within the European institutions it is common practice to sum up incomes and assets of all household members and of the household as a whole, and to notionally attribute an equal share of this sum to each household member. In the European context, such putative income becomes the equivalent income through the adoption of an equivalence scale aimed at allowing for economies of scale in consumption. A major drawback of this approach is that the underlying assumptions of equal contribution to the household's resources and of equal sharing of the household's means are criticized by the scientific literature.

The alternative, as recently done for example by Bárcena-Martín and Moro-Egido (2013), is to let gender gaps emerge by limiting the analysis to a minority of the population, such as single-adult households, which satisfies the condition of exhibiting a different number of adult men and women for each household. However, the generalizability of the ensuing results is unclear, as specific trends may characterize these parts of the population (in our case, concerning poverty). To overcome this limitation, we consider the whole population and removing any hypothesis on intra-household sharing of resources, we limit the analysis to household as collective entities. Accordingly, we define as men-headed (MH) households those in which a man declares earning the highest income, and women-headed (MH) households those in which it is a woman to earn most.

EU SILC database is also characterized by some errors deriving from conceptual and measurement (collection and processing) sources leading to patterns differing across countries. Due to the violation of the normality assumption of income variables required by the standard Grubbs test (Grubbs 1969 and Stefansky 1972), we apply the absolute deviation around the median criterion (Leys et al. 2013) to detect and eliminate outliers in the database. Compared to the standard deviation, the choice of the median as central tendency indicator

Table 3.2 Households' budget composition by source of income

Wage (sum for all household members of gross employee cash or near cash income)[5]
Labour income (sum of cash benefits or losses from self-employment and wage)[6]
Income from capital (restricted) (interest, dividends, profit from capital investments in unincorporated business, income from rental of a property or land, pensions received by individual private plans)
Income from capital (interest, dividends, profit from capital investments in unincorporated business, income from rental of a property or land, imputed rent, pensions received by individual private plans)[7]
State transfers (sum of family/children related allowances, social exclusion not elsewhere classified, housing allowances, regular inter-household cash transfers received, unemployment benefits, old-age benefits, survivor' benefits, sickness benefits, disability benefit)[8]

does not assume a normal distribution of the data; furthermore, while the mean and standard deviation are strongly impacted by outliers, the median is insensitive to the presence of outliers (Hampel 1974, Huber 1981).[9] This procedure permits to eliminate extreme values, but we still allow for the possibility of negative incomes deriving from self-employment, capital or net income after taxes.[10] However, outliers, defined as observations greater than five times the median absolute deviation, have been removed. 620,017 households in 27 European countries compose the final database for three years (2007, 2010, 2012).[11] We define the different sources of households' incomes as shown in Table 3.2.

Gender and class during the crisis

In the EU-SILC database, income from capital includes also money from rent of properties and imputed rent being a sort of in-kind house advantage impacting on household well-being. Even if the inclusion of imputed rent produces effects of income re-ranking among households, it represents an indirect income from property. In our analysis, we consider the indirect income from housing property as a source of capital income in order to define the functional "positioning" of the household between capital and labour, however the family position in the income distribution will be defined without the inclusion of the imputed rent.[12] Household budget shares are computed as ratios of real yearly quantities of wage, capital and state transfer on the total gross household income.[13]

Table 3.3 shows the composition of the sample in terms of typology of households and individuals.

As expected, over time the percentage of women-headed households has increased probably due to "forced" women's participation in the labour market in consequence of massive job cuts experienced by male-concentrated sectors such as manufacturing. In our sample, more than 60 per cent are men-headed households where the earner (in case of single) or major income earner (in case of households with more adults) is a man. The gender of households based on the "bread-winner hypothesis" introduces a bias in the sample, namely it changes the proportion of women and men in the sample. In terms of individuals, we have an equal distribution between men and women. As stated before, the focus of our analysis on sources of income requires a household approach leading to a different gender proportion in the sample.

At European level more than 50 per cent of households depend on labour income as prevailing source, 40 per cent on wages (dependent work); while the so-called "capitalist"

Table 3.3 Distribution of individuals and households by gender over years[14]

	2007		2010		2012	
Gender	*Individuals (%)*	*Households (%)*	*Individuals (%)*	*Households (%)*	*Individuals (%)*	*Households (%)*
Men / men headed households	47.85	61.46	47.77	60.78	47.89	60.52
Women / women headed households	52.15	36.74	52.23	38.25	52.11	38.5
Zero income[15]		1.8		0.97		0.98

Source: elaboration on EU-SILC 2007, 2010, 2012 cross sectional data.

households represent a small proportion of the sample, less than 4 per cent including imputed rent and private pensions. However, 0.1 per cent of households exclusively rely on profit and rent becoming 1 per cent if we consider profits and capital as the prevailing source of income.

Looking at the distribution of households according to the exclusive source of income, we detect an increasing proportion of "wage" and "labour income" households over time. Labour income households whose income exclusively comes from dependent jobs and self-employment are about 2 per cent of European households in 2007 and 3.4 per cent in 2012. The same increasing pattern has been verified for "wage" households shifting from 1.5 per cent in 2007 to 2.8 per cent in 2012. The proportion of State dependent households has been increasing over the period too, almost doubling. Overall, while pure-income households – defined as those households depending on one typology of income – have been increasing over the period 2007–2012, the proportion of mixed-income households decreases with the exception of households depending on State transfers. A smooth trend towards polarization of sources of income arises, mostly for State transfers and labour income.

Table 3.5 allows comparing mean and median income by source and gender. A consistent divergence between men-headed and women-headed households arises. Women-headed households earn on average less than men-headed households.[16] This pattern is consistent over time, however, the difference in wage and labour income between typologies of households seems to decrease over 2007–2012, probably due to job losses in male oriented sectors. Men-headed households earn higher wages compared to women households, even if the absolute wage has declined over the period (2007–2012), the "wage-gap" between households is still verified. The same pattern has been detected for capital income, which is systematically higher for men-headed households over the period and for State transfers.

The analysis of median values suggests further insights on the distribution of earnings between households over the period. From this point of view, the median value of wage, labour income, capital and State transfers is always below the mean underling a major concentration of households in the lower part of the distribution. Most households receive wages, capitals and State transfers below the average value. This pattern is more evident for women-headed households.

Capital income is characterized by a higher level of dispersion compared to wage or labour income, namely few households register a high amount of capital, but the median value is equal to zero. This pattern of capital concentration is particularly evident for

Table 3.4 Distribution of households by source of exclusive or prevailing source of income

	Exclusive source of income					Prevailing source of income				
	Wage	*Labour income*	*Capital restricted*	*Capital*	*State transfers*	*Wage*	*Labour income*	*Capital restricted*	*Capital*	*State transfers*
2007	1.57%	1.95%	0.09%	0.44%	2.91%	44.04%	55.98%	0.85%	3.80%	40.13%
2010	3.00%	3.60%	0.13%	0.40%	4.63%	43.82%	54.52%	1.14%	3.49%	41.87%
2012	2.87%	3.42%	0.16%	0.42%	4.84%	43.16%	54.10%	1.15%	3.29%	42.43%

Source: elaboration on EU-SILC 2007, 2010, 2012 cross sectional data.

Table 3.5 Sources of income by household type in euros (EU SILC, 2007, 2010, 2012)

			Wage	Labour income	Capital restricted	Capital	State transfer
2007	Men-headed households	mean	15957.5	18562.0	977.7	4979.5	8683.2
		median	8422.3	12177.5	7.0	4257.6	3481.0
		CV	1.2	1.1	3.5	1.1	1.4
		Gini index	0.433	0.426	0.747	0.479	0.54
	Women-headed households	mean	11232.8	12601.3	757.9	4234.4	8274.7
		median	2687.0	4280.0	0.8	3131.7	4987.8
		CV	1.4	1.4	3.8	1.2	1.2
		Gini index	0.457	0.459	0.772	0.503	0.477
2010	Men-headed households	mean	14632.5	16732.1	1122.2	3640.7	8996.0
		median	7799.8	11085.8	5.7	1713.3	3962.3
		CV	1.2	1.1	3.7	1.5	1.3
		Gini index	0.422	0.415	0.758	0.577	0.527
	Women-headed households	mean	10582.0	11767.0	904.8	3274.1	8147.8
		median	3048.0	4506.6	0.0	1332.8	5110.4
		CV	1.4	1.3	3.7	1.6	1.2
		Gini index	0.44	0.442	0.784	0.589	0.47
2012	Men-headed households	mean	14029.6	16164.2	1036.6	3430.0	8905.0
		median	6984.6	10295.4	0.0	1602.8	3873.0
		CV	1.2	1.1	3.5	1.5	1.3
		Gini index	0.428	0.421	0.772	0.582	0.526
	Women-headed households	mean	10333.9	11480.9	836.9	3086.0	8209.1
		median	2898.6	4382.4	0.0	1239.4	5029.8
		CV	1.4	1.3	3.8	1.5	1.2
		Gini index	0.444	0.445	0.793	0.592	0.467

Source: elaboration on EU-SILC 2007, 2010, 2012 cross sectional data

women-headed households compared to men-headed ones. The distribution of incomes for women-headed households is more unequal compared to men-headed ones for each source of income, with the only exception of State transfers. Finally, in terms of intertemporal dynamics, we register a decrease in the median and mean value of wage for both households counterbalancing the increase in 2007–2010 of the mean value of capital (without imputed rent) for both households.

If we look at the budget composition, men-headed households depend more on income from work compared to women households, which are surprisingly more dependent on capital incomes including in our definition both imputed rent and pensions from private

Table 3.6 Shares of income by household type (EU SILC, 2007, 2010, 2012)

			Share Wage	Share Labour income	Share Capital restricted	Share Capital	Share State transfer
2007	Men-headed households	mean	45.3%	53.0%	2.2%	13.6%	33.3%
		median	51.7%	67.6%	0.0%	11.7%	15.8%
		CV	0.86	0.72	2.88	0.97	1.08
	Women-headed households	mean	36.3%	40.6%	2.1%	15.9%	43.4%
		median	24.9%	37.9%	0.0%	13.0%	41.9%
		CV	1.05	0.96	3.01	0.99	0.85
2010	Men-headed households	mean	44.8%	51.6%	2.6%	12.6%	35.8%
		median	48.3%	64.3%	0.0%	9.1%	19.9%
		CV	0.89	0.76	2.97	1.15	1.03
	Women-headed households	mean	37.1%	41.2%	2.7%	14.7%	43.9%
		median	25.8%	37.5%	0.0%	10.1%	42.2%
		CV	1.05	0.97	3.18	1.15	0.85
2012	Men-headed households	mean	44.3%	51.4%	2.5%	12.5%	36.1%
		median	46.4%	64.7%	0.0%	8.9%	19.4%
		CV	0.90	0.77	3.15	1.18	1.04
	Women-headed households	mean	37.2%	41.3%	2.5%	14.3%	44.3%
		median	25.7%	37.0%	0.0%	9.6%	43.2%
		CV	1.05	0.97	3.32	1.17	0.86

Source: elaboration on EU-SILC 2007, 2010, 2012 cross sectional data.

plans. As expected, although women-headed households receive a lower amount of income from State compared to men headed households, their budget is composed by almost 40 per cent by transfers from State. Systematic differences arise between both typologies of households in terms of budget composition, mostly for wage, labour income and State transfers. Surprisingly the share of capital covers 2 per cent of income for both households with a higher dispersion for women headed households. Overall, households budget composition does not change very much over 2007–2012, namely crisis does not reshape households budget. From this point of view, given a household budget that is stable over time, we aim to investigate the typology of income and households more hit during the crisis. Hence, different patterns of household budget shares can be related to household characteristics in terms of occupation, education, age and civil status of the principal earner.

Tables A1 and A2 in the annex synthetize main features by source of income. As expected, elderly people, with an educational level lower than secondary school, mainly compose households receiving State transfers. Over 35 per cent are widowed. In this group we found both men- and women-headed households. "Capital-income" households are headed both by women and men, mainly professionals (over 20 per cent) both married or single. In this group we find a higher concentration of secondary and tertiary educational levels corresponding to the major proportion of managerial occupations (ISCO88COM 1, 2, 3). The "labour group" is the most heterogeneous both for education and professional levels. Compared to the "capital group", labour-income households are headed mostly by men. A

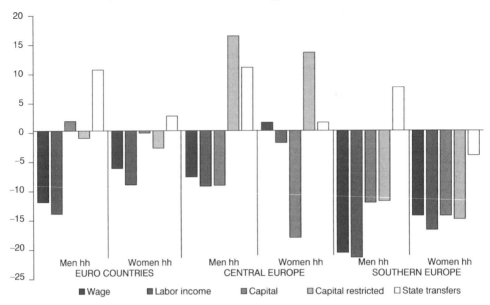

Figure 3.1 Changes in income by gender and geographical area (per cent, 2007–2012)

Note: Euro countries: BE, DE, EE, IE, GR, ES, FR, IT, CY, LU, NL, AT, PT, SI, SK, FI. Central Europe: DE, NL, AT, FI. Southern countries: IE, GR, ES, IT, PT.

more nuanced picture emerges from the analysis of household characteristics matched with the prevailing source of income. Still wage and labour income households are the most heterogeneous for education and professions, but they are more uniform in terms of gender. While both women and men headed households rely on capital and State transfers income, men headed households mostly depend on self-employment and wage.

Finally, we analyse changes in income by typology of households and geographical areas. The wage and labour incomes have been the most hit over 2007–2012, mostly in Southern Europe. Capital income keeps growing at least in terms of profits and rents for both women- and men-headed households in central Europe. Conversely, with the exception of State transfers for men-headed households, Southern Europe registers a decrease for all income sources. State transfers have increased mostly for men-headed households.

In terms of shares of income, we detect an overall stability of capital share, with the exception of Southern Europe where the share of capital has decreased on average at household level by 2 percentage points. Southern Europe registers the highest increase in State transfers share by almost 6 percentage points, while the wage share uniformly decreases by 3 percentage points across Europe. Overall, in terms of gender, men-headed households register major reduction in wage and labour share compared to women-headed households.

From the descriptive analysis above, we can conclude that major differences in terms of income exist between men-headed and women-headed households, namely the latter register on average a lower amount of wage, capital, labour income and State transfers over the entire period. These differences are evident over the entire period consolidating the income gap existing between households. However, in terms of dependence, women-headed households present lower shares of wages and labour suggesting a major dependence from State transfers than men headed households. In aggregate terms, both wage and capital distributions shifted over the period 2007–2012 suggesting a decrease in the average amount

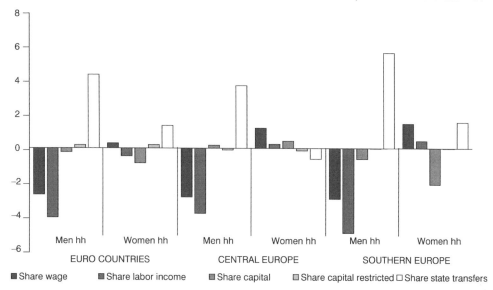

Figure 3.2 Changes in shares of income by gender and geographical area (2007–2012)

Note: Euro countries: BE, DE, EE, IE, GR, ES, FR, IT, CY, LU, NL, AT, PT, SI, SK, FI. Central Europe: DE, NL, AT, FI. Southern countries: IE, GR, ES, IT, PT.[17]

of capital and wage earned by households. The decrease in the mean and median wage (and labour income) is bigger than the capital one impacting mostly on men-headed households being more dependent on labour income that women ones.

Conclusions: a need to re-examine gender and the crisis?

We have computed percentage changes of average incomes for men-headed and women-headed households over the period 2007–2012, as well as for households' capital and labour incomes separately. To approximate the impact of economic recession and of austerity for 27 European countries we have computed the cumulative rate of change of GDP and a measure of fiscal consolidation (the average yearly rate of change of the General Government primary surplus/deficit).

As shown in Figure 3.3, the correlation between GDP growth (or recession) and households' incomes growth in the period considered is obviously positive. Furthermore, the relation is remarkably similar for MH and WH households, with a simple correlation of 0.5 for MH and 0.46 for WH (both statistically significant at the 5 per cent confidence level). No significant differences emerge between the relation of GDP growth and men-headed versus women-headed households' labour and capital incomes (for both WH and MH households, labour income only is significantly correlated to GDP growth). On the contrary, for both MH and WH households' labour incomes are significantly correlated with GDP growth (0.49 for MH and 0.44 for WH households), whereas capital incomes are not.

Austerity measures seem to be correlated in a similar way with the average incomes of men-headed and women-headed households. Similarly to the impact of GDP growth, marked differences arise, both for men and women, in their correlation with labour and capital incomes.[18] As shown in Figure 3.4, fiscal consolidation seems to exhibit a negative correlation with both average total incomes and average labour incomes of MH

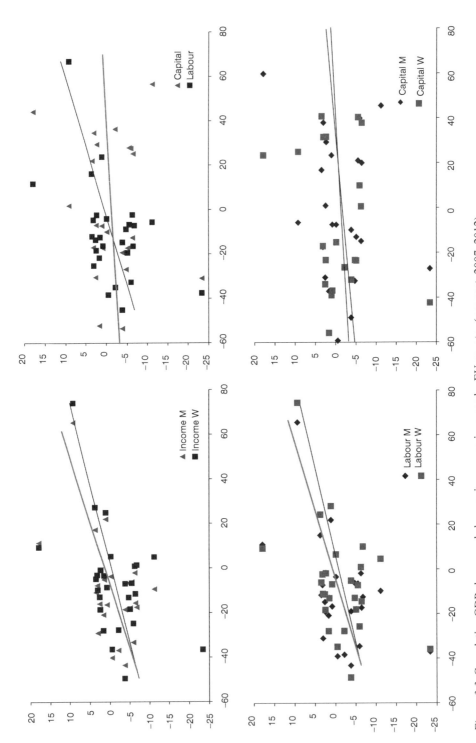

Figure 3.3 Cumulative GDP change and changes in average incomes by EU country (per cent, 2007–2012)

Source: elaboration on EU-SILC 2007, 2010, 2012 cross sectional data and European Commission, AMECO database.

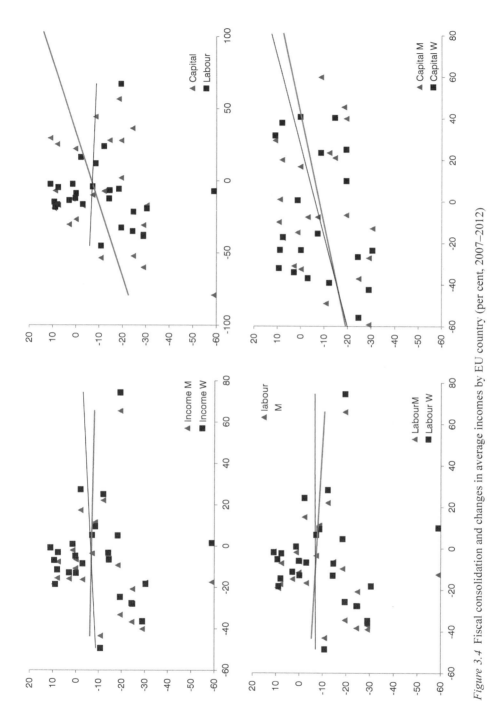

Figure 3.4 Fiscal consolidation and changes in average incomes by EU country (per cent, 2007–2012)

Note: fiscal consolidation is measured by the average yearly percentage change in the primary surplus (+) or deficit (–) of General Government.

and WH households. However, due to the high variability between countries, none of these correlations is statistically significant. By contrast, the only statistically significant correlation (with value 0.45) is that between fiscal consolidation and the capital incomes of women-headed households. For men-headed households, the international heterogeneity seems of a comparable size to WH households', but the estimated coefficient is smaller (0.29) and thus at the 95 per cent confidence level it cannot be excluded that the apparent negative correlation is not in fact nil. Evidently, given the significantly smaller mean and median values of women-headed households' capital incomes (and their higher variability) than men-headed households', it cannot be said that women stand to profit more (or loose less) from austerity than men. However, what can be said is that, especially as owners of capital assets, not all women are net losers in the period considered.

Notes

1 Croatia is not considered here because it only joined the EU in 2014.
2 Similarly for the USA, Grown and Tas (2010) show that in the case of the Great Recession a basic comparison of unemployment rates for men and women adopted in the "man-cession representation" of the crisis led to partial results and biased policy responses. By exploring a collection of different labour market indicators, job loss for women was over 10 times higher in the current recession than in the previous 1990–1991 and 2000–2001 recessions, compared to a 2.3 times higher job loss for men.
3 Public administration, education, health and social work activities are the NACE sectors proposed by Rubery (2013) as a proxy for the public sector.
4 Monetary values are expressed in euro and deflated with the Consumer Price Index (CPI) provided by Eurostat. All values are expressed in euros 2007.
5 Wage is given by the sum of individual income from dependent job ($py010g$).
6 Income from self-employment corresponds to variable $py050g$, which is defined as the income received, during the income reference period, by individuals, for themselves or in respect of their family members, as a result of their current or former involvement in self-employment jobs.
7 Income for capital is the sum of the following variables: $hy090g$, $hy030g$, $hy040g$, $py080g$. Income from capital includes also money from rent of properties and imputed rent being a sort of in-kind house advantage impacting on household well-being. Even if the inclusion of imputed rent produces effects of income re-ranking among households, it represents an indirect income from property. In our analysis, we consider the indirect income from housing property as a source of capital income in order to define the functional "positioning" of the household between capital and labour. For a detailed discussion on the effect of the inclusion of the imputed rent in the income distribution with EU SILC data, make reference to Maestri (2012). A potential re-ranking bias can emerge including income from imputed rent due to the diversity of estimation methods applied among countries.
8 State transfers is the sum of $py090g$, $py100g$, $py110g$, $py120g$, $py130g$, $py140g$, $hy060g$, $hy070g$, $hy080g$.
9 After computing the median absolute deviation (MAD), we drop those incomes greater or lower than five times the MAD, two times more than the rejection criterion suggested by Miller (1991).
10 Given to the high incidence of negative values for Denmark, about half of the sample, we eliminate Denmark from the analysis. However, as underlined by Verma et al. (2010), even if in Denmark half of capital income values are negative, this component accounts for around 20 per cent of total income of households, which is equivalent to the average value of capital share over EU countries. The large number of negative values in Denmark is in fact made up of numerous small amounts because register countries tend to record small values exhaustively, while in personal interviews only larger amounts are likely to be recorded (Verma et al., 2010, p. 62).
11 The original sample is composed by 651,210 households.
12 For a detailed discussion on the effect of the inclusion of the imputed rent in the income distribution with EU SILC data, make reference to Maestri (2012). A potential re-ranking bias can emerge including income from imputed rent due to the diversity of estimation methods applied among countries.

13 In Eurostat the gross household total income is defined as the sum for all household members of gross personal income components (gross employee cash or near cash income), gross non-cash employee income, employers' social insurance contributions, gross cash benefits or losses from self-employment (including royalties), value of goods produced for own consumption, pensions received from individual private plans, unemployment benefits, old-age benefits, survivor' benefits, sickness benefits, disability benefits and education-related allowances, income from rental of a property or land, family/children related allowances, social exclusion, housing allowances, regular inter-household cash transfers received, interests, dividends, profit from capital investments in unincorporated business, and imputed rent.

14 Only adults have been considered.

15 Zero income is referred to households with zero income for which the max income criterion cannot be applied. These households cannot be classified in terms of gender.

16 We can reject the null of equality of mean and median values for all incomes between men- and women-headed households at 5 per cent of significance level (T test analysis allowing for unequal variance). Results available upon request.

17 Iceland, Norway and 25 EU member states, excluding Croatia, Malta and Denmark due to the lack of adequate microdata in the EU-SILC dataset.

18 The results are not qualitatively different using alternative definitions of fiscal consolidation. The use here of the percentage change in primary surpluses, rather than e.g. the sum of primary surpluses/deficits expressed as a percentage of GDP, is aimed at capturing the impact of the policy change only, rather than the compound impact of fiscal policy and its impact on the size of the national economy. Further details are available from the authors upon request.

References

Adler, M. and Schmid, K.D. (2013) Factor shares and income inequality – evidence from Germany 2002–2008. *Journal of Applied Social Science Studies*, 2(133), 121–132.

Arpaia, A., Perez, E. and Pichelmann, K. (2009) *Understanding Labour Income Share Dynamics in Europe*. Economic Papers, 379, European Commission.

Atkinson, A.B. (2009) Factor shares: the principal problem of political economy? *Oxford Review of Economic Policy*, 25 (1), pp. 3–16.

Atkinson, A.B. and Brandolini, A. (2008) *On Analysing the World Distribution of Income*, Working Papers, 97, ECINEQ, Society for the Study of Economic Inequality.

Atkinson, A.B. and Brandolini, A. (2011) *On the Identification of the "Middle Class"*. Working Papers 217, ECINEQ, Society for the Study of Economic Inequality.

Bárcena-Martín, E. and Moro-Egido, A. I. (2013) Gender and poverty risk in Europe. *Feminist Economics*, 19 (2), pp. 69–99.

Bazillier, R. and Héricourt, J. (2014) *The Circular Relationship between Inequality, Leverage, and Financial Crises: Intertwined Mechanisms and Competing Evidence*. CEPII Working Paper, No. 2014-22, Paris.

Bettio, F., Corsi, M, D'Ippoliti, C., Lyberaki, A., Lodovici, M. S. and Verashchagina, A. (2012) *The Impact of the Economic Crisis on the Situation of Women and Men and on Gender Equality Policies*. European Commission, FGB – Fondazione Giacomo Brodolini, IRS – Istituto per la Ricerca Sociale, December 2012.

Checchi, D. and Garcia-Penalosa, C. (2010) Labour market institutions and the personal distribution of income in the OECD. *Economica 77* (307), 413–450.

Cho, Y. and Newhouse, D. (2013) How Did the Great Recession affect different types of workers? Evidence from 17 middle-income countries. *World Development*, 41, 31–50.

Glyn, A., (2009) Functional distribution and inequality. In: W. Salverda, B. N., Smeeding, T. M. (eds), *Oxford Handbook of Economic Inequality*. Oxford: Oxford University Press.

Green, J. and Lavery, S. (2014) *Britain's Post-Crisis Political Economy: A 'Recovery' through Regressive Redistribution*. SPERI Paper, No. 11, The University of Sheffield.

Grown, C. and Tas, E. (2010) *Gender Equality in the US Labor Markets in the Great Recession of 2007–2010*. Working Papers 2010–15, American University, Department of Economics.

Grubbs, F. (1969) Procedures for detecting outlying observations in samples. *Technometrics*, 11 (1), 1–21.

Mckay, A., Campbell, J., Thomson, E. and Ross, S. (2013) Economic recession and recovery in the UK: What's gender got to do with it?. *Feminist Economics*, 19 (3), 108–123.

Milkman, R. (1976) Women's Work and economic crisis: some lessons of the Great Depression. *Review of Radical Political Economics*, 8, (1), pp. 71–97.

Hampel, F. R. (1974) The influence curve and its role in robust estimation. *Journal of the American Statistical Association*, 69 (346), pp. 383–393.

Hein, E. (2012) *The Crisis of Finance-dominated Capitalism in the Euro Area: Deficiencies in the Economic Policy Architecture and Deflationary Stagnation Policies*. Economics Working Paper Archive wp_734, Levy Economics Institute.

Hein, E. (2013) The crisis of finance-dominated capitalism in the euro area, deficiencies in the economic policy architecture, and deflationary stagnation policies. *Journal of Post Keynesian Economics*, 36 (2), pp. 325–354.

Huber, P. J. (1981) *Robust Statistics*. New York: John Wiley.

ILO (2013) *Global Wage Report 2012/13: Wage and Equitable Growth*. Geneva: ILO.

Jenkins, S. P., Brandolini, A.,Micklewright, J. and Nolan, B. (2013) *The Great Recession and the Distribution of Household Income*. Oxford: Oxford University Press.

Karamessini, M. and Rubery, J. (2014a) The challenge of austerity for equality a consideration of eight European countries in the crisis. In A. Eydoux, A. Math. and H. Perivier. (eds.) *European Labour Markets in Times of Crisis. A Gender Perspective*. Debate and Policies 133, Revue de l'OFCE, http://www.ofce.sciences-po.fr/publications/revue.htm

Karamessini, M. and Rubery, J. (2014b) *Women and Austerity: The Economic Crisis and the Future for Gender Equality*. London: Routledge.

Leys, C., Klein, O., Bernard, P., and Licatet, L. (2013) Detecting outliers: Do not use standard deviation around the mean, use absolute deviation around the median. *Journal of Experimental Social Psychology*, http://dx.doi.org/10.1016/j.jesp.2013.03.013

McKay, A., Campbell, J., Thomson, E. and Ross, S. (2013) Economic recession and recovery in the UK: What's gender got to do with it? *Feminist Economics*, 19(3), 108–123.

Maestri, V. (2012) *Imputed Rent and Income Re-ranking. Evidence from EU-SILC Data*. GINI Discussion Papers 29, AIAS, Amsterdam Institute for Advanced Labour Studies.

Miller, J. (1991) Reaction time analysis with outlier exclusion: Bias varies with sample size. *The Quarterly Journal of Experimental Psychology*, 43 (4), 907–912.

OECD (2008) *Growing Unequal? Income Distribution and Poverty in OECD Countries*. Paris: OECD

OECD (2011) *Divided We Stand. Why Inequality Keeps Rising*. Paris: OECD.

Palley, T. (2013) Cambridge and neo-Kaleckian growth and distribution theory: comparison with an application to fiscal policy. *Review of Keynesian Economics*, 1(1), 79–104.

Périvier, H. (2014) *Men and Women during the Economic Crisis: Employment Trends in Eight European Countries*. Revue de l'OFCE/Debates and policies – 133.

Perry, M. J. (2010) The Great Mancession of 2008–2009. Paper presented at the Statement before the House Ways and Means Committee Subcommittee on Income Security and Family Support On Responsible Fatherhood Programs, American Enterprise Institute for Public Policy Research, June.

Rubery, J. (2013) Public sector adjustment and the threat to gender equality. In D. Vaughan-Whitehead (ed.) *Public Sector Shock*. Cheltenham: ILO and Edward Elgar.

Schlenker, E. and Schmid, K. (2015) Capital income shares and income inequality in 16 EU member countries, *Empirica*, 42(2), 241–268.

Sierminska, E. and Takhtamanova, E. (2011) Job flows, demographics, and the Great Recession. In H. Immervoll, A. Peichl and K.Tatsiramos (eds) *Who Loses in the Downturn? Economic Crisis, Employment and Income Distribution*, Bingley: Emerald Group Publishing.

Signorelli, M., Choudhry, M. and Marelli, E. (2012) The impact of financial crises on female labour. *European Journal of Development Research*, 24, 413–433.

Stefansky, W. (1972) Rejecting outliers in factorial designs. *Technometrics*, 14, 469–479.

Stockhammer, E. (2013) *Why Have Wage Shares Fallen? A Panel Analysis of the Determinants of Functional Income Distribution.* Conditions of Work and Employment Series No. 35. Geneva: International Labour Organization.

Summers, L. H. and Balls, E. (2015) *Report of the Commission on Inclusive Prosperity.* Washington, DC: Center for American Progress.

Thompson, D. (2009) It's not just a recession. It's a man-cession! *The Atlantic.* July 9.

Todorova, Z. (2009) *Money and Households in a Capitalist Economy.* Cheltenham: Edward Elgar.

Van der Hoeven, R. (2014) Profits without labour benefits: The impact of financial globalization on work. *The Broker* http://www.thebrokeronline.eu/Articles/Profits-without-labour-benefits

Verma, V., Betti, G., and Gagliardi, F. (2010) *An Assessment of Survey Errors in EU-SILC,* Eurostat. Methodologies and Working Papers, Luxembourg: Eurostat.

Villa, P. and Smith, M. (2012) *Gender Equality, Employment Policies and the Crisis in EU Member States.* EGGE Report for the European Commission, DG Employment, Social Affairs, and Equal Opportunities, Brussels.

Wall, H. (2009) The "man-cession" of 2008–2009: it's big, but it's not great. *The Regional Economist,* 18(4), 4–9.

Women Budget Group (2010) *The Impact on Women of the Coalition Spending Review.* www.wbg.org.uk/RRB_Reports_4_1653541019.pdf

Annex

Table 3.A1 Household characteristics by exclusive income source

	2007	2010	2012
Labour income			
Gender	69% (men headed) 31% (women headed)	64.68% (men headed) 35.32% (women headed)	64.66% (men headed) 35.34% (women headed)
Age	42	43	43
Education	No secondary (20.93%) Secondary (42.02%) Tertiary e (37.05%)	No secondary (15.81%) Secondary (41.29%) Tertiary (42.89%)	No secondary (13.94%) Secondary (42.06%) third level (44%)
Marital status	Married or consensual union (48.75%) Separated (2.34%) Divorced (9.73%) Widowed(1.45%) Never married (37.72%)	Married or consensual union (39.38%) Separated (2.35%) Divorced (11.98%) Widowed(1.52%) Never married (44.78%)	Married or consensual union (39.92%) Separated (2.54%) Divorced (11.74%) Widowed(1.5%) Never married (44.31%)
Occupation	Legislators, senior off. and managers (9.44%) Professionals(18.21%) Tech. and ass. professionals (17.61%) Clerks (10.35%) Workers and shop assistant (9.02%) Skilled agr. (2.67%) Craft w. (16.03%) Plant and machine operators (9.54%) Elementary occupations (7.13%)	Legislators, senior off. and managers (8.87%) Professionals(20.05%) Tech. and ass. professionals (21.62%) Clerks (10.98%) Workers and shop assistant (9.56%) Skilled agr. (2.19%) Craft w. (13.42%) Plant and machine operators (8.02%) Elementary occupations (5.29%)	Legislators, senior off. and managers (6.51%) Professionals(21.65%) Tech. and ass. professionals (23.34%) Clerks (7.35%) Workers and shop assistant (9.75%) Skilled agr. (2.77%) Craft w. (13.96%) Plant and machine operators (9.72%) Elementary occupations (4.95%)
Dual earners	44.4%	40.7%	42.5%
Capital			
Gender	36.21% (men headed) 63.79% (women headed)	44.27% (men headed) 55.73% (women headed)	52.95% (men headed) 47.05% (women headed)
Age	46	45	44
Education	No secondary (33.53%) Secondary (40.4%) Tertiary (26.07%)	No secondary (23.77%) Secondary (44.26%) Tertiary (31.96%)	No secondary (15.46%) Secondary (48.44%) Tertiary (36.11%)
Marital status	Married or consensual union (28.22%) Divorced (13.02%) Widowed (19.59%) Never married (39.16%)	Married or consensual union (36.04%) Divorced (27.04%) Separated (0.47%) Widowed (7.37%) Never married (29.08%)	Married or consensual union (36.46%) Divorced (17.5%) Separated (10.27%)- Never married (35.77%)

	2007	*2010*	*2012*
Occupation	Legislators, senior off. and managers (8.82%) Professionals (56.21%) Tech. and ass. professionals (5.71%) Clerks (8.71%) Workers and shop assistant (0.8%) Craft w. (1.5%) Plant and machine operators (18.24%)	Legislators, senior off. and managers (13.21%) Professionals (20.74%) Tech. and ass. professionals (18.53%) Clerks (7.02%) Workers and shop assistant (8.01%) Skilled agr. (1.68%) Craft w. (19.29%) Plant and machine operators (3.42%) Elementary occupations (8.12%)	Legislators, senior off. and managers (6.35%) Professionals (23.49%) Tech. and ass. professionals (17.65%) Clerks (16.49%) Workers and shop assistant (10.70%) Skilled agr. (2.5%) Craft w. (14.2%) Plant and machine operators (3.4%) Elementary occupations (5.22%)
Dual earners	0.5%	0.3%	0.8%

Capital restricted

	2007	*2010*	*2012*
Gender	62.03% (men headed) 37.97% (women headed)	47.47% (men headed) 52.53% (women headed)	56.8% (men headed) 43.2% (women headed)
Age	41	39	38
Education	No secondary (9.68%) Secondary (61.97%) Tertiary (28.36%)	No Secondary (4.55%) Secondary (56.56%) Tertiary (38.89%)	No secondary (4.60%) Secondary (54.56%) Tertiary (40.84%)
Marital status	Married or consensual union (0.51%) Separated (42.96%) Divorced (23.31%) Never married (33.22%)	Married or consensual union (25.56%) Divorced (36.51%) Never married (37.93%)	Married or consensual union (35.49%) Divorced (23.24%) Never married (41.27%)
Occupation	Legislators, senior off. and managers (48.39%) Tech. and ass. professionals (20.76%) Clerks (13.55%) Workers and shop assistant (0.46% Elementary occupations (16.84%)	Legislators, senior off. and managers (13.81%) Professionals (28.70%) Tech. and ass. professionals (26.84%) Clerks (8.07%) Workers and shop assistant (1.86%) Craft w. (15.64%) Elementary occupations (5.08%)	Legislators, senior off. and managers (2.81%) Professionals (31.58%) Tech. and ass. professionals (20.97%) Clerks (20.99%) Workers and shop assistant (7.90%) Skilled agr. (1.57%) Craft w. (12.83%) Plant and machine operators (0.67%) Elementary occupations (0.70%)
Dual earners	0.1%	0.9%	0.9%

(Continued)

Table 3.A1 Continued

	2007	2010	2012
State transfers			
Gender	51.86% (men headed)	53.73% (men headed)	54.45% (men headed)
	48.14% (women headed)	46.27% (women headed)	45.55% (women headed)
Age	69	70	70
education	No secondary (58.13%)	No secondary (49.29%)	No secondary (47.44%)
	Secondary (28.01%)	Secondary (31.56%)	Secondary (32.35%)
	Tertiary (13.86%)	Tertiary (19.20%)	Tertiary (20.21%)
Marital status	Married or consensual union (39.80%)	Married or consensual union (38.54%)	Married or consensual union (39.67%)
	Separated (1.68%)	Separated (1.71%)	Separated (1.78%)
	Divorced (8.37%)	Divorced (9.82%)	Divorced (9.95%)
	Widowed(38.74%)	Widowed(37.58%)	Widowed(36.7%)
	Never married (11.4%)	Never married (12.34%)	Never married (11.9%)
Occupation	Legislators, senior off. and managers (7.6%)	Legislators, senior off. and managers (8.95%)	Legislators, senior off. and managers (6.63%)
	Professionals (8.08%)	Professionals (11.18%)	Professionals (12.69%)
	Tech. and ass. professionals (10.15%)	Tech. and ass. professionals (13.6%)	Tech. and ass. professionals (16.93%)
	Clerks (10.27%)	Clerks (11.28%)	Clerks (7.53%)
	Workers and shop assistant (9.72%)	Workers and shop assistant (8.62%)	Workers and shop assistant (9.80%)
	Skilled agr. (8.34%)	Skilled agr. (6.24%)	Skilled agr. (7.07%)
	Craft w. (17.21%)	Craft w. (16.71%)	Craft w. (14.61%)
	Plant and machine operators (12.01%)	Plant and machine operators (10.48%)	Plant and machine operators (11.28%)
	Elementary occupations (16.63%)	Elementary occupations (12.94%)	Elementary occupations (13.45%)
Dual earners	29.5%	32.3%	33.0%

Source: elaboration on EU-SILC 2007, 2010, 2012 cross sectional data.

Table 3.A2 Households' characteristics by prevailing income source

	2007	2010	2012
Wage			
Gender	68.13% (men headed) 31.87% (women headed)	66.13% (men headed) 33.87% (women headed)	65.56% (men headed) 34.44% (women headed)
Age	41	42	42
Education	No secondary (18.94%) Secondary (44.92%) Tertiary (36.14%)	No secondary (17.67%) Secondary (45.1%) Tertiary (37.23%)	No secondary (15.46%) Secondary (45.7%) Tertiary (38.84%)
Marital status	Married or consensual union (52.43%) Separated (2%) Divorced (10.25%) Widowed(1.91%) Never married (33.41%)	Married or consensual union (47.45%) Separated (1.88%) Divorced (11.31%) Widowed(2.14%) Never married (37.22%)	Married or consensual union (46.62%) Separated (2.31%) Divorced (11.17%) Widowed(2.14%) Never married (37.76%)
Occupation	Legislators, senior off. and managers (6.29%) Professionals(15.74%) Tech. and ass. professionals (19.68%) Clerks (11.13%) Workers and shop assistant (9.70%) Skilled agr. (1.12%) Craft w. (16.84%) Plant and machine operators (11.12%) Elementary occupations (8.38%)	Legislators, senior off. and managers (6.62%) Professionals(15.69%) Tech. and ass. professionals (19.66%) Clerks (11.74%) Workers and shop assistant (10.89%) Skilled agr. (1.13%) Craft w. (15.35%) Plant and machine operators (10.84%) Elementary occupations (8.09%)	Legislators, senior off. and managers (5.18%) Professionals(18.13%) Tech. and ass. professionals (22.74%) Clerks (7.44%) Workers and shop assistant (9.73%) Skilled agr. (1%) Craft w. (15.62%) Plant and machine operators (12.46%) Elementary occupations (7.70%)
Dual earners	50.9%	50.5%	50.2%
Labour income			
Gender	68.92% (men headed) 31.08% (women headed)	66.8% (men headed) 33.2% (women headed)	66.43% (men headed) 33.57% (women headed)
Age	42	42	43
Education	No secondary (20.17%) Secondary (44.51%) Tertiary (35.32%)	No secondary (18.65%) Secondary (44.81%) Tertiary (36.55%)	No secondary (16.30%) Secondary (45.40%) Tertiary(38.20%)
Marital status	Married or consensual union (54.74%) Separated (2%) Divorced (9.43%) Widowed(1.99%) Never married (31.81%)	Married or consensual union (49.7%) Separated (1.9%) Divorced (10.6%) Widowed(2.20%) Never married (35.61%)	Married or consensual union (49.05%) Separated (2.26%) Divorced (10.54%) Widowed(2.14%) Never married (36.01%)

(Continued)

Table 3.A2 Continued

	2007	2010	2012
Occupation	Legislators, senior off. and managers (7.65%) Professionals(15.72%) Tech. and ass. professionals (18.7%) @@ Clerks (10%) Workers and Shop assistant (9.42%) Skilled agr. (2.92%)- Craft w. (17.31%) Plant and machine operators (10.35%) Elementary occupations (7.92%)	Legislators, senior off. and managers (8.04%) Professionals(15.88%) Tech. and ass. professionals (19.11%) Clerks (10.58%) Workers and Shop assistant (10.51%) Skilled agr. (2.34%)- Craft w. (16.03%) Plant and machine operators (10.02%) Elementary occupations (7.5%)	Legislators, senior off. and managers (5.57%) Professionals(17.93%) Tech. and ass. professionals (21.58%) Clerks (6.85%) Workers and Shop assistant (10.13%) Skilled agr. (2.97%)- Craft w. (16.3%) Plant and machine operators (11.6%) Elementary occupations (7.09%)
Dual earners	52.6%	52.3%	52.2%

Capital income

Gender	46.36% (men headed) 53.64% (women headed)	50.19% (men headed) 49.81% (women headed)	51.65% (men headed) 48.35% (women headed)
Age	56	55	56
Education	No secondary (42.67%) Secondary (34.68%) Tertiary (22.64%)	No secondary (38.9%) Secondary (35.31%) Tertiary (25.79%)	No secondary (35.11%) Secondar (37.62%) Tertiary (27.27%)
Marital status	Married or consensual union (30.47%) Separated (3.59% Divorced (10.95%) Widowed(29%) Never married (26%)	Married or consensual union (34.36%) Separated (2.99%) Divorced (11.72%) Widowed(22.77%) Never married (28.15%)	Married or consensual union (33.8%) Separated (3.38%) Divorced (13.35%) Widowed(22.4%) Never married (27.07%)
Occupation	Legislators, senior off. and managers (11.53%) Professionals(9.92%) Tech. and ass. professionals (12.12%) Clerks (11.26%) Workers and shop assistant (12.93%) Skilled agr. (5.96%) Craft w. (13.62%) Plant and machine operators (6.99%) Elementary occupations (15.67%)	Legislators, senior off. and managers (14.78%) Professionals(10.44%) Tech. and ass. professionals (13.88%) Clerks (9.44%) Workers and shop assistant (12.24%) Skilled agr. (7.65%) Craft w. (14.05%) Plant and machine operators (6.89%) Elementary occupations (10.68%)	Legislators, senior off. and managers (6.17%) Professionals(13.06%) Tech. and ass. professionals (14.64%) Clerks (8.09%) Workers and shop assistant (17.50%) Skilled agr. (8%) Craft w. (11.52%) Plant and machine operators (7.2%) Elementary occupations (13.81%)
Dual earners	16.6%	21.9%	20.8%

	2007	*2010*	*2012*
Capital income restricted			
Gender	58.43% (men headed) 41.57% (women headed)	53.85% (men headed) 46.15% (women headed)	54.64% (men headed) 45.36% (women headed)
Age	58	59	59
Education	No secondary (27.68%) Secondary (37.90%) Tertiary (34.42%)	No secondary (33.01%) Secondary (37.32%) Tertiary (29.67%)	No secondary (30.87%) Secondary (39.17%) Tertiary (29.96%)
Marital status	Married or consensual union (44.46%) Separated (2.63%) Divorced (9.22%) Widowed(21.65%) Never married (22.03%)	Married or consensual union (40.67%) Separated (1.35%) Divorced (12.39%) Widowed(24.77%) Never married (20.82%)	Married or consensual union (36.45%) Separated (1.56%) Divorced (13.07%) Widowed(26.25%) Never married (22.67%)
Occupation	Legislators, senior off. and managers (21.35%) Professionals(15.25%) Tech. and ass. professionals (14.16%) Clerks (11.73%) Workers and shop assistant (8.85%) Skilled agr. (6.36%) Craft w. (11.52%) Plant and machine operators (3.36%) Elementary occupations (7.42%)	Legislators, senior off. and managers (21.32%) Professionals(13.61%) Tech. and ass. professionals (16.01%) Clerks (8.99%) Workers and shop assistant (7.7%) Skilled agr. (10.2%) Craft w. (11.9%) Plant and machine operators (5.64%) Elementary occupations (4.62%)	Legislators, senior off. and managers (7.61%) Professionals(14.38%) Tech. and ass. professionals (17.49%) Clerks (10.11%) Workers and shop assistant (17.76%) Skilled agr. (10.13%) Craft w. (9.11%) Plant and machine operators (5.06%) Elementary occupations (8.33%)
Dual earners	22.1%	27.2%	23.7%
State transfers			
gender	54.99% (men headed) 45.01% (women headed)	55.15% (men headed) 44.85% (women headed)	54.97% (men headed) 45.03% (women headed)
Age	64	64	64
Education	No secondary (45.45%) Secondary (34.22%) Tertiary (20.33%)	No secondary (45.81%) Secondary (34.74%) Tertiary (19.45%)	No secondary (43.22%) Secondary (36.14%) Tertiary (20.64%)
Marital status	Married or consensual union (41.67%) Separated (1.75%) Divorced (10.8%) Widowed(28.96%) Never married (16.82%)	Married or consensual union (38%) Separated (1.92%) Divorced (12.01%) Widowed(29.77%) Never married (18.31%)	Married or consensual union (38.56%) Separated (1.98%) Divorced (12.45%) Widowed(29.16%) Never married (17.85%)

(Continued)

Table 3.A2 Continued

	2007	2010	2012
Occupation	Legislators, senior off. and managers (6.51%) Professionals(9.9%) Tech. and ass. professionals (13.42%) Clerks (11.41%) Workers and shop assistant (10.37%) Skilled agr. (6.88%) Craft w. (16.22%) Plant and machine operators (10.49%) Elementary occupations (14.8%)	Legislators, senior off. and managers (7.41%) Professionals(10.16%) Tech. and ass. professionals (13.33%) Clerks (11.12%) Workers and shop assistant (10.86%) Skilled agr. (5.63%) Craft w. (16.21%) Plant and machine operators (10.66%) Elementary occupations (14.61%)	Legislators, senior off. and managers (5.32%) Professionals(11.78%) Tech. and ass. professionals (16.28%) Clerks (7.47%) Workers and shop assistant (11.41%) Skilled agr. (6.30%) Craft w. (14.34%) Plant and machine operators (12.19%) Elementary occupations (14.91%)
Dual earners	34.7%	34.5%	34.4%

Source: elaboration on EU-SILC 2007, 2010, 2012 cross sectional data.

4 Economic inequality, political power and political decision-making

The case of the "middle-income trap"

Svenja Flechtner and Stephan Panther

This chapter discusses political and economic consequences of unequally distributed wealth, income and economic power for economic development in middle-income countries. In recent years, the "middle-income trap" has received increasing attention among economists. Some middle-income economies, many of which are Latin American, have not achieved the transition into high-income status for many years and are allegedly trapped in middle-income status. While most authors give technical advice to overcome this trap, we introduce a political economy perspective to the discussion. We argue that high inequality in the access to economic resources and political power will increase the likelihood of entering a middle-income trap, since under these conditions the position of narrow elites is incompatible with the institutional changes and policies needed to overcome middle-income status. We use comparative cases of two Latin American countries, the Dominican Republic and Brazil, in order to illustrate how the high concentration of economic power and ties of the business elite with political regimes has influenced policy choices.

Introduction

South Korea is a striking development success. One of the poorest countries in the world in the 1950s, it was assigned middle-income status for the first time in 1969 by the World Bank. In 1995, it was listed as a high-income country, remaining a middle-income country for no more than 26 years. Other countries, many of which are Latin American, have attained middle-income status decades and even centuries ago, but have either been unable to converge with high-income economies ever since or have taken a very long time for the process. Chile, recently hailed as a "Latin American tiger", became a middle-income country as early as 1891 (Felipe 2012), but was part of the World Bank's high-income group for the first time only in 2012, thus taking 121 years or almost 5 times as long as South Korea to traverse middle-income status.

The academic debate over the reasons for such differences in the ability of countries to leave behind middle-income status has intensified over the last years under the heading of the so-called "middle-income trap". The cases of success-stories like that of South Korea or Taiwan have been analysed in detail, and by and large the policy changes necessary to overcome middle-income status are by now fairly well understood and technical policy-advice on how to overcome middle-income status is increasingly abundant.

However, the question of why some countries were able and willing to implement favourable policies and why others were not able to do so has not been resolved. We argue that in order to understand the dynamics behind such divergent development processes, one

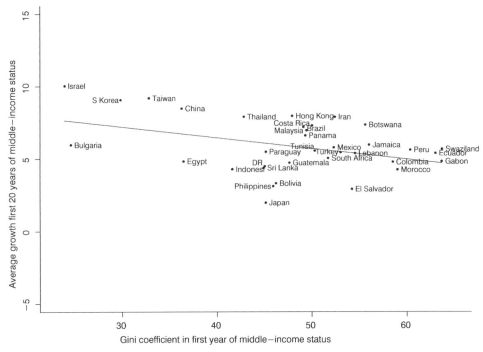

Figure 4.1 Gini coefficient in first year of middle-income status and 20-year average growth rate

Data source: UNU-WIDER (2014) and World Bank (2014c)

needs to adopt a political economy perspective. Our key argument is that the concurrence of multiple high inequalities – in terms of income distribution, ownership of productive assets and access to political power – leads to low institutional quality and prevents the adoption of favourable policies and the emergence of institutional structures which would be necessary for the transition into a high-skill, high-productivity economy.

Figure 4.1 shows the average growth rates of middle-income economies during the first 20 years after they attained middle-income status and the Gini coefficient at the year of entry. The entry years vary greatly, from 1882 (Uruguay) to 2002 (India).[1] For middle-income economies, the average growth rate during the first 20 years as middle-income country and the degree of inequality at transition is significantly correlated (Spearman correlation coefficient: 0.33). Countries with lower inequality at transition have higher average growth rates. This simple correlation does of course not take account of the different moments in time the transition to middle-income status occurred and the different technological and external economic and policy conditions which this entails, and can tell us nothing about causality. Still it is an interesting point of departure for our analysis.

We proceed as follows. The second section characterizes the middle-income trap and the policy advice to overcome or avoid it in a more systematic fashion. The next develops our theoretical argument on the political economy of the middle-income trap. In the following section, we confront this view with case study evidence from two Latin American countries, the Dominican Republic and Brazil, before the final section concludes.

The middle-income trap: A brief summary of the literature

In recent years, the contrasting growth experiences of Latin American and some East Asian economies have been discussed in development research under the heading of the "middle-income trap" (Griffith 2011; Felipe 2012; Agénor et al. 2012; Eichengreen et al. 2013; Woo 2012; Lin and Treichel 2012).[2] The concept refers to the problems or failure of middle-income countries to transition into a high-income economy. While many countries have achieved growth from a low-income to a middle-income economy since the 1950s, very few have reached high-income status (Agénor and Canuto 2012).

There is a fair amount of consensus that the step from low-income to middle-income is comparatively easy as countries undergo Lewis-type structural changes, shifting labour from low-productivity sectors like traditional agriculture and informal services to sectors with higher productivity, benefiting from imported technologies. This is regularly accompanied by specializing in low-cost, low-skill activities. When these productivity gains are exhausted, countries face the challenge to further increase their per capita income – and this means: wages – without losing competitiveness.

On a first level, it is fairly straightforward to name the changes necessary in order that countries can overcome a middle-income trap or avoid falling into it in the first place. By analysing both successes and failures to leave middle-income status, the literature emphasizing structural change has reached consensus that the key for a successful transition to high income status is the diversification of economic activity and its development toward high-quality activities, where much more of the product "design", be it technological or in other areas (like marketing and branding), is undertaken inside the country, by country nationals and by firms owned by country nationals. Thus innovation and investment, especially into education, are essential to create further productivity growth and fuel the increased wage level (Griffith 2011, Paus 2011, Ohno 2009, Agénor et al. 2012). Policies discussed to support this include investment in high quality infrastructure (Agénor et al. 2012) and R&D (Lin and Treichel 2012),as well as improvements regarding the efficiency and rationality of policy formation and implementation (Ohno 2009).

Put very generally, it is necessary on the one hand to mobilize creative talent through education. On the other hand, it is decisive to give talent the right incentives so that it is used to assimilate best-practice technologies and organizational routines, adapt and apply them to local tasks and create cutting edge innovations in technology, management, design, marketing, etc. (Agénor et al. 2012, Rodrik 2013). While the details of doing so will depend on the local circumstances, a few elements of how these two tasks may be achieved are undisputed. In education, this includes a clear shift from quantity to quality. Yes, higher enrolment rates in secondary and tertiary education will be necessary, but what is more important, education on all levels should be of a high quality, building up cognitive and social skills for mastering cutting edge science and unleashing creativity. In order to get there, it may be necessary to change the training of the teaching profession accordingly, to work on the prestige of school teachers, to raise their pay, to improve the teaching materials, etc. Such an argument has been modelled recently by (Cantoni and Yuchtman 2013).[3] Such policies will be able to "harvest" the larger an amount of excellent talent, the more comprehensive they will be socially. Discriminating access to high quality education along lines of gender, ethnicity or social class will inevitably reduce the pool of talent a country can draw upon.

When it comes to the incentives necessary to transform educated talent into the mastering of cutting edge technologies and the creation of innovation, it is essential that doing exactly that is the way to richness and prestige in a society. Put differently, creation of wealth must be rewarded, and gaining wealth by taking it from others must be made as difficult as possible. Robinson and Torvik (2011) provide a general model on this; Acemoglu (1995) is a classic. There is no clear consensus among economists about the extent to which market forces on their own or assisted by a deliberate technology policy are required to do the job. In any case, the task for countries aspiring to attain high-income status can be described as constructing their own national innovation systems (Paus 2014; Vivarelli 2014). It is clear what is not beneficial for talent to be rewarded: ample opportunities to accumulate riches by either grand or petty corruption, by using public funds or political power for private enrichment or by any other kind of rent seeking.

While the discussion on the middle-income trap is relatively new, the policies described in the previous paragraphs have been discussed for a considerable time. Policy advice for Latin American countries today repeats many aspects that have been central in policy advice from the 1950s already. Moreover, some governments had applied them before they were discussed and recognized in academia. What prevented other governments to try and find their own successful policy mix using the experience of others and policy advice?

A political economy perspective

Underlying approaches

Acemoglu (2006), Acemoglu and Robinson's (2012; 2008; 2006; AR henceforth) and Acemoglu et al. 2005 political economy framework is the starting point for our analysis of middle-income economies from a political economy perspective. In their 2005 chapter in the *Handbook of Economic Growth* with Simon Johnson, AR summarize their general approach using the diagram in Figure 4.2.

By making the economic performance at any point in time depend on the institutions regulating the economic sphere, AR reaffirm the prevailing institutionalist orthodoxy which has been established over the last two decades. By emphasizing their distributional preconditions and consequences, they transform it into a political economy: Any economic outcome implies a certain distribution of income and wealth. The distribution of material resources, in turn, is a key determinant of the distribution of political power in a society. The second key determinant of this "de facto political power" is the ability of a group to overcome the collective action problem. While the latter ability is a kind of shift parameter for their analysis, the distribution of resources is a cornerstone. AR recognize the – partial – autonomy of the political sphere, the sphere of collective decision-making about the rules of the game. Hence, political power is determined also by constitutional rules – "political institutions" in the AR parlance – resulting in "de iure political power".

Actors use their de iure and de facto political power to influence decisions about economic institutions and about the rules of future rule-making – that is, political institutions. In AR

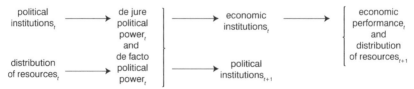

Figure 4.2 AR's political economy of development approach

Source: Acemoglu et al. (2005)

(2008), the authors propose a model that studies how political institutions and the de facto practice can diverge: when a democracy is "captured", political institutions are changed, but actors invest resources in de facto political power. The model explores interactions of the de iure and de facto levels and concludes that changes at the institutional level do not necessarily change behaviour, if not accompanied by a change in the distribution of de facto political power.

Given the recursive dynamic nature of the system, it will gravitate towards certain more or less stable configurations of the component factors. As a first approximation, AR describe two such configurations, which they name inclusive and extractive institutions, respectively. Inclusive economic institutions are those that feature "secure private property, an unbiased system of law, and a provision of public services that provides a level playing field in which people can exchange and contract; it also must permit the entry of new businesses and allow people to choose their careers" (AR 2012, p. 74–75). Inclusive political institutions are both "sufficiently" pluralistic and centralized, where pluralism is defined as a relatively broad diffusion of political power combined with considerable constraints on the use of that power, and centralization is defined as monopoly of the legitimate use of violence. Extractive institutions, both economic and political, are characterized by the absence of the characteristics of inclusive institutions. AR call them extractive "because such institutions are designed to extract incomes and wealth from one subset of society to benefit a different subset" (AR, p. 76). Inclusive institutions will generate and will be supported by a relatively equal distribution of income and wealth and high average income, while exclusive institutions will be associated with highly unequal distributions of income and wealth and low average income.

Key to the inefficient low-level equilibrium in the AR framework is what they call the non-existence of a political Coase theorem[4] (Acemoglu 2003): certain technological or economic changes leading to an increased national income may threaten the economic or political position (or both) of the dominant group, which then has the choice between having a large share of a small pie or a smaller share of a larger pie – and may well go for the former. In other words: a systematically unequal distribution of political and economic resources may be a stumbling block for economic growth.

Samuel Bowles (2012) comes to similar conclusions. Discussing the benefits of egalitarian societies for economic performance, he argues that high inequality is bad for productivity because it dilutes incentives, discourages trust, and diverts resources from productive uses to the enforcement of the rules of the game. Inequality is an "impediment to economic performance when it precludes the implementation of productivity-enhancing governance structures" (Bowles 2012, p. 6). Moreover, unproductive governance structures reproduce inequality (see Figure 4.3) and may endure, despite their being unbeneficial or even undesired, "because they are favoured by powerful groups for whom they secure a large slice of a given pie, not because the structures foster the growth of the pie itself" (p. 5).

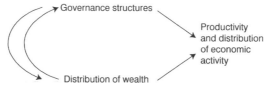

Figure 4.3 Governance structure, wealth inequality, productivity, and inequality of opportunity
Source: Bowles (2012), p. 5

AR's and Bowles' approaches to institutional lock-in situations where institutions favour the interests of a ruling elite in unequal societies are both compatible and convincing. Note also that in both cases we have multiple feedback loops opening up the possibility of multiple equilibrium and extensive covariation of the different features involved.

This is also the case in a third general approach underlying our argument, Besley and Persson (2011, BP from now on). Indeed, the covariation of different forms of political violence, weak state institutions and low incomes per capita motivates this research. More specifically, the monograph of BP develops a family of models centring on the explanation of two forms of institutional variables and two forms of political violence which are seen to be central for the explanation of income per capita. The institutional variables are the ability of the state to mobilize resources, "fiscal capacity".[5] Political violence may be one-sided in the form of repression by the state or two-sided in the form of civil unrest or even civil war. Both co-vary negatively with the two institutional measures of state capacity and income per capita. As stated above, one key result of BP is the explanation of this co-variation of all of these factors in a model of self-interested political actors.

Among the different exogenous factors determining the equilibria of this co-varying system – resource dependence, development aid, cohesiveness of political institutions and common vs. redistributive interests – the latter two help our analysis in this chapter. Fundamentally, "cohesiveness of political institutions" expresses the idea that the power of any political incumbent to redistribute resources from one group to another is constitutionally limited. This adds a characteristic to de-iure power which does not feature explicitly in AR, i.e. the ability to commit to restrict state power. Indeed, North, Wallis and Weingast (2012) have made this feature a cornerstone of their approach. Relevant for our analysis below, they interpret this as the ability of elite coalitions to commit to binding agreements among themselves.

The other exogenous factor in the BP approach, common vs. redistributive interests, reinforces rather than complements the insights by AR and Bowles. BP model this factor as the common interest in the provision of public goods by those groups of society which may conceivably become political incumbents. If these groups value the same public goods highly, investments in state capacity will be likely, if they value them differently or not at all, redistributive motivations dominate government action. BP do not consider rich and poor sections of society valuing public goods differently in a systematic fashion in their analysis.[6] They do, however, explicitly analyse the effect of income inequality on investment in fiscal capacity, which turns out to be negative: bearing a larger share of the costs of the establishment of state capacity and facing the risk of adverse redistributive results, rich incumbents do not invest into fiscal capacity of the state and do not use existing fiscal capacity fully.[7]

A political economy explanation of the middle-income trap

The institutional level

To create a political economy of the middle-income trap against this theoretical background, let us first look at the institutional requirements specific to the policies needed to overcome or avoid the middle-income trap. First, providing high-quality education to as large as possible a section of the population will always require a highly capable bureaucracy. This is obvious in the case of public provision of education, where the state controls both the rules of the educational system and also trains and staffs it. However, regulating a system where part of the provision of education is private in order to achieve high-quality education in all parts of the system is certainly not less challenging, if anything it is more.

The establishment of the right incentives and opportunities for technological and market innovation, the "liberal component" of a successful national innovation system – free entry into markets, which are kept as competitive as possible – certainly is not harmed by a capable and well-financed bureaucracy. Nevertheless, the focus here is on the ability of a state apparatus to institutionally commit to respect private property rights and refrain from idiosyncratically protecting political supporters from the forces of competition. Recall, however, that according to BP, investment in market supporting regulation and fiscal capacity will be complementary in any case.

When it comes to the more activist elements of an innovation policy – the establishment of technical universities, the financing of strategically important basic research, the subsidization of technologies at an early stage, the provision of key infrastructures, etc. – the picture is very similar to the one sketched when discussing education. Institutionally, a state capable to finance the necessary expenditure and to direct these finances effectively using a capable bureaucracy is the base of the necessary policies.

Overall, a fiscally potent and bureaucratically and legally capable state which is able to institutionally commit to self-restraint is the institutional base for avoiding or overcoming a middle-income trap. This is certainly compatible with the concept of inclusive institutions as described by AR, and very much so with the concept of "state capacity" in BP (2011). Legal capability is incompatible with extractive institutions almost by definition. As to the determinants of a capable, "Weberian" bureaucracy, it is obvious that this needs meritocratic recruitment procedures. However, increasing the meritocratic element in the staffing of government bureaucracies in order to provide the complementary public goods needed by a thriving private sector reduces the basis of power of a clientelistic regime. The incentives to install a clientelistic regime in the first place are particularly strong in high-inequality countries[8] (Robinson and Verdier (2013). Finally, as stated above, BP (2011) find that increased inequality of income and wealth will reduce the likelihood of a fiscally and legally capable state. Overall, there are good arguments to conjecture that the institutional prerequisites of the policies needed to avoid or overcome a middle-income trap are less likely to exist in countries with high economic inequality.

The policy level

Leaving the institutional level and turning to the policies, there are additional lines of arguments strongly suggesting that the policies discussed above have a large potential to undermine a regime based on the concentration of political and economic power in the hands of a narrow elite. Broad-based education has historically been regularly associated with the demand for greater participation in political decision-making, and this is likely to be true for broad-based quality education with a vengeance (Glaeser et al. 2007, Campante and Chor 2012). More equitable access to educational opportunities increases the competition over, and, therefore, reduces scarcity rents from, whatever income opportunities education might lead to, to the disadvantage of those with formerly privileged access to education. In other words, extending quality education to the poor is exactly that kind of public expenditure which is of little (immediate) benefit to the dominating wealthy elites, while being highly beneficial to disadvantaged sections of society: A constellation leading to decreased investment in state capacity according to BP (2011).

Some of the complementary infrastructure needed in an innovative economy may furthermore threaten the power of the privileged directly. Improved transport may threaten the hold of local monopolies on the local labour market, improved information may do so too, and the role of the internet in recent revolutionary uprisings has been documented by a lot of anecdotal evidence. Moreover, one obvious way to finance the necessary expenditures on education and research, namely the reduction of tax privileges for the well-to-do, closes the doors to redistribution from the poor to the rich.

Finally, the very nature of a dynamic high-income economy itself, with its permanent threats to any established income and social position due to rapid technological and social change, might be perceived as a threat by those benefiting from a narrowly based regime (North et al. 2012). Overall there are good reasons to believe that also the policies necessary to achieve high-income status are high-risk steps for any elite based on excluding others from the access to wealth and political power. By their very nature they will tend to level the economic playing field and lead to increased demands for political participation.

On rationality and perfect foresight

AR (2012) give wonderful anecdotal evidence of European monarchs consciously acting on an understanding of their situation akin to the picture described so far, consciously trying to stop growth-generating policies due to the threat they would pose to their power. However, we do not claim conscious decisions of elite members are the usual channel through which the regularities conjectured above are created. In a complex system, it is likely that actors do not realize how they contribute to system logics. Thus, elites may desire economic modernization and embark on the road to it, only to be confronted with the challenges to their power during the process. This then may lead to increased political instability or outright social unrest and repression, to coups and civil wars, thus decreasing investment in state capacity and income, as explained in the BP framework. Thus, the middle-income trap is not unlikely to be associated with political violence in one form or another.

Second, institutional equilibria may be complementary in the sense of Aoki (2007): agents do not consciously coordinate their choices and expected payoffs across domains, but consider institutions in other domains (taken as given) and make choices in other domains under consideration of them, and vice versa. This way, interdependent and mutually reinforcing institutions may arise. Schneider (2009a, 2009b) and Schneider and Soskice (2009) have argued forcefully that this is indeed responsible for the mediocre performance of Latin American economies over time.

An illustration with the Dominican and the Brazilian case

This section briefly discusses and compares two country cases. According to Felipe (2012), both countries are in the middle-income trap: Brazil attained middle-income status in 1957 and the Dominican Republic in 1972. Before proceeding to the comparison and discussing how economic distribution and political power are related with economic and political decision-making and policies in both countries, helping to perpetuate their middle-income status, the next paragraph lays out commonalities and differences between both countries and motivate our choice.

Brazil and the Dominican Republic: differences and commonalities of two middle-income countries

In 2014, the World Bank issued a development report about the Dominican Republic (DR) titled *When prosperity is not shared*, criticizing low economic mobility and non-inclusive

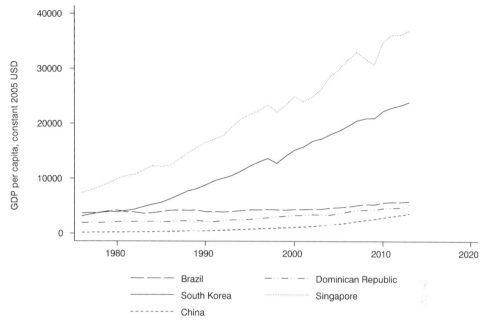

Figure 4.4 GDP per capita in five countries, 1976–2013

Data source: World Bank (2014d)

growth and revealing serious issues with equity and equal access to opportunities, despite high economic growth rates (World Bank 2014a). Brazil, a country with traditionally extremely high levels of inequality has caught attention for its considerable reduction of inequality during the 2000s (Lustig et al. 2013) but still figures among the most unequal countries of the world. Thus, both countries seem to be good candidates for a middle-income trap explained by the factors we emphasize.

This is confirmed by a look at Figure 4.4. In terms of GDP per capita, both countries still have a long way ahead when compared with middle-income success stories like South Korea or Singapore. Starting at roughly comparable levels in the 1970s, South Korea and Singapore's GDP per capita growth exceeded that of the Latin American countries many times. China is still below in terms of levels, but shows a more rapid upwards tendency.

However, looking at the growth story somewhat more closely, neither Brazil nor the DR rank high on the list of development "problem children". Figure 4.5 witnesses that their growth rates have been above regional and world averages more often than not during the last 15 years. After an internal crisis in 2004, the DR experienced very high rates until the global economic crisis of 2008, recovering more rapidly than Latin America and the world economy thereafter. Brazil has not seen such extreme rates, but has been above average for nearly 10 years now. In addition, Brazil has risen as a new, global power (Dauvergne and Farias 2012).

Looking somewhat closer again resolves the apparent puzzle. We have characterized countries in the middle-income trap not only by their GDP per capita, but as well, and more importantly, by their productive structures. In terms of total factor productivity (TFP), both countries perform relatively well in regional comparison, but lag behind the successful Asian countries (see Figure 4.6) again. Moreover TFP has decreased in the Dominican Republic over the course of the decades and only improved slightly in Brazil. Thus, growth in both countries seems to have been extensive, driven by

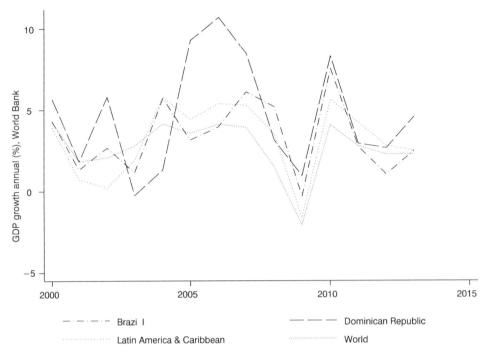

Figure 4.5 GDP growth rates in four countries, 2000–2013

Data source: World Bank (2014c)

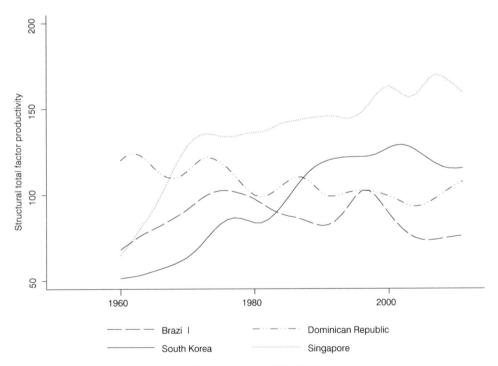

Figure 4.6 Total factor productivity in four countries, 1960–2013

Data source: Fernández-Arias (2014a)

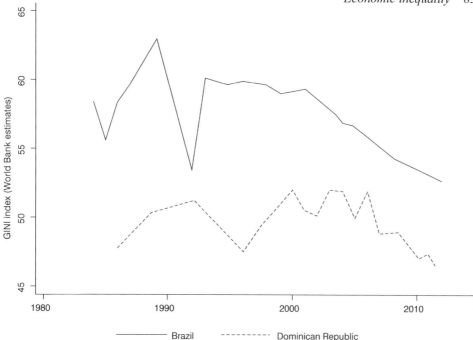

Figure 4.7 Gini coefficients in Brazil and the Dominican Republic, 1984–2012
Data source: World Bank (2014b)

factor accumulation, not least the strong population growth, and not by an increase in technical capabilities.

Looking at technological capabilities of both countries goes into the same direction. According to Hausman et al. (2011), Brazil is the fourth most diversified economy in Latin America (after Mexico, Panama and Costa Rica) and has diversified its production significantly since the 1960s. Nevertheless, Brazil's exports rely heavily on mineral products (24 per cent in 2013) as well as vegetable products (17 per cent) and foodstuffs (14 per cent). More sophisticated products like cars and transportation goods including platforms and even aircrafts (12 per cent) play a role as well.

The DR's most important export products in 2013 were gold and precious minerals (around 20 per cent), textiles such as t-shirts (around 8 per cent), cigars (7 per cent), bananas and plantains (6 per cent), electrical apparatus (6 per cent) and medical instruments (5 per cent). While the share of textiles has decreased considerably from over 50 per cent in the 1990s, it has been replaced by products which are equally not very demanding in terms of human capital or technical abilities. Earlier than other countries in the region, the Dominican Republic tried to get away from its comparative advantage in primary products, and the first Free Trade Zone (FTZ) was created in 1969. Although dependency on primary exports (sugar, coffee, bananas) was ended in the 1990s, new dependencies on the *maquila* sector (39 per cent of total exports in 2002, Sánchez-Ancochea 2004) and on tourism (50 per cent of exports in 2005, Dominican Central Bank 2014) emerged. The export manufacturing industry accounts for higher shares of total exports than in other Central American countries, including Mexico (Padilla et al. 2008).

Overall, at a first level of concreteness, both economies tend to confirm the predicted correlation between high inequality and the inability to upgrade technologically sufficiently. Let us look at the underlying political economy more closely.

Maximizing the cake or maximizing one's piece of the cake?

This section discusses how the distribution of economic power and interests has possibly shaped policy-making in both countries from a general perspective. We inquire how the general goals of economic policies have been influenced, before looking into a more concrete policy field – education – in the next section.

Legacies from the early 20th century

Brazil's history of economic development is particular in some regards because Brazil belongs to those Latin American countries with early experiences of populism: Getúlio Vargas, Brazilian president from 1930–1945 and from 1950–1954, is counted among the "classical populists" (Cardoso and Helwege 1992). Populism is usually associated with redistribution and thus establishes a crucial break with usual elitist policies. Populism in general and in Latin America and Brazil in particular is subject of intense discussion, and we do not aim to romanticize in any regard. Still, we think that Getúlio Vargas' *Estado Novo* regime provoked a series of long-lasting effects in the Brazilian economy. He incorporated the Brazilian *povo* (the working class) into the political system as political agents for the first time in Brazilian history. In addition to the political integration of non-elites, classical populists endorsed industrialization as a means of developing the country's economy.

Of course Brazil was a highly unequal society, too, with large parts of the population living under poor conditions.[9] But workers were at least able to benefit from Getúlio Vargas' populist policies: according to Giambiagi et al. (2011), his policies aimed at contenting large parts of the population without, however, tackling real structural reforms.[10] The government played a strong role in the economy, for instance through public enterprises: the Brazilian Development Bank (BNDE, today BNDES) as well as Petrobras were created under Vargas' presidency (Cardoso and Helwege 1992; Giambiagi et al. 2011). These policies, despite of being 'leftist' did not chase industrialists or exporters thanks to public subsidies, investment and industry protection. As long as ISI policies worked, distributional conflicts were attenuated because the interests of more than one interest group were blended (Cardoso and Helwege 1992). This might reflect a somewhat specific Brazilian path: 'leftist' policies were not as radical as to be against capitalist reform or integration into world markets, for instance. Overall, Brazilian policy in 1950s and 1960s can be interpreted as an attempt to grow nationally without fundamentally changing the underlying social imbalances.

Likewise in the DR, economic policy since the second half of the 20th century aimed at domestic capital accumulation and the creation of new investment opportunities in new sectors. This began during Trujillo's dictatorship, which had created large inequalities, notably between cities and rural areas/agricultural production, through the concentration of capital in the inner circle of the regime, a strong urban bias, repression of labour and weak institutionalization of bureaucracy and administration (Sánchez-Ancochea 2004). However there were some differences compared to Brazil. The Dominican economic system under Trujillo was highly concentrated and remains to be so until today. Trujillo himself and his family were the leading political and economic force, with only few co-existing industrialists (Hoetink 1982). He controlled 80 per cent of industrial production in 1961 and employed 45 per cent of the labour force through his firms and 15 per cent through the state (Moya Pons 2010). If at all, business organizations were a weak political actor. If Trujillo pushed and achieved significant industrial production, he did so in exploitive, capital-accumulating ways without redistribution or participation in income generation of the working class. In contrast to Brazil, the DR did not pursue corporatist policies and aimed at the demobilization of the business organizations as political actor (Espinal 1998).

Political regimes after the big figures

After Vargas, industrialization remained a topic on the political agenda. According to Cardoso and Helwege (1992), Vargas' policy and notably the concentration on the Brazilian industry would influence Brazil for decades. In other words, the agreed-upon Brazilian development strategy was increasing the size of the economy, and not to increase one's share of the cake. This was, again, part of the public discourse: in this presidential campaign (1956), Juscelino Kubitschek emphasized the structural change from a rural to an urbanized and industrialized society the country was running through and the active role of the state in this process, which was necessary for a large economy's development (Giambiagi et al 2011). Later on, the military regime kept the overall goal of increasing the economy's scope and size. For all the ruling groups since the 1930s, the means of increasing welfare and wealth, be it for a narrow or a broader group, was economic growth and industrialization. Time horizons were reasonably long as to have a rational interest in this higher-level goal.

In 1956, Kubitschek created a development program focussing on industrial development. It comprised expenses of 5 per cent of the GDP (1957–1961) and was directed to investment in energy and transport (about 70 per cent), basic industries (around 20 per cent) and nutrition and education (6 per cent). Although education was not key in this programme, it needs to be read against the context of the times: human capital was not yet emphasized when it came to industrial policy and development. Nevertheless, illiteracy was decreased as a side-effect of these measures (Giambiagi et al. 2011). Redistributional effects of these policies were aimed at urban labour groups and middle classes, but not the poorest. Social security programmes and state universities did not tackle poverty. The most neglected group at that time was represented by the rural poor (Cardoso and Helwege 1992). This would perhaps have changed with a measure proposed by Celso Furtado in his function as Minister for Planning in 1962–1963. Having identified the domestic market as prerequisite for industrialization, Furtado wanted to increase domestic purchasing power by means of redistributional policies and, notably, a land reform (Giambiagi et al. 2011). Agrarian reforms, of course, are a truly equity-creating policy measure that require broad acceptance in the face of costs for the privileged groups. In Brazil, (prospects of) land expropriations and occupations went beyond the acceptable realm for conservative and wealthy groups and led to political radicalization. On 31 March, a *golpe civico-militar* substituted João Goulart as president. This event shows that while a certain extent of redistributive policies was acceptable and in the own interest of the better-off groups society – industrialization needed workers and consumers – but there were limits as well.

The subsequent military regime's economic policy reflected conservative interests more openly. While the promotion of industrialization as a general policy goal was not put into question, concrete policies were generally more profit-oriented and less wage-oriented (Giambiagi et al. 2011). For instance, a tax reform was carried out which increased tax revenue, but in a regressive fashion, since most taxes were indirect. However, the military government seems to have been aware of potential pressure for redistribution: despite restrictive wage policies, for instance, wages were increased as much as to compensate for inflation, in order to avoid distributional conflicts. Overall it can be interpreted as an attempt to maintain the earlier growth model, while repressing demands for more fundamental changes in underlying inequalities.

The economic miracle certainly made political decision-making relatively easy. The growth model led to increased external dependence and structural changes were necessary. Geisel (1974–1978) reacted with a *II Plan de Desenvolvimento Nacional* (PND) in order to maintain economic growth. Here, again, increasing national income remained the primordial goal. In the first place, public investment was able to maintain growth rates, albeit with increasing inflationary pressure. Figueireido, Geisel's successor, finally started to employ restrictive monetary policies at the beginning of the 1980s. At the end of 1982, Brazil signed the first accord with the IMF, which certainly reinforced this tendency, but first steps had been made beforehand.

In the DR, the polarization of the economy during the era of Trujillo changed less than one may have expected, as the business class became an increasingly organized actor and a few dominant families were able to divide Trujillo's legacy among them. Since then, family-owned conglomerates are a dominant political actor with strong de facto power with significant and long-lasting impacts on economic policy during the decades to come (Alemán 2012; Hoetink 1982). In 1962, the Industrialists's Association of the Dominican Republic came into existence and became a strong political actor promoting the interests of the capital's industrialist elite (Espinal 1998). Family heads of the oligarchic elite were closely connected with government organs, for instance as advisers or through family members who served there (Rosario 1988). The economy was strongly dualist with a very large and poor working and peasant class and a very small and very rich upper class (Moya Pons 2010).

One major attempt to overcome these structures in 1962 remained unsuccessful. Juan Bosch and allies had ideas opposed to this industrial establishment and expressed themselves in favour of social spending and redistributive policies (Sánchez-Ancochea 2004, Espinal 1998). However, Bosch's elected presidency was overthrown, mainly because worker movements and social reforms went strongly against the interests of the newly emerging, post-Trujillo business elite. This happened in spite of non-radical procedures, e.g. the inclusion of *trujillistas* in the government or the postponement of a land reform. Still, in 1963, the business elite grouped with the Catholic church and other conservative forces and organized a coup against Bosch. The role of the US intervention, in fear of communist powers, was also influential in this conflict (Sánchez-Ancochea 2004, Sánchez 1992).

Balaguer's subsequent government (1966–1978) was a "golden age for business" (Espinal 1998, p. 104). The government intensified its close ties with large, family-owned conglomerations that concentrated large fractions of economic power across sectors in few hands and who became a major political force and dominant interest group (Sánchez-Ancochea 2004). Authoritarianism and clientelism were important pillars of this system (Espinal 1998). According to Sánchez-Ancochea (2004), this domination accounts for a development model that aims at concentrating capital instead of human development. In other words, it was not in the interest of the elite to promote educational or health policies. In 1966, Balaguer constituted a National Commission for Development, the majority of members coming from the business elite (Espinal 1998, Rosario 1988). In this council, personalist and particularist policy favours and privileges were exchanged against political support (Espinal 1998). Overall, Balaguer's policies favoured the business elite, on which his political survival relied to large extents (Sánchez-Ancochea 2006).

On the other hand, policies promoted industrial production for foreign markets through FTZs. For example, FTZ firms were exempted from taxes, and credits at preferential conditions were provided by the state for the domestic firms. The Corripio family with *Industrias Corripio* and *Pinturas Tropical* is one example of a family conglomerates that benefited from ISI policies (Sánchez-Ancochea 2004). In contrast to these policies,

Balaguer's regime clearly discriminated against labour, for instance through laws that kept wages low. In addition, low levels of social spending affected the working force negatively. Low levels of overall spending allowed Balaguer to desist from taxing the business elite. In addition, major parts of public spending went into infrastructure (roads, school, housing, hydroelectricity). In 1975, public investment was 400 per cent of the amount invested in health and education (Sánchez-Ancochea 2004). This benefited newly created construction firms. Circular developments occurred when these firms became large enough to lobby effectively for new public investments.

These exclusionary policies were, in the beginning, considered successful economic policy. On the other hand, unequal socio-economic structures were cemented through these policies. In the 1970s, discontent grew on behalf of the business associations and excluded groups, which were not favoured through the personalist systems. Balaguer's policies were never corporatist, but favoured single persons or families (Espinal 1998). In addition, productivity increases did not need to be achieved through increasing labour productivity, since labour was cheap due to labour laws, and because ISI saved firms from international competition (Sánchez-Ancochea 2004). This policy mix, made investments in human capital – education and health – appear unnecessary.

The recent decades

In the first years of post-military governments, the *Estado Novos*'s major problem was increasing inflation. In the public debate among parties and Brazilian economists, different analyses and plans were raised. One of the interpretations, put forward by economists from the *Partido do Movemento Democrático do Brasil* and *Unicamp*, blamed high inequality and polarization for high inflation. Their policy proposal, the *Pacto Social* was however not adopted (Giambiagi et al. 2011). Yet it is interesting that high inequality was discussed as an underlying cause of economic problems, which did not play major roles in the debates before.

Several plans tried to get a grip on high inflation, albeit without lasting success. Only after several years and attempts, the *Plano Real* was able to provide some stability. Several features of this period are relevant for our analysis. First, Brazil adopted Washington Consensus policies as of 1989. For instance, in 1990, a national expropriation plan was implemented. However, these policies were much more moderate than those experienced by other Latin American and Asian countries. One reason was the protection of the national industry's interests; also there was public opposition to such measures. Furthermore, a new Constitution had been adopted in 1988, which did not allow certain privatizations (Giambiagi et al. 2011).

Important structural changes were prepared and executed during Cardoso's presidency from 1995–2003. At the same time that the economy was restructured further, relatively advanced (in regional comparison) social policies were put into place. Despite positive economic assessments of the policies, all the more in the medium run, Cardoso's party was substituted by Lula Inácio Lula da Silva, the working party's candidate, in 2003. When he took office, some interesting developments occurred. In the first place, relatively radical leftist policies which were expected from Lula did not materialize, but gave way to processes of moderation within his party and person. When a development strategy was proposed in 2003, this strategy emphasized that stabilizing policies needed to be maintained and complemented with social policies. This cannot be compared to other Latin American leftist regimes which came up with much more radical policies. During the last years, of course, the expansion of access to schooling via programs such as *Bolsa Família* are famous social policies beyond Brazilian frontiers (Giambiagi et al. 2011). While it is a matter of intense debate if and to what extent these policies have actually provoked structural changes in the Brazilian society or if they are rather assistentialist and populist policy programs, it is clear that questions of economic distribution and social justice have rarely figured as prominently in the political debate in Brazil before.

The Dominican economy grew at very fast rates in the 1990s, which was commonly attributed to liberalization and structural adjustment policies. Balaguer had been forced to adopt these policies by both the capitalist class and international actors like the IMF. As Espinal puts it, these policies "brought peace to the relationship between business and government (Espinal 1998, p. 115). Laws for TNCs were designed such that the large groups were either able to compete with them or became important partners. The concentration of capitalist power among few large firms in the DR made it risky for foreign firms to enter the market alone and most opted for a partnership with the big ones instead. In the construction sector, political pressure was such that foreign firms ended up being obliged to invest through joint ventures only (Sánchez-Ancochea 2004). Tax reforms both in the early 1990s under Balaguer and under Mejía (2000–2004) were based on raising value added tax and other regressive reforms. Trade liberalization, which brought transnational corporations into the country, benefited the large conglomerates the most. In the 1990s, all the major players had close ties to the financial sector (Sánchez-Ancochea 2004, p. 239). At the same time, the large groups achieved significant diversification and expanded to new activities and sectors. Living standards, however, improved only disproportionately, and labour continued to be marginalized.

Economic interests and education policies

The previous paragraphs have illustrated how Brazilian politicians since the 1960s pursued, in general terms, the objective of industrializing their economy and to achieve economic growth. Second, there were certain continuities in their politics. For instance, ISI was maintained by the military regime although this policy was not originally theirs. In a similar way, Lula Inácio da Silva did not interrupt structural reforms executed by his predecessor. These are important factors for explaining Brazil's trajectory: Brazil shows a very clear inclination towards statist corporatism and developmentalist policies.

On the other hand, Brazil has had a tradition of neglecting public education since colonial times. In 1937, Brazil had four universities (Levy 1986). Some authors refer to this scarcity of higher education as Brazil's "original sin" (ibid., p. 176). The first private university that received official recognition was founded in 1940. Not surprisingly, we can observe that access to education has been considerably increased since then. On the other hand, extremely high enrolments rates in primary education (World Bank 2014b) testify poor quality education and high repetition rates. No numbers are available for recent years, but this tendency has increased between 1970 and 1997. If especially higher education was an elite issue in 1950, this was much different in the 1990s (Levy 1997). But still in the 1970s, tertiary enrolment rates were very low with 4.73 per cent of the age group five years after graduation from secondary schooling.

Brazil's human capital accumulation is comparatively low, even within the region. The graph in Figure 4.8 provides data on the human capital both countries dispose of, in comparison again with South Korea and Singapore. Data come from Fernández-Arias (2014a) and refer to a human capital index and to the average years of schooling of the population over 15 years.[11] The graph illustrates that average years of schooling have increased at least

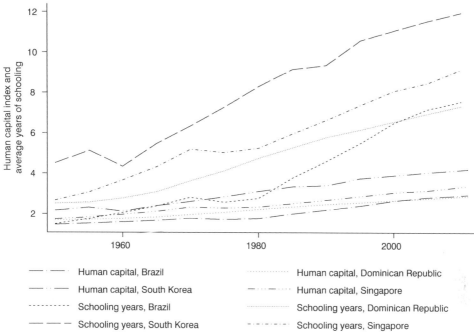

Figure 4.8 Human capital index and average years of schooling, 1950–2013

Data source: Fernández-Arias (2014a)

since 1980 in Brazil, but that in terms of absolute levels, Brazil lags behind South Korea and Singapore and, in fact, behind many others like Chile, Argentina, Mexico or Panama as well and is comparable to Nicaragua or Honduras. The same can be said about human capital.

Moreover, the observed expansion of participation in higher education did not stem from planned policy initiatives, but rather resulted as unintended consequences. Furthermore, much of the increase comes from private higher education. Through strict entrance rules for public universities, this development was indirectly pushed because private institutes were founded as substitutes (Levy 1997). The strict access rules for public universities, which are of high quality in Brazil, is still a considerable mechanism of redistribution from the poor to the rich, since graduates from many public schools have low chances of succeeding in the *vestibular*, the highly selective entrance test by which students for public institutions are selected. Only recently, quotas for certain disadvantaged groups have been installed.

Overall, it seems fair to conclude that industrialization and development occurred due to corporatist development policies, but not due to massive education. This is congruent with the observation that certain middle-class groups participated in these developments and benefited, but inequality throughout the whole country is still very high because other groups did not. This has been a development trajectory that worked since the 1950s. However, it is clear that this trajectory was possible not because of educational policies, but rather despite of them. As stated above, it is unlikely, however, that such policies will take Brazil into the ranks of high-income countries.

In the DR, educational and human capital indicators are similarly low. Average years of schooling and human capital have increased over the last years, but even countries like Bolivia, El Salvador, Jamaica or Nicaragua have slightly higher levels (Fernández-Arias 2014a). While values are higher than for small Central American countries like Guatemala or Nicaragua, the DR falls behind Costa Rica and Panama. Even though expected years of schooling for younger generations show that improvements in enrolment are expected, these are as well more limited than in Panama, Mexico, Cuba and El Salvador (CEPAL 2011). According to Census data from 2002, there is an upward tendency for tertiary education. However, the shares of persons with graduate or doctoral degrees are low and quite constant: the highest share is reached in the age group 40–44, where 1.66 per cent hold a specialization, 0.96 per cent a *Maestría* and 0.46 per cent a doctoral degree. Not surprisingly thus, based on a survey with enterprises from different industrial sectors, Miranda and Toirac (2010) find that the lack of qualified personnel is identified as major problem by more than one third of interviewed enterprises.

Social spending has traditionally been low in the DR, even in regional comparison. In 1966, only 2.3 per cent of the GDP were dedicated to education. During a short period in the late 1970s, the PRD administration under Antonio Guzmán envisaged redistributive policies. However, protests of the business elite aroused and pressure was put on the government (Sánchez-Ancochea 2004, Espinal 1998). Education received at its maximum 1.7 per cent of GDP in 1981 (Sánchez-Ancochea 2004). The percentages even fell until the 1990s, attaining 0.9 per cent for education and 3.8 per cent of GDP for total social spending. At that time, Costa Rica and Panama invested already 15.6 per cent and 16.2 per cent, and among the Central American countries, only Guatemala spent as little as the DR. No other country in the region spends as little as 2.5 per cent of GDP (2007–2008) for education. This is in part due to generally low levels of public spending, but as well to the circumstance that small shares of total public spending are reserved for education. While Honduras dedicated 34.6 per cent of total public spending to education in 2007–08, the share was only 15.8 per cent in the DR. The poorer Central American countries tend to compensate for smaller public budgets with larger shares for education than the DR. In absolute terms, Costa Rica spent $289 for education per inhabitant and year in 2007–2008, Panama $212, Mexico $287, Honduras $72, Nicaragua $48 and the DR $69 (CEPAL 2011).

Sánchez and Senderowitsch (2012) see one reason for this in weak collective action, especially on behalf of the middle class. Middle and upper classes easily opt for private health and educational options instead of demanding better public services. So the DR has relatively high enrolment rates in private educational institutes (Sánchez and Senderowitsch 2012). After private tertiary institutes had come into existence in the 1960s, enrolment rates already amounted to 46 per cent in 1979 (Levy 1986). Only Brazil and Colombia reached higher levels. The number of students studying at universities was only about 3,500 in 1960, but 90,000 in 1979, without public spending following the rhythm, and many new private institutes were created (Levy 1986). These private institutes were to a large extent controlled by members of the oligarchic elite, for instance as members of the boards, taking influence on policies and teaching contents (Rosario 1988). Low social spending fits well with low taxation. From 2003–2008, tax burden averaged 16.6 per cent of GDP. This level is lower than the Latin American average (21 per cent). During the last 25 years, tax income increased by only 5 per cent of GDP. This is associated with large indirect tax incidences on the hand and exemptions for rich sectors on the other (CEPAL 2009).

Conclusion

In this chapter, we have attempted to show that distributional patterns can significantly influence policy decisions and development trajectories of an economy. Using the case of the middle-income trap, we have conjectured that policies allowing a country to increase

GDP per capita and productivity easily conflict with the economic and political interest of dominant elite groups and are therefore opposed politically.

For the case of middle-income economies, this means that the policies conjectured to lead a country into high-income status – continuous investment into market and innovation supporting infrastructure, broad based quality education, easy entry into markets, protection of the returns to risky investments and complementary support for R&D by the state, all requiring high investments into fiscal, legal and administrative state capacity – are severely hampered in economic and political regimes based on the highly unequal access to political and economic resources. Elites have decreased incentives to implement the necessary measures, the state capacities to do so are weak and the danger of political violence counteracting any possible advances is high.

We have discussed the case of broad-based quality education with two cases, Brazil and the Dominican Republic. Their development over the last 50 years or so is in line with our argument. While in both countries industrialization has resulted from conscious development efforts, repression of demands for greater political participation and redistribution was an essential part of the resulting social dynamics. While education expanded in both countries, this happened hesitantly, and a strong bias towards serving and maintaining the privileges of a limited section of society is clearly visible. Overall, productivity stagnated or increased only slowly.

Despite all similarities, we found important differences between both countries. Even if total factor productivity in Brazil remains lower than in the Dominican Republic, it seems clear that with some optimism, a nascent own technological base is visible in Brazil, whereas the Dominican Republic depends on the exploitation of resources and low-qualified labour in tourism and services.

One aspect we think is distinctive here is country size and population. Hirschman argued that economies with monopolistic structures of production are less likely to adopt new technologies and, in this case, to industrialize: when only few firms dominate a market, they themselves have more interest in the status quo than in buying new technologies, equipment etc. (Hirschman 1958). Despite potential gains through technical innovation, technological adoption can be slow if that means that few producers without competitive pressure would have to renew existing production sites (Ferranti et al. 2001). In a large economy like Brazil, such dominant monopolistic structures are more difficult to imagine than in smaller ones. In contrast, in the Dominican Republic, a few families have strived to maintain control over the small, national economy.

The aspect of size is linked with the fragmentation of the private sector's interests. Brazil's business class has been fragmented ever since it came into existence: there has not been an all-embracing peak association, but regional and sectoral associations prevailed and competed with one another, "acting at cross-purposes" (Weyland 1998, p. 74). Reasons are to be found in the heterogeneity of the sectors and the large country size. Historically, state-corporatism and considerable state interventions under Getúlio Vargas did not foster the internal organization but helped disaggregate the business class further: the road to entrepreneurial access was through particularistic attention and links to politicians. It was necessary to lobby for specific advantages on behalf of a bureaucracy with large discretionary power. As well under the military regime, singular groups and entrepreneurs had personalist and particularistic access to political decision-making. However, there were no unified demands for specific policies or reforms (Weyland 1998). This contrasts with the much more tightly knit, but also personalist network of "families" in the Dominican Republic which makes for a much stronger grip of a narrow section of society on political decisions.

The current economic and political situation in both countries may be interpreted as on the one hand a confirmation of the problematic configuration we describe and on the other hand as containing the possible seeds for overcoming it. In the Dominican Republic, the sustained civil society effort of the 4% movement[12] shows the awareness of the general public of the importance of broad based educational improvements for the advance of the country. The continuous resistance against such a shift in public spending, on the other hand, shows the strong entrenchment of the present constellation. In Brazil, the end of the commodity boom has lowered growth dramatically and confronts the country with the lack of internally created dynamics. On the other hand, the political polarization experienced in the 2014 presidential election and the corruption scandals surfacing in its aftermath could, once again, provide the fuel for more coordinated efforts of Brazilian civil society and indeed, business, to press for more systematic efforts to broaden education and realize the existing technological potential of the country.

Notes

1 Later entries into middle-income status are not included in the graph because of the interest in medium-term growth averages of at least 10 years.
2 See Paus (2014) for a recent survey of the literature. She distinguishes two groups of authors, a larger group emphasizing structural change issues and a smaller group discussing the growth-slowdowns. This chapter takes the structural change approach as its base.
3 Hanushek and Woessmann (2012) recently found that school attainment has been relatively high in Latin America, but educational achievement has remained low. In other words, relatively high quantity of schooling has not come along with high quality of schooling. The authors argue that this lack of quality accounts for Latin America's poor overall growth performance.
4 A political Coase-theorem fails due to the inability of political parties to commit not to use a major shift in political power implied by a political deal to renege on it. Under these conditions distributional issues may adversely affect efficiency and, therefore, growth.
5 To those two dimensions, we would add "administrative capacity" in the sense of a "Weberian" capable bureaucracy. Cingolani (2013) provides an overview of the history, the present use and different dimensions of the concept of state capacity in the social sciences.
6 Heterogeneity of group interests in their discussion is much more related to ethnic or ideological differences (see Besley and Persson, 2011).
7 The incentive of poor incumbents to invest in the fiscal capacity of the state is reduced also, since the effectiveness of fiscal capacity, not used by rich incumbents, is reduced. See Besley and Persson, 2011).
8 This can be connected to Greif's "administrative power": is the administration to some extent independent of the government and a real political countervailing power? This requires a certain level of preparation and education (Greif 2008).
9 Unfortunately, inequality data for this time in Brazil are not easily available. The earliest date in the UNU-WIDER (2014) data base is from 1958, citing an income Gini coefficient of 49.1. For 1960, a range of different coefficients is available from different data sources and of different qualities. They range from 42.3 to 68.9, with an arithmetic mean of 54.2.
10 Nevertheless, these policies were sufficient for certain circles to contemplate a coup against him.
11 Please see the data description file that is downloadable with the data set for a more detailed description (Fernández-Arias, 2014b).
12 A broad coalition of civil society actors has tried to push through that 4% of the national budget be allocated to education for five years.

References

Acemoglu, D. (1995), Reward structures and the allocation of talent, *European Economic Review*, 39(1): 17–33.

Acemoglu, D. (2003), Why not a political Coase theorem? Social conflict, commitment, and politics, *Journal of Comparative Economics*, 31: 620–652.

Acemoglu, D. (2006), A simple model of inefficient institutions, *Scandinavian Journal of Economics*, 108(4): 515–546.

Acemoglu, D. and Robinson, J.A. (2006), *Economic origins of dictatorship and democracy*, Cambridge, New York: Cambridge University Press.

Acemoglu, D. and Robinson, J.A. (2008), Persistence of power, elites, and institutions, *American Economic Review*, 98(1): 267–293.

Acemoglu, D. and Robinson, J.A. (2012). *Why nations fail: The origins of power, prosperity, and poverty*. New York: Crown Publishers.

Acemoglu, D., Robinson, J.A. and Johnson, S. (2005), Institutions as a fundamental cause of long-run growth. In P. Aghion and S.N. Durlauf (eds), *Handbook of economic growth*, Amsterdam: Elsevier.

Agénor, P.-R. and Canuto, O. (2012), *Middle-income growth traps*, World Bank Policy Research Working Paper 6210.

Agénor, P.-R., Canuto, O. and Jelenic, M. (2012), *Avoiding middle-income growth traps*, World Bank Economic Premise 98.

Alemán, J.E. (2012), *Economía política dominicana (2003–2006)*, Santo Domingo: Centro Pedro Francisco Bonó.

Amable, B. (2003), *The diversity of modern capitalism*, Oxford: Oxford University Press.

Aoki, M. (2007), Endogenizing institutions and institutional changes, *Journal of Institutional Economics*, 3(1): 1–31.

Besley, T. and Persson, T. (2011), *Pillars of prosperity: The political economics of development clusters*. The Yrjö Jahnsson Lectures. Princeton, NJ: Princeton University Press.

Bowles, S. (2012), *The new economics of inequality and redistribution*. Federico Caffè lectures. Cambridge: Cambridge University Press.

Campante, F.R. and Chor, D. (2012). Schooling, political participation, and the economy, *Review of Economics and Statistics*, 94(4): 841–859.

Cantoni, D. and Yuchtman, N. (2013), *The political economy of educational content and development: Lessons from history*, CESifo Working Paper 4221.

Cardoso, E.A. and Helwege, A. (1992), *Latin America's economy: Diversity, trends, and conflicts*, Cambridge, MA: MIT Press.

CEPAL (2009), *La República Dominicana en 2030: Hacia una nación cohesionada*, Mexico: CEPAL.

CEPAL (2011), *Indicadores sociales básicos de la Subregión Norte de América Latina y el Caribe*, Edición 2010–2011, no. 1019.

Cingolani, L. (2013), *The state of state capacity: a review of concepts, evidence and measures*, MERIT Working Paper 53.

Dauvergne, P. and D. Farias (2012), The rise of Brazil as a global development power, *Third World Quarterly*, 33(5): 903–917.

Dominican Central Bank (2014), *Producto interno bruto (PIB) 1991–2012, año de referencia 1991*, Work sheet: PIB-Corriente Anual 1991–2012.

Eichengreen, B., Park, D. and Shin, K. (2013), *Growth slowdowns redux: new evidence on the middle-income trap*, NBER Working Paper 18673.

Espinal, R. (1998), Business and politics in the Dominican Republic, in F. Durand and E. Silva (eds), *Organized business, economic change, and democracy in Latin America*, Coral Gables, FL: North-South Center Press.

Felipe, Jesus (2012), *Tracking the middle-income trap*, Levy Economics Institute Working Paper 715.

Fernández-Arias, E. (2014a), Productivity and factor accumulation in Latin America and the Caribbean: A database (2014 update). Inter-American Development Bank, http://www.iadb.org/research/pub_desc.cfm?pub_id=DBA-015

Fernández-Arias, E. (2014b), Productivity and factor accumulation in Latin America and the Caribbean: Description of the database (2014 update). Inter-American Development Bank, http://www.iadb.org/research/pub_desc.cfm?pub_id=DBA-015

Ferranti, D. de; Guillermo E., P., Lederman, D. and Maloney, W.F. (2001), *From natural resources to the knowledge economy: Trade and job quality*, Washington, DC: World Bank.

Giambiagi, F., Villela, A. and Castro, L.B. de (2011), *Economia brasileira contemporánea: 1945–2010*, Rio de Janeiro: Elsevenir and Editore Campus.

Glaeser, E.L., Ponzetto, G.A.M. and Shleifer, A. (2007), Why does democracy need education?, *Journal of Economic Growth*, 12(2): 77–99.

Greif, A. (2008), The impact of administrative power on political and economic developments. toward a political economy of implementation. In E. Helpman (ed.), *Institutions and economic performance*, Cambridge, MA: Harvard University Press.

Griffith, B. (2011). Middle-income trap. In R. Nallari (ed.), *Frontiers in development policy*, Washington, DC: World Bank.

Hanushek, E.A. and Woessmann, L., (2012), Schooling, educational achievement, and the Latin American growth puzzle, *Journal of Development Economics*, 99(2): 497–512.

Harvey, D. (2005), *The new imperialism*, Oxford, New York: Oxford University Press.

Hausmann, R., Hidalgo, C.A., Bustos, S., Coscia, M., Chung, S., Jimenez, J., Simoes, A. and Yıldırım, M.A. (2011), *The atlas of economic complexity*, Hollis, NH: Puritan Press.

Hirschman, A.O. (1958), *The strategy of economic development*, New York: Norton.

Hoetink, H. (1982), *The Dominican people, 1850–1900: Notes for a historical sociology*, Baltimore, MD: Johns Hopkins University Press.

Levy, D.C. (1986), *Higher education and the state in Latin America: Private challenges to public dominance*, Chicago, IL: University of Chicago Press.

Levy, D.C. (1997), Latin America and the Change in Change, in M.F. Green, *Transforming higher education*, American Council on Education/Oryx Press series on Higher Education, Phoenix, AZ: Oryx Press.

Lin, J.Y. and Treichel, V. (2012), *Learning from China's rise to escape the middle-income trap: a new structural economics approach to Latin America*, World Bank Policy Research Working Paper 6165.

Lustig, N., Lopez-Calva, L.F. and Ortiz-Juarez, E. (2013), Declining inequality in Latin America in the 2000s: The cases of Argentina, Brazil, and Mexico, *World Development*, 44: 129–141.

Mehlum, H., Moene, K. and Torvik, R. (2006), Institutions and the resource curse, *The Economic Journal*, 116(508): 1–20.

Miranda, J. and Toirac, L. (2010), Indicadores de productividad para la industria Dominicana, *Ciencia y Sociedad*, XXXV: 235–290.

Moya Pons, F. (2010), *The Dominican Republic: A national history*, Princeton, NJ: Markus Wiener Publishers.

North, D.C., Wallis, J.J. and Weingast, B.R. (2012), *Violence and social orders: A conceptual framework for interpreting recorded human history*, Cambridge: Cambridge University Press.

Ohno, K. (2009), Avoiding the middle-income trap: renovating industrial policy formulation in Vietnam, *ASEAN Economic Bulletin*, 26(1): 25–43.

Padilla, R., Corderio, M., Hernández, R. and Romero, I. (2008), *Evolución reciente y retos de la industria manufacturera de exportación en Centroamérica, México y República Dominicana: Una perspectiva regional y sectorial*, México, D.F.: CEPAL.

Paus, E. (2011), Latin America's middle income trap, *Americas Quarterly*, 5(1): 71–76.

Paus, E. (2014), Latin America and the middle-income trap, *Financing for Development Series*, No 250. Santiago, ECLAC.

Robinson, J.A. and Torvik, R. (2011), Institutional comparative statics. Paper prepared for the 2010 World Congress of the Econometric Society and Shanghai. url: http://scholar.harvard.edu/files/jrobinson/files/econometricsocietymay28. pdf

Robinson, J.A. and Verdier,T. (2013), The political economy of clientelism, *Scandinavian Journal of Economics*, 115(2): 260–291.

Rodrik, D. (2003), *Growth strategies*, NBER Working Paper 10050.

Rodrik, D. (2013), *The past, present, and future of economic growth*, Global Citizen Foundation Working Paper 1.

Rosario, E. (1988), *Los dueños de la República Dominicana*, Santo Domingo: Editora Búho.

Sánchez, P.M. (1992), The Dominican case. In J. Higley and R. Gunther (eds), *Elites and democratic consolidation in Latin America and Southern Europe*, Cambridge: Cambridge University Press.

Sánchez-Ancochea, D. (2004), Leading coalitions and patterns of accumulation and distribution in small countries: A comparative study of Costa Rica and the Dominican Republic under globalization. Dissertation New School for Social Research.

Sánchez-Ancochea, D. (2006), Development trajectories and new comparative advantages: Costa Rica and the Dominican Republic under globalization, *World Development*, 34(6): 996–1015.

Schneider, B.R. (2009a), A comparative political economy of diversified business groups, or how states organize big business, *Review of International Political Economy*, 16(2): 178–201.

Schneider, B.R. (2009b), Hierarchical market economies and varieties of capitalism in Latin America, *Journal of Latin American Studies*, 41(3): 553–575.

Schneider, B.R. and Soskice, D. (2009), Inequality in developed countries and Latin America: coordinated, liberal and hierarchical systems, *Economy and Society*, 38(1): 17–52.

UNU-WIDER (2014), World Income Inequality Database (WIID3.0b), September 2014.

Vivarelli, M. (2014), *Structural change and innovation as exit strategies from the middle income trap*, IZA Discussion Paper 8148.

Weyland, K. (1998), The fragmentation of business in Brazil. In F. Durand and E. Silva (eds), *Organized business, economic change, and democracy in Latin America*, Coral Gables, FL: North-South Center Press.

Woo, W.T. (2012), China meets the middle-income trap: the large potholes in the road to catching-up, *Journal of Chinese Economic and Business Studies*, 10(4): 313–336.

World Bank (2014a), *When Prosperity is not Shared: The weak links between growth and equity in the Dominican Republic*, Washington D.C.: World Bank.

World Bank (2014b), *GINI Index*, PovcalNet.

World Bank (2014c), *GDP Growth Annual (%)*, Annual percentage growth rate of GDP at market prices based on constant local currency, constant 2005 U.S. dollars.

World Bank (2014d), *GDP per capita (%)*, constant 2005 US$.

Part II
Empirical evidence and policy suggestions

5 Welfare models, inequality and economic performance during globalisation

Pasquale Tridico

Globalisation: causes and consequences, a brief overview

Globalisation has been one of the most debated topics in at least the last two decades by scientists of different disciplines such as economics, politics, sociology, business, anthropology, engineering and transport studies, and environmental studies, among others. In fact, the emergence of globalisation is widely relevant to the subject of human lives from different perspectives concerning incomes, wealth, consumption habits, production, institution, governance, infrastructures, transports, and technology, etc. However, globalisation is still a generic term, which, in most of the definitions, is identified as a process of the *intensification* of, for instance, trade, capital mobility, finance, and labour. By contrast, there are authors such as Hay and Wincott (2012) who disagree with such a definition of globalisation and would rather define globalisation as a process not only of the intensification of those flows but also of *extensive* increase at a planetary level of trade, capital and labour mobility, and technological exchange (Held et al., 1999). Because evidence of this second type of definition of globalisation is missing and not all countries in the globe are part of the globalisation process (quite the opposite; globalisation interests a limited, yet increasing, number of countries), they conclude that it would be more appropriate to speak about regionalisation rather than globalisation. For instance, trade, capital and labour mobility particularly increased in the European Union (Europeanisation), among advanced and emerging economies (trans-regionalism), or among North American countries (with regional agreements such as NAFTA), etc. Hence, the interpretation of globalisation remains quite controversial and remains an on-going and evolutionary process. The figure below attempts to show the asymmetry of globalisation or essentially the intensification of the process in primarily advanced economies during 1980–2006 (i.e., until the eve of the financial crash in 2007), which is considered the period during which globalisation intensified tremendously.[1]

Nonetheless, while it is true that globalisation interests more advanced (and increasingly more emerging economies, typically BRIC countries)[2] and less poor economies, it is objectively impossible to deny the intensification of this process and the increase in the number of countries involved in the global economy in the last two decades. The figure below is the simplest representation of this kind of globalisation. In particular, a first big wave of globalisation, identified purely according to the *intensive* definition, took place after 1970, which a new international monetary scenario, the change in oil prices and the beginning of the European Monetary Systems, may have generated. However, this first wave of globalisation was unstable and the process of intensification declined during the 1980s. Finally, the process of intensive globalisation, accompanied often by the extensive inclusion

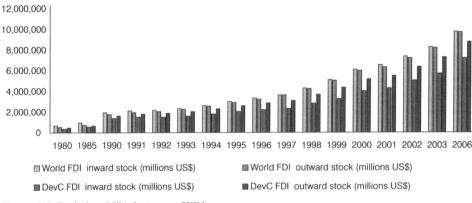

Figure 5.1 Capital mobility in terms of FDI
Source: The World Bank database

of more and more countries in the process, steadily took place at the end of the 1980s, when several institutional, geopolitical and technological changes occurred. I tend to particularly underline the importance of the following six changes to the process of globalisation:

1   The political (and to some extent also ideological) change that occurred during the 1980s, particularly in the United States and Great Britain with the new administrations of Reagan and Thatcher. These two political leaders were able to shape the international political consensus to some extent that the change towards globalisation required. This change occurred initially in the USA and the UK and later was promoted with the help of the major international organisations such as the International Monetary Fund and the World Bank, which were very close to the Washington administration (Stiglitz, 2002) at the international level, along with a new political economic doctrine which became known as the "Washington Consensus".
2   The financial deregulation that occurred in particular under the stimulus and the policies of the two administrations of Reagan and Thatcher mentioned above, first in the USA and in Great Britain and later in many advanced and developing economies. The financial deregulation contributed to both extend capital globally in search of higher profits and intensify the economy with finance and financial tools so that economies across the world soon became attracted to the process of financialisation.
3   The fall of Berlin Wall in 1989 (and the following dissolution of the Soviet Union in 1991), which caused the end of the Cold War and the end of the division between the East and West of Europe (and in a way of the East and West of the World) with the significant inclusion of the former communist economies in the global economy (or to be more precise, in the economic system of Western Europe, North America and other few advanced economies).
4   The deepening of the process of integration of the European Union (which in a way is connected with the previous item), which culminated with the Maastricht Treaty, introducing capital mobility along with the liberalisation of trade, service, goods and labour in an important and large market such as the European Union.
5   The tremendous challenges posed by the technological progress that brought about the ICT revolution and all the other great innovations introduced in transport and in telecommunications then contributed to reduce transportation costs enormously.

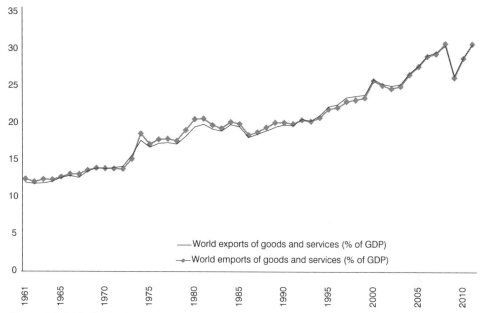

Figure 5.2 Globalisation in terms of trade intensification
Source: The World Bank database

6   The take-off (during the 1980s and 1990s) of several emerging economies in terms of economic growth, often identified with the term BRIC.

Theoretically, globalisation, or to be more precise, openness, was and is supported by the so-called mainstream neoclassical approach. Lewis (1980) and many economists such as Lucas (1993) and Bhagwati (2004) believed that trade is the engine of economic growth. Nevertheless, the experience of globalisation so far has shown that the performance of opened economies can vary consistently. The hypothesis that we are supporting in the paper is that openness *per se*, although it may be one of the indicators of competitiveness, is not an engine of economic growth. Openness (defined as imports and exports as a percentage of GDP) and integration in the world economy should be accompanied by institutions, state strategies and particularly by a consistent welfare state that support internal cohesion and maintain external competitive advantages. According to Rodrik (1999), the best-performing countries are the ones that are integrated in the world economy with appropriate institutions that are able to support the impact of globalisation on the domestic market and social domestic issues. Countries with poor social institutions, weak conflict management institutions (which means poor welfare states) and strong social cleavages suffer external shocks and do not perform well in the world economy. Nevertheless, for most of the globalisation period, the USA has been an example of neoclassical economics, showing that globalisation does not necessarily need a strong welfare state. However, the current financial and economic crisis which started in the USA in 2007 and its consequences that are currently propagated in many advanced economies seems to show that the Rodrik argument still holds true:

The world market is a source of disruption and upheaval as much as it is an opportunity for profit and economic growth. Without the complementary institutions at home – in the areas of governance, judiciary, civil liberties, social insurance, and education, one gets too much of the former and too little of the latter

(Rodrik, 1999:96).

For Lucas (1993), international trade contributes to stimulate economic growth through a process of structural change and capital accumulation, as in the case of Ireland, where according to Walsh and Whelan (2000), a structural change had already taken place during the 1970s and created conditions that allowed the Irish economy to grow considerably in the 1990s and later in the 2000s. Capital accumulation is determined by "learning by doing" and "learning by schooling" in a process of knowledge and innovation spillovers. A country that protects its goods from international competition by raising tariffs on goods made with intensive skilled work will have as an effect a domestic increase in the price of goods that use intensive skilled work. Skilled workers' wages will increase and R&D will be more expensive. Consecutively, investments in R&D will decrease, and growth will be affected negatively. On the contrary, deleting tariffs on those goods will cause a reduction in the price of goods that use intensive skilled work. R&D will cost less, and investments in R&D will increase, with positive effects on growth (Lucas, 1993). Policies should, therefore, address such problems and should create conditions for effective and substantial R&D investments.

This argument, however, does not take into consideration the inequality and uneven development caused mainly by liberalisation and trade intensification via wage differentials. This risk was already raised by Stolper and Samuelson: according to the Stolper-Samuelson theorem, market integration increases economic inequality and vulnerability because increased international trade raises the incomes of the owners of abundant factors and reduces the incomes of the owners of scarce factors. Since advanced industrial countries are more capital-intensive economies and abundant with skilled labour, trade is expected to be beneficial for capital-intensive economies and skilled labour and detrimental for unskilled labour, increasing income inequality, and for labour-intensive economies, increasing regional disparities.

Similarly, increased capital flows are expected to raise income inequality in advanced industrial economies because capital outflows from capital-rich countries to LDCs reduce domestic investment and lower the productive capability and demands for labour in these economies (Ha, 2008; Tsebelis 2002). Because a reduction in total capital in the production process increases the marginal productivity of capital and reduces the marginal effect of labour, capital outflows increase the income of capital relative to labour, increasing income inequality. In particular, because foreign direct investment (FDI) outflows from advanced industrial countries tend to be concentrated in industries with low-skilled labour in the home country (Lee 1996), rapidly rising FDI outflows often reduce the demand for low-skilled labour and increase income gaps in industrialised countries. In fact, several studies find that trade with less developed countries is associated with expanded income inequality in industrialised countries (Wood, 1994; Leamer, 1996; Rodrik, 1996; McKeown, 1999).

Empirically, it is interesting to observe FDI expansion, which experienced a strong increase in the 1990s due to liberalisation of capital mobility and then a collapse at the beginning of the 2000s due to the global uncertainty caused by the international events of September 11, 2001. A further and bigger increase in FDI flow can be observed immediately later and until the financial crash of 2007, with a peak in the FDI flows in 2006–07. The current crisis, marked by financial instability and depression, caused a further squeeze in FDI, which, however, remains at a much higher level than at the beginning of 1990s.

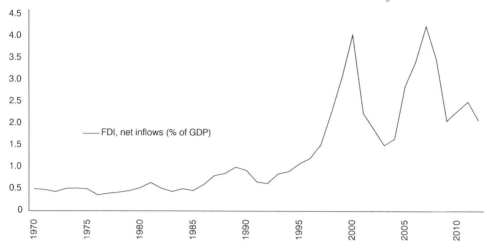

Figure 5.3 FDI in the world economy
Source: The World Bank database

Welfare, inequality and economic performance

Globalisation poses several challenges to national economies and governments. One of the most important is the consequence on inequality, both within countries and between countries, and its impact on welfare state sustainability (Hay and Wincott, 2012).

During globalisation, inequality increased consistently in most advanced and emerging economies, particularly during the 1990s and the 2000s. A simple look at the Gini coefficients across countries shows the worsening of income distribution within countries. The reasons for this are various (Atkinson, 1999; Milanovic, 1988; Tridico, 2012; Galbraith, 2012).

The debate is very lively, and it has produced two main interpretations of the problem. The first one states that globalisation reduces the share of welfare states because it constitutes a cost for firms. Higher levels of welfare states produce higher income tax levels, social costs and contributions, which reduce profit prospective and increase costs for firms. Firms would be hence pushed to go abroad unless government retrenched welfare state spending and reduced taxes. Hence, in order to maintain higher levels of investments, firms and employment in the country, the welfare state needs to be reduced under the process of globalisation, with bad consequences for inequality. This interpretation is well known as "the efficiency thesis". This thesis was developed within the neoclassical (or neoliberal) paradigm, and it argues that globalisation has forced (or should force) states to retrench social welfare in order to achieve a market-friendly environment and attract increasingly mobile international capital and competitiveness (Blackmon, 2006; Castells, 2004; Allan and Scruggs, 2004).

The efficiency thesis is contrasted by "the compensation thesis", which argues that because globalisation increases inequality, welfare states need to increase. In other words, globalisation pressured governments to expand welfare expenditures in order to compensate for the domestic "losers" of the globalisation process (Brady et al., 2005; Rodrik, 1998; Swank, 2002). In a way, it can be also argued following the compensation argument that welfare expansion would allow states to further pursue globalisation. An extensive interpretation would then see welfare expansion not as a result but as a condition of globalisation, so that in order to continue (or to start) with the process of globalisation, policy makers must expand social safety nets.

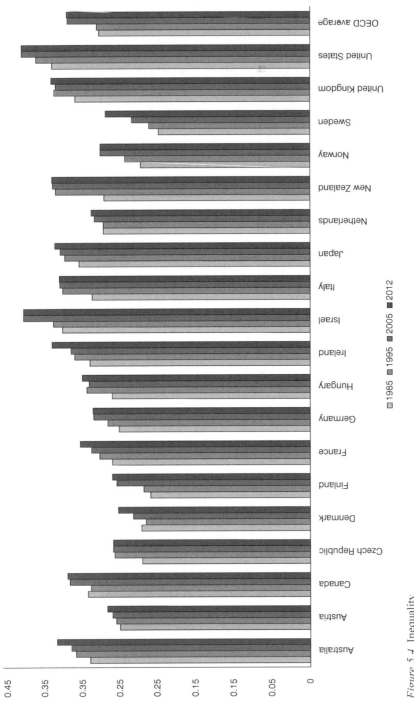

Figure 5.4 Inequality
Source: OECD database

Empirical evidence concerning the relation between globalisation (intensification) and welfare (expansion/retrenchment) is often found to be inconsistent and mixed.

Certainly, with the introduction of outsourcing practices and FDI outflows, globalisation has improved the bargaining position of capital relative to labour in higher-income countries. As Feenstra (1998, p.46) observes, the impact of globalisation on changing the bargaining position of labour and capital has far-reaching consequences. The decline in union power, particularly within trade-oriented industries, may well account for a portion of the increased wage inequality in the United States and in other countries (Borjas and Ramey, 1995). The decision of firms to move capital and production across countries has distributional effects: the position of low-skilled workers in industrial countries is worsened by a combination of 1) globalisation and 2) new technology (Tisdell and Svizzero 2003). The first increases the bargaining power of capital against labour, with the consequence that it is easier for capital to obtain tax reductions and welfare retrenchment. The states are willing to embark on tax competition among them in order to keep investments and production at home. The second has a direct and negative impact on unskilled labour and income distribution without welfare support and social institutions.

In this context, wage shares declines dramatically, with negative consequences on the aggregate demand, as the figure below suggests. The figure reports the average data aggregate by group of countries. Anglo-Saxon economies (later included in the liberal competitive market economy model) and Mediterranean economies suffered the most from the restructuring process that occurred since the 1980s and intensified during the 1990s and 2000s.

As far as socio-economic model classification is concerned, I used a revised and updated version of the approach used by Esping-Andersen (1990) according to whom welfare models can be divided into three groups, Liberal, Continental and Scandinavian models.[3] This classification, although methodologically still very relevant, was based on data from before 1990. Therefore, I updated that classification to the new evidence, following in particular the work of Hay and Wincott (2012). Hay and Wincott follow more or less the same methodology as Esping-Andersen (1990), taking into consideration the evolution of these models in the last two decades. They extended this classification to five models: the three models used by Esping-Andersen plus the Mediterranean group and the

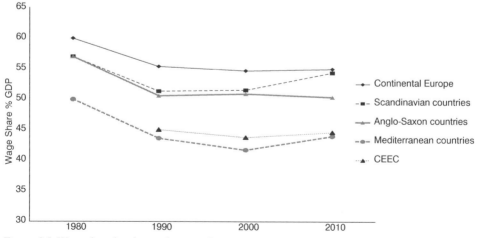

Figure 5.5 Wage share in advanced economies

Note: The unadjusted wage share is calculated as total labour compensation of employees divided by value added.
Source: own elaboration on the ILO (2013)

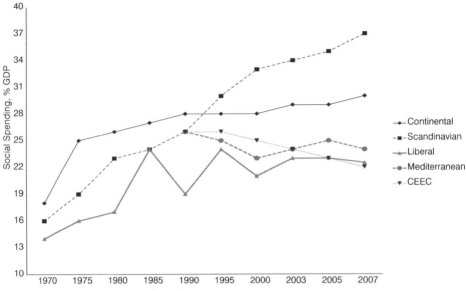

Figure 5.6 Welfare expenditure by models

Source: Own calculation on the OECD database. See also Adema and Ladaique (2009).

Note: Social spending (% of GDP): is the sum of "social benefits in-kind" and "social transfers other than in-kind" as defined as well before (OECD definition). Continental: Belgium, Germany, Luxembourg, the Netherlands, Austria; Scandinavian: Denmark, Finland, Sweden, Norway; Liberal: UK, Ireland, USA, Australia, Canada, New Zealand; Mediterranean: Greece, Spain, Italy, Cyprus, Malta, Portugal; CEEC): Czech Republic, Estonia, Latvia, Lithuania, Poland, Slovenia, Slovak Republic, Romania and Bulgaria.

Central and East European Countries (CEEC) group, claiming that a strong difference can be observed among these groups in general patterns. Moreover, since 1990, welfare patterns are diverging even more with the Scandinavian model, which seems to clearly have followed a compensation thesis in order to cope with the challenge of globalisation; the continental model, which maintained stable or increased slightly the level of welfare spending in the same period; and the other three groups, the Liberal, the Mediterranean and the CEEC, which converge among themselves in the sense that they reduced the level of welfare spending clearly following a sort of efficiency thesis during the last two decades of globalisation, as the figure below suggests.

The evolutionary path of welfare models under the condition of globalisation presented a challenge for all countries involved in the process. Some countries, typically the Mediterranean countries, did not manage to increase welfare spending, and they ended up with both higher inequality levels and the worst performance in terms of GDP and labour market performance. The case of Scandinavian economies shows exactly the contrary: the challenges and the threats to income distribution and competitiveness of globalisation could be better coped with by increasing welfare spending.

In fact, once we compare welfare spending data with the economic performance in the years of the crisis (2007–13) we discover interesting results that confirm our hypotheses: countries that had better performance are those that managed not to retrench the welfare state under the process of globalisation and, therefore, reached the eve of the crisis in 2007 better equipped in terms of the welfare state, as Figure 5.7 shows.

In the graph below, I used a so-called Performance Index (PI) that combines GDP growth, "g", and labour market performances (employment growth "n", and unemployment levels

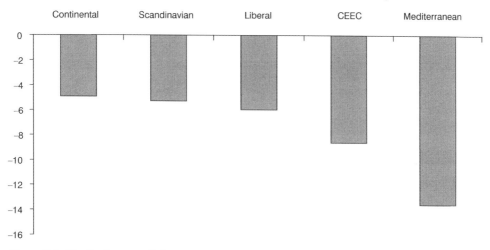

Figure 5.7 The Performance Index

Source: own elaboration on the WEO IMF, and OECD database

Note: The Performance index here is built simply by aggregating GDP and labour market performance in the following way: (Average GDP growth in 2007–13 + Average Employment growth in 2007–13) – Unemployment rate (average 2007–13)

"U") for the period 2007–2013. The PI allows to avoid biases and to look at the economic performance from a wider perspective: in fact, some countries can have relatively better GDP dynamics but very bad employment performance (and vice versa), in particular during unstable periods like the current one.

The compensation approach seems to have contributed, in these best performing countries, to both maintaining lower levels of inequality and to having better performance in terms of GDP and the labour market. These countries' comparative economic performance, measured in this paper with the Performance Index since 2007 has been considerably better.

Moreover, if from one side it is true that inequality, as we argued before, increased everywhere during globalisation, from another side there are important differences among countries and models: Scandinavian and Continental models maintain lower levels of inequality, along with higher levels of social spending. On the contrary, the countries of the Liberal and Mediterranean models, which in the last two decades retrenched the welfare state or did not increase it, also experienced increasing inequality.

On the contrary, the efficiency thesis seems to provide an alternative explanation: advanced economies that embarked on globalisation had to reduce their welfare expenditures in order to satisfy firms' needs and requests and to increase their competitiveness. However, as I will show, this explanation is not appropriate to understand which countries in the end actually had better economic performance. In particular, we will see that countries that reached a relatively higher level of welfare expenditures and where cuts did not occur, or occurred relatively less, had better economic performance during the crisis that started in 2007 and continued until today. On the contrary, countries that at the eve of the crisis were found to have poorer welfare states and cut welfare expenditures more profoundly during the 1990s and 2000s had a worse economic performance. These results will be shown in the following section.

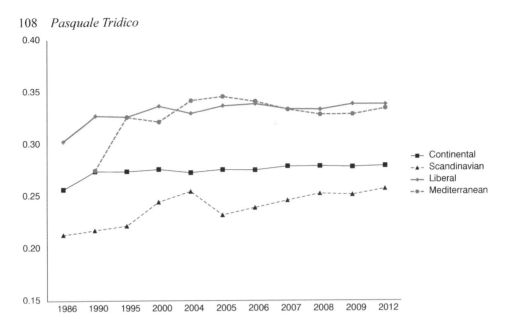

Figure 5.8 Inequality by welfare models

Note: Because of the lack of historical data, is not possible to reconstruct the variables for the CEEC group.
Source: OECD database

The model

In order to test my hypothesis, according to which countries which followed the compensation approach managed not only to have lower inequality but also better economic performance, (contrary to the "efficiency thesis countries"), I used a sample of 42 advanced economies, OECD countries and EU members. The equation to test is the following:

$$GDP = \alpha + \beta_1 \, SocialSub. + \beta_2 \, EducationExpendit. - \beta_3 \, Import + \beta_4 \, Export + \varepsilon$$

The model predicts that countries have higher income if they invest more in welfare (*SocialSub.*), invest more in Education (*EducationExpendit.*), import less and export more (var *Import* and *Export*); a term of error, ε is added to the equation.

The model uses longitudinal panel data of six years for the period between 2007 and 2012. These were the years where most of the advanced economies fell into economic crisis and stagnation. The results, presented in the following regression table, confirm the predicted model of the above equation, according to which GDP per capita in 2012 is higher if countries invest more in welfare (as a percentage of the social subsidies on GDP), in education (as a percentage of education expenditures on GDP) and manage to import less and to export more (Import and Export as percentages of the GDP). All the data refer to the period 2012–2007, for a total of 240 observations.

The method used, a regression model on a longitudinal panel data, with a "between-group effects" is more relevant in this case, since I am mostly interested in the differences between groups of countries. Moreover, the Hausman test, which checks for the validity of the between effect (BE) against both the fixed effect (FE) and the random effect (RE), produces positive results in the sense that the hypothesis zero (H_0), of consistency of the BE, is accepted with the maximum level of significance, against the alternative hypothesis (H_a) of consistency of BE and RE.

Table 5.1 Regression results

Regression model on a longitudinal panel
Dependent variables: GDP per capita (log natural)

Variable	Coefficient (standard errors)	P values
Public Social subsidies (% of GDP)	.0085532 (.0029786)	0.008
Education_Expend. (public), % of GDP	.1323674 (.0372624)	0.001
Import, % GDP	−.026967 (.0068556)	0.001
Export, % GDP	.0223626 (.0061447)	0.001
Investment (capital formation), % GDP	−.0041776 (.0034335)	0.234
FDI (out), % GDP	−.0008266 (.0005231)	0.126
FDI (in), % GDP	−.000998 (.0085615)	0.908
Constant	10.34326 (.7078016)	0.000

Time dummies (Years 2007, 2008, 2009, 2010, 2011, 2012): YES

R^2 (between) = 0.8097
sd(u_i + avg(e_i.))= .1875238 Prob > F = 0.0000

Number of observations = 240;
Number of groups = 42 Panel (2007–2008–2009–2010–2011–2012)
Between-group effects (BE)

Hausman Test (BE vs FE):
b (BE) = consistent under H_0 and H_a; obtained from xtreg
B (FE) = inconsistent under H_a, efficient under H_0; obtained from xtreg
Test: H_0: difference in coefficients not systematic
$\chi^2(12)$ = (b-B)'[(V_b-V_B)^(-1)](b-B) = 138.73 Prob>χ^2 = 0.0000

Hausman Test (BE vs RE):
b (BE) = consistent under H_0 and H_a; obtained from xtreg
B (RE) = inconsistent under H_a, efficient under H_0; obtained from xtreg
Test: H_0: difference in coefficients not systematic
$\chi^2(11)$ = (b-B)'[(V_b-V_B)^(-1)](b-B) = 97.00 Prob>χ^2 = 0.0000

Note: In the sample, there are 39 Countries: Australia, Austria, Belgium, Bulgaria, Canada, Switzerland, Chile, Cyprus, Czech Republic, Germany, Denmark, Spain, Estonia, European Union, Finland, France, the United Kingdom, Greece, Croatia, Hungary, Ireland, Iceland, Israel, Italy, Japan South Korea, Lithuania, Luxembourg, Latvia, Malta, Netherlands, Norway, New Zealand, OECD members, Poland, Portugal, Romania, Slovak Republic, Slovenia, Sweden, and the United States, plus average values for the Euro area, European Union and OECD members. Total: 42 observations. Public Social subsidies are subsidies, grants, and other social benefits including all unrequited, non-repayable transfers on current account to private and public enterprises; grants to foreign governments, international organisations, and other government units; and social security, social assistance benefits, and employer social benefits in-cash and in-kind (World Bank definition, see World Bank database).

As the regression table suggests, social subsidies and education expenditures, both with positive and significant coefficients, are functional to higher GDP. Positive coefficients and significance are noted for the variable Export (as a percentage of GDP), while a negative significant coefficient is noted for the variable Import (as a percentage of GDP). Hence, richer countries export and are more competitive than countries that import more instead. However, they also have a stronger welfare state. Moreover, other openness variables used as control variables such as FDI (inward and outward) and Investments (as a percentage of GDP) are not significant. In this sense, the "compensation hypothesis" is confirmed: regulated globalisation and an expanded welfare state are better able to produce higher GDP per capita. In other words, countries that perform the best during this period

(2007–2012), results suggest, invested more in welfare state (social subsidies and public education expenditures) and adopted mercantilist policies, importing less and exporting more without being as open towards FDIs. These countries do not properly represent an orthodox model of liberal capitalist economy. On the contrary, they represent a corporative or social market economy model: in fact, most of these best-performing countries are Continental and Scandinavian European economies.[4]

In other words, from these results, it follows that richer countries are those that rely on a corporative socio-economic model rather than on a liberal competitive model. This means that countries that managed to keep higher levels of public expenditure on the welfare state in the global economy are better off today.

The compensation thesis proves to be stronger because it confirms that investing in the welfare dimension, not only reduces inequality, is not a drain on competitiveness or a barrier to economic efficiency as the efficiency thesis advocates would argue. The most generous of Europe's welfare states are also the most efficient and successful economies.

Conclusions

In this chapter, I argued that globalisation posed important challenges to countries on several domains of economics, particularly in the last two decades. I investigated the challenges of income distribution and welfare states. In this context, I indicated that countries that reacted to these challenges by the implementation of the efficiency thesis, according to which globalisation needs to be accompanied by the retrenchment of welfare states in order for firms to be competitive, did not achieve better economic performance and, particularly during the current economic crisis, suffered the most (these countries belong to the Liberal and Mediterranean market economy models). Moreover, their income distribution worsened and inequality increased. On the contrary, our econometric exercises show that the "compensation thesis" (i.e., regulated globalisation and an expanded welfare state) was better able to produce higher economic growth along with better labour market performance and better income distribution.

Some lessons can be learned from that. First of all, there is a strong and steady correlation between welfare spending and inequality. Countries in the Scandinavian and Continental models maintain higher levels of social spending along with lower levels of inequality. On the contrary, the countries of the liberal and Mediterranean models, which in the last two decades retrenched the welfare state or did not increase it, also experienced increasing inequality. Second, the evolutionary path of welfare models under the condition of globalisation presented a challenge for all countries involved in the process. Some countries, typically the Mediterranean countries, did not manage to increase welfare spending, and they ended up with both higher inequality levels and the worst performance in terms of GDP and labour market performance. The case of Scandinavian economies shows exactly the contrary: the challenges and the threats to income distribution and competitiveness of globalisation could be better coped with by increasing welfare spending.

Notes

1 Advanced economies mostly correspond to OECD countries, termed in Figure 5.1 as DevC (Developed Countries).
2 Brazil, Russia, India and China.
3 Esping-Andersen (1990) ranks welfare models mainly according to the level of social spending, to the level of (de)commodification of welfare and to degree of extension of welfare among citizens.

4   One can obtain similar results if we consider as dependent variables in a cross-section regression the cumulative rate of growth (instead of the per capita GDP in 2012) that countries experienced during the last years, when the crisis occurred (2007–2012). It is clear again in this context that countries that implemented unconventional policies managed to get better results in terms of growth. In fact, the cross-section regression shows that countries that performed better implemented their own way of globalisation that is more regulated, with higher levels of tax on trade, and always with higher levels of welfare expenditures and education expenditures. The results suggest that these countries followed mercantilist policies typical of the corporative model pursued in Germany (and other countries such as Switzerland, Austria, Luxembourg and Netherlands), then reaching higher levels of imports and surplus in the balance of payment.

References

Adema, W. and Ladaique, M. (2009), *How Expensive is the Welfare State?: Gross and Net Indicators in the OECD Social Expenditure Database (SOCX)*, OECD Social, Employment and Migration Working Papers 92, OECD Publishing. http://www.oecd-ilibrary.org/social-issues-migration-health/how-expensive-is-the-welfare-state_220615515052

Allan, J. P. and Scruggs, L. (2004), "Political Partisanship and Welfare State Reform in Advanced Industrial Societies". *American Journal of Political Science*, 48(3): 496–512.

Atkinson, A. (1999), Is Rising Inequality Inevitable? A Critique of the Transatlantique Consensus. WIDER Annual Lectures No. 3, Helsinki.

Basso, P. (1998), *Tempi moderni, orari antichi. Il tempo di lavoro a fine secolo*, Milan: FrancoAngeli.

Bhagwati, J. (2004), *In Defense of Globalization*, Oxford: Oxford University Press.

Borjas G.J. and Ramey V.A. (1995), "Foreign Competition, Market Power, and Wage Inequality," *The Quarterly Journal of Economics*, 110(4): 1075–1110.

Blackmon, P. (2006), "The State: Back in the Center of the Globalization Debate." *International Studies Review*, 8(1): 116–119.

Brady, D., Beckfield, J. and Seeleib-Kaiser, M. (2005), "Economic Globalization and the Welfare State in Affluent Democracies, 1975–1998." *American Sociological Review*, 70: 921–48.

Castells, M. (2004), "Global Informational Capitalism." In D. Held and A.G. McGrew (eds). *The Global Transformations Reader: An Introduction to the Globalization Debate* Malden, MA: Blackwell.

Esping-Andersen, G. (1990), *The Three Worlds of Welfare Capitalism*, Cambridge: Polity.

Feenstra, R. C. (2004), *Advanced International Trade: Theory and Evidence*, Princeton, NJ: Princeton University Press.

Feenstra, R. C. (1998), "Integration of Trade and Disintegration of Production in the Global Economy". *Journal of Economic Perspectives*, 12(4), pp. 31–50.

Galbraith J. K. (2012), *Inequality and Instability*, Oxford: Oxford University Press,

Greenspan, A. (2007), *The Age of Turbulence: Adventures in a New World*, London: Allen Lane.

Ha, E. (2008). "Globalization, Veto Players, and Welfare Spending." *Comparative Political Studies*, 48(6): 783–813.

Hay, C., and Wincott, D. (2012), *The Political Economy of Eruopean Welfare Capitalism*, Basingstoke: Palgrave Macmillan.

Held D., McGrew A., Goldblatt D. and Perraton J. (1999), *Global Transformations: Politics, Economics and Culture*. Cambridge: Polity.

ILO (2013), *Global Wage Report 2012/13: Wages and Equitable Growth*, Geneva: ILO.

Leamer, E. (1996), "Wage Inequality from International Competition and Technological Changes: Theory and Country Experience." *The American Economic Review*, 86: 309–314.

Lewis A., (1980), "The Slowing Down of the Engine of Growth: Nobel Lecture" *American Economic Review*, 70(4): 555–564.

Lucas R. (1993), "Making a Miracle", *Econometrica*, 61: 251–257.

McKeown, Timothy J. (1999), "The Global Economy, Post-Fordism, and Trade Policy in Advanced Capitalist States." In H. Kitschelt (ed.). *Continuity and Change in Contemporary Capitalism*. Cambridge: Cambridge University Press.

Milanovic, B. (1988), *Explaining the Increase in Inequality during the Transition*, Policy Research Working Paper Series 1935, The World Bank.

OECD (2012), Social Expenditure database www.oecd.org/els/social/expenditure

OECD (various years), Employment Outlook (online database).

Rodrik, D. (1996), *Why Do More Open Economies Have Bigger Governments?* NBER Working Papers 5537. Cambridge, MA: National Bureau of Economic Research.

Rodrik, D. (1999), *Making Openness Work*, Baltimore, MD: John Hopkins University Press.

Rodrik, D. (1998), "Why Do More Open Economies Have Bigger Governments?" *Journal of Political Economy*, 106: 997–1032.

Stiglitz, J. E. (2002), *Globalization and Its Discontents*, New York: W.W. Norton & Company.

Stolper, W. F. and Samuelson, Paul A. (1941), "Protection and Real Wages", *Review of Economic Studies,* 9 (1): 58–73

Swank, D. (2002)., *Global Capital, Political Institutions, and Policy Change in Developed Welfare States.* New York: Cambridge University Press.

Tisdell, C. and Svizzero, S. (2003), *Globalization, Social Welfare, and Labour Market Inequality*, Working Paper 20, The University of Queensland.

Tridico, P. (2012), "Financial Crisis and Global Imbalances: Its Labor Market Origins and the Aftermath, *Cambridge Journal of Economics* 36(1): 17–42.

Tsebelis, G. (2002), *Veto Players: How Political Institutions Work.* Princeton, NJ: Princeton University Press.

Walsh, P. and Whelan, C. (2000), "The Importance of Structural Change in Industry For Growth", *Journal of the Statistical and Social Inquiry Society of Ireland*, XXIX: 1–32.

Wood, A. (1994), *North-South Trade, Employment and Inequality*. Oxford: Clarendon Press.

6 Labour market institutions and wage inequality within education groups in Europe

Cristiano Perugini and Fabrizio Pompei

Introduction

Earnings inequality between education and skill cohorts in Europe has traditionally been one of the main focuses of theoretical and applied research. In particular, the skill-biased technical change (SBTC) theory traces back the origin of the skill premia for highly educated workers in a race between education and technology, in which the winner is a technology complementary to higher education and skills (Goldin and Katz, 2008). Relatively little effort has been devoted to analyse the size of within group disparities and their drivers. However, especially under certain structural and institutional conditions, which may favour incomes polarisation and the persistence into low-pay traps, this dimension of inequality may be relevant.

This chapter aims at shedding light on the drivers of earnings inequality within education levels in EU countries focusing on individual, economic, employment and demographic characteristics of dependent workers and on country-wide institutional settings. In particular, for the reasons spelled out in the next section, we focus on the importance of employment status (particularly temporary/permanent positions) in connection with employment protection regimes. The use of quantile regression techniques allows investigating the effect of individual and institutional features at different parts of the wage distribution within each education pool.

The chapter adds to the existing literature by: (i) providing a descriptive comparative picture of hourly earnings disparities in Eastern and Western EU countries by education and employment status before (2007) and during (2011) the crisis; (ii) showing and explaining the importance of institutional factors in shaping the wage gap between temporary and regular workers within each education pool and at different parts of the wage distribution. The chapter proceeds as follows: in the next section we provide a summary of the reference literature on the topic. Then we present the data and the descriptive evidence. In the last three sections we describe the econometric approach, the outcomes of our regression analysis and we provide some concluding remarks.

Inequality within education groups and labour market institutional settings

Wage and income inequality has been increasing remarkably in most developed countries over the last 3 decades, mainly driven by changes at the top and the bottom of the distribution (OECD, 2011). These trends have been explained by changes in taxation which reduced progressivity of the tax schedule at the top of the distribution (e.g., Atkinson et al., 2011), globalisation and technical change which increased relative skill premia (e.g., Autor and Katz, 1999; Atkinson, 2007; Goldin and Katz, 2008; Machin, 2008; Chusseau et al., 2008; Van Reenen, 2011) and a generalized weakening of labour market institutions and policies intended to support lower incomes (Fortin and Lemieux, 1997; Checchi and Garcia-Penalosa, 2008). The incapacity of the trade theories and of SBTC hypothesis to fully explain the evolution of wage distributions and labour demand, particularly job polarisation (Goos and Manning, 2007), has led to a more nuanced formulation of the SBTC theory. The main explanation of the polarisation patterns, observed in the US and UK first and recently confirmed for all main European countries (Goos et al., 2009), relies on the so-called routinisation hypothesis (Autor et al., 2003; Acemoglu and Autor, 2012). It maintains that routinary manual and cognitive tasks, placed at the middle of the wage distribution, tend to be easily replaced by computers; non-routinary (conceptual) cognitive tasks are instead complemented by technologies, the introduction of which increases their demand. Technology is also neutral towards employment in those elementary low-paid service workers and elementary occupations which, by own nature, cannot be replaced by computers (personal care services, cleaners, domestic helpers). As a consequence, routine workers will lose in their wage position both relative to abstract workers and to elementary non-routine occupations.

This approach has the advantage of complementing the between education groups inequality explanation with a within education groups one, related to tasks performed by workers with the same endowment of formalized human capital. Yet, this approach only partially contributes explaining the remarkable pay differences existing within education groups; it does not help providing, for example, any justifications of the presence of mature highly educated workers in the low-wage sector, i.e., of the fact that they are either not employed in abstract tasks or, if they are, they receive a low pay. This drives the attention towards the role played by labour market institutional settings (Levy and Murnane, 1992), especially those that favour a weakening of wage compression mechanisms (connected to the declining role of unions and collective bargaining) and an increase in the bargaining power on the side of employers (deregulation of labour markets and dismissal of minimum-wage provisions). One visible outcome of these processes, observable in particular throughout Europe in the last two decades, is the proliferation of new contractual forms and the increasing use (and mis-use) of temporary jobs (Boeri and Garibaldi, 2007).

Generally speaking stronger wage-setting institutions are expected to compress the wage structure and inhibit discriminatory practices (Card, 1992; Freeman, 1993; Dustmann et al., 2009). However, in the presence of asymmetric distributions of unions between different workers statuses (with permanent workers being typically more unionized and better organized), between-group (unionized/non-unionized workers) effects might prevail over within-group ones, leading to an increase in inequality (Firpo et al., 2010). In the framework of insider/outsiders models, collective wage setting institutions can also reinforce the existence of dual segments in the labour market (incumbent/new-hire or temporary/permanent workers) (Booth et al., 2002). Similarly, stronger wage-setting centralisation and coordination are expected to reduce inter-firm and inter-industry wage variation. However, the weaker tradition of collective bargaining practices in certain sectors and occupations, and for different working status, may result in an increase of the wage gap (see Ponzellini et al., 2010, for Hungary). Lastly, and of particular interest here, labour market deregulation patterns also contribute to shaping wage disparities. On the side of wages, the impact of employment protection legislation (EPL) depends on the bargaining strength of workers vis-à-vis employers. Changes in EPL may contribute to re-shaping wage disparities, especially in the presence of asymmetries in EPL for different segments of workers that may favour new dual labour market structures (Boeri and Garibaldi, 2007; Belot et al., 2007). In case of substantial firing and hiring costs for permanent contracts and low protection for fixed-term positions, firms will prefer placing new entrants into temporary jobs, irrespective of other workers' characteristics, including education. Deregulation of temporary work may, therefore, lead to a higher incidence of temporary employment aimed at reducing present and future labour costs, with consequent expansion of experience/informal skills gaps and, ultimately, an increase of the wage gap (Ponzellini et al., 2010). This may lead to a strengthening of a new labour market duality between secure jobs and temporary positions, in which both employers and employees have little incentive to invest in the accumulation of firm-specific skills; the likely final outcome is a polarization of fixed-term workers into traps of repeated short-duration/low-productivity/low-pay positions (Nickell and Layard, 1999; Arulampalam et al., 2007).

Data

The datasets used for the empirical analysis are the 2008 and 2012 releases of the EU-Silc (European Union Statistics on Income and Living Conditions) cross-section samples, with reference years 2007 and 2011, respectively, which allow comparing inequality levels and drivers before and after the outburst of the global crisis. We focus here on 19 EU countries, 6 from Central and Eastern Europe (the Czech Republic, Estonia, Hungary, Poland, Slovenia and the Slovak Republic) and 13 Western EU members (EU-17 minus UK, Denmark, Malta and Cyprus, due to missing information on key variables). The remaining new EU members from Eastern Europe could not be included due to missing information on labour market institutional variables (OECD employment protection legislation) considered crucial for the aims of the analysis. For the same reason, Slovenia, Estonia and Luxemburg are part of our econometric analysis only with data for 2011 (being the OECD data available for this reference year only).

The two samples are composed of 225,148 (2007) and 253,279 (2011) individuals aged between 16 and 65 years. Of them, 122,810 and 131,025, respectively, are employed as dependent workers and are the object of our empirical analysis of wage drivers. The remaining individuals (not in employment, in education, self-employed or retired) are used in the estimates to account and correct for sample selection bias. The focus on dependent work is motivated by our interest in the role of the workers' status (temporary *versus* permanent) in shaping wage differences within education levels. Of course the size of the sample is also influenced by data availability of the variables we use in the econometric analysis.

Employees' income (variable PY010G) is defined as the gross total (yearly) remuneration, in cash or in kind, payable by an employer to an employee in return for the work done in the reference period. It includes wages and salaries paid in cash, holiday payments, thirteenth month payment, overtime payment, profit sharing, bonuses and productivity premia, allowances paid for transport or for working in remote locations, as well as the social contributions and income taxes payable by employees. The use of gross wages is common in the literature that considers within-countries wage and earnings inequality (Antonczyk et al., 2010). Brandolini et al. (2010) explain in detail why the use of gross wages is, in fact, the only alternative when EU-SILC data are employed for the countries of interest here. In order to account for differences in hours worked, we compute all earning measures on an hourly basis using the information on the number of hours usually worked per week in the main job and the number of months spent at work. The top and bottom 1 per cent of the hourly wage distributions in each country and year were trimmed in order to avoid distortions by outliers. All monetary values are expressed in 2005 Euro PPPs.

In order to investigate the drivers of wage differentials within education levels, we have split the sample into three subsamples corresponding to primary-, secondary- and tertiary-educated workers, corresponding to the ISCED classification levels 0–2, 3–4, and 5–6, respectively. As explanatory variables, besides the employment status (temporary or permanent), we used a large set of individual information which include gender, age (and its square), marital status, self-reported health status (on a 1-very good to 5-very bad scale), localization (urban/non-urban region), presence of a second job, control for part-time employment, type of occupation, sector and size of the firm in which the individual is employed.[1]

As regards the analysis of the impact of labour market institutional variables, we consider the widely used OECD indicators on the strictness of employment protection legislation for regular (EPL_r) and temporary (EPL_t) employment. Specifically, EPL_r is the OECD synthetic indicator defining conditions under which both individual and collective dismissals are possible (provisions for notice periods, involvement of third parties, such as courts and works' councils, specification of severance payments and additional provisions in the case of collective dismissals). EPL_t describes the conditions under which workers can be hired on fixed-term or temporary work agency contracts. These rules usually concern the type of jobs and activities in which these contracts are allowed, their maximum duration, and the conditions for their renewal or termination. For each year, indicators refer to regulation in force on the 1st of January. Data range from 0 to 6 with higher scores representing stricter regulation (see *OECD Indicators of Employment Protection* for more information[2]). The choice of the two indicators is due to the specific focus of the analysis and aimed at capturing the evolution of institutional settings related to temporary workers and to asymmetries in their protection compared to permanent employees.

Descriptive evidence

As shown in the first two columns of Table 6.1, average hourly wages (in 2005 Euro PPPs) vary remarkably across countries, with Slovakia, Estonia and Hungary being positioned at the bottom of the distribution (between 4 and 5 Euros per hour) and the Netherlands at the top (around 22 Euros per hour). As expected, in all countries under scrutiny higher levels of education correspond to higher wages.

It is worth noting that hourly wage declined between 2007 and 2011 in 11 out of 19 countries and both Eastern (the Czech Republic, Estonia and Hungary) and Western EU members (Greece, Spain, Portugal, Italy, Luxemburg, Germany, the Netherlands, Sweden) are part of this picture. The persistent unemployment after the 2008 crisis is indicated as the responsible factor for this downward pressure on the aggregate hourly wages (OECD, 2014). Moreover, in the majority of countries with declining wages, the fall between 2007 and 2011 was observed throughout all education groups (see columns 3–8 in Table 6.1).

As regards wage inequality, Figure 6.1 provides a comparative picture of the way the wage gap between regular and temporary workers is linked to the level of regular workers' wage (data on the wage gaps are reported in Table 6.A1 in the Appendix). These gaps are built on the basis of country-level raw averages, i.e., they are calculated not controlling for other workers (such as gender, age, etc.) or job (sector, occupation, etc.) characteristics that may affect wage levels. Nonetheless, an interesting piece of information emerges. First of all, the

Table 6.1 Hourly wages by education level, 2007 and 2011

	All ISCED levels		Primary		Secondary		Tertiary	
	2007	2011	2007	2011	2007	2011	2007	2011
AT	15.56	16.52	10.34	11.67	14.97	15.44	20.56	22.41
BE	16.18	16.41	13.64	13.44	14.86	14.39	18.53	19.06
CZ	6.31	6.29	4.49	4.43	5.99	5.85	8.96	8.63
DE	15.98	15.8	11.79	11.3	13.91	13.61	19.12	19.36
EE	5.1	4.93	4.42	4.37	4.73	4.48	6.09	5.86
EL	11.47	9.04	8.52	6.92	9.78	7.77	16.09	11.74
ES	10.87	10.45	8.55	8.14	10.3	9.56	13.91	12.98
FI	13.81	14.33	11.44	12.17	11.91	12.31	16.7	16.76
FR	12.77	13.48	10.81	11.5	11.63	12.08	15.61	15.94
HU	4.58	4.4	3.08	3	3.98	3.87	7.15	6.34
IE	16.88	18.07	12.87	14.19	14.3	14.53	22.5	21.58
IT	12.45	12.38	10.26	10.16	12.66	12.4	16.8	15.89
LU	18.81	18.52	12.36	12.48	18.01	17.6	26.32	26.18
NL	22.6	21.76	17.75	16.42	20.18	19.26	28.15	26.49
PL	6.06	6.39	4.21	4.48	5.3	5.5	8.97	8.87
PT	7.83	7.4	6	5.71	8.8	7.53	15.82	13.2
SE	16.27	13.94	14.49	12.32	15.25	13.14	18.59	15.4
SI	9.8	10.03	6.9	7.04	8.81	8.59	14.73	14.18
SK	4.67	5.6	3.4	4.13	4.4	5.21	6.04	6.9
Total	11.9	11.87	9.76	9.51	10.22	10.14	16.47	15.83

Source: own elaboration on EU-Silc data

scatter plots disclose a non-linear relationship, since the regular/temporary workers' wage gap increases as the average level of the regular workers' remuneration grows only until a certain threshold (around 15 Euros per hour); beyond the threshold, the higher the rewards for secure jobs, the lower the gap. This non-linear relationship holds for all workers (all ISCED levels of education), and it is especially apparent for workers with primary and tertiary education. We find all Eastern countries at the bottom and the Mediterranean countries and Germany at the top of the upward sloping part of the curve; for them, the higher the regular workers' wage, the higher the regular/temporary workers' wage gap. In contrast, the Netherlands is located on the downward sloping part of the relationship, where the opposite holds: the higher the regular workers' wage, the lower the wage gap. However, in this part of the curve things are more differentiated when we look into different education levels. Within the group of workers with primary education the Netherlands is on the descending part of the curve together with France, Belgium and Sweden, whereas in the case of workers with tertiary education the Netherlands joins Austria, Ireland and Luxemburg.

It is worth noting that after the outbreak of the crisis the average regular/temporary workers' wage gap remarkably declines within the group of workers with primary education in France, Belgium, Germany, Greece and Finland, and slightly decreases in the Czech Republic, Estonia and Poland (see Table A1 in the Appendix). The number of countries that shows a declining wage gap after the crisis grows if we consider the highly educated

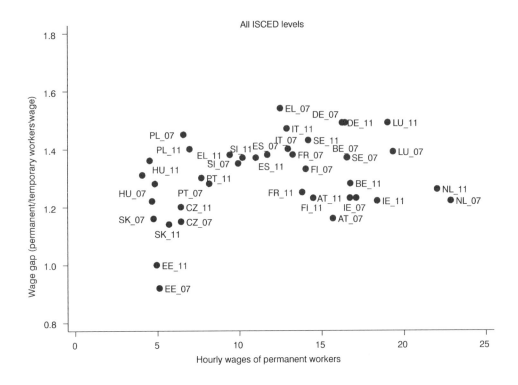

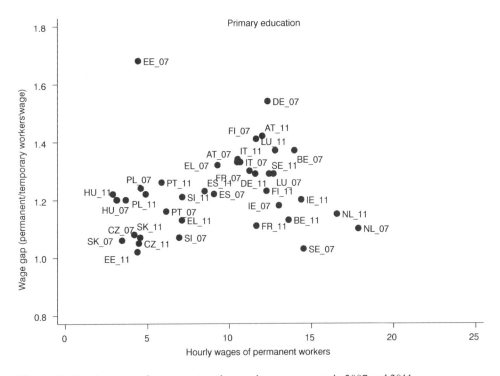

Figure 6.1 Hourly wages of permanent workers and raw wage gaps in 2007 and 2011

Source: own elaboration on EU-Silc data

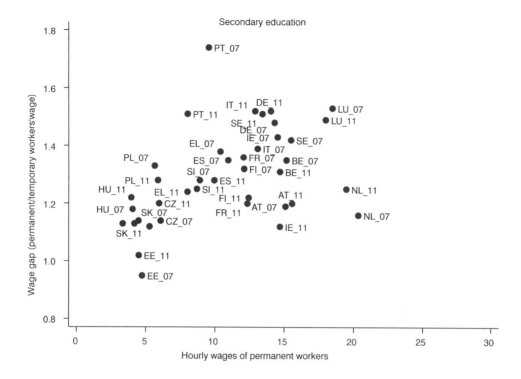

Secondary education

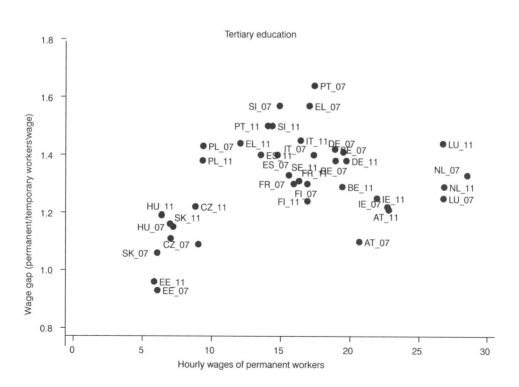

Tertiary education

workers. In this case, the Netherlands, Portugal, Sweden and Slovenia add to the countries mentioned above.

Figure 6.2 shows the distribution of countries according to their level of employment protection legislation (EPL) measured by OECD for regular (individual and collective dismissals) and temporary workers in 2007 and 2011. As expected, very little changes occurred in these labour market institutions over the short period considered here. By adding to the diagrams averages levels of employment protection, we can identify three quadrants of interest in which the countries are classified. The Mediterranean countries, plus France, Belgium and Luxemburg, show highly regulated labour markets both for regular and temporary workers (North-East quadrant). The majority of Eastern countries, plus Ireland, Austria, Finland and Sweden are located in the opposite quadrant (low regulated labour markets). Eventually, Germany, the Netherlands, the Czech Republic and Slovenia fall in an area of asymmetry in which high protection levels against individual and collective dismissals are accompanied by high deregulation for temporary jobs.

By combining these different employment protection regimes with the aggregate wage inequality between regular and temporary workers reported above, we can only have partial, preliminary evidence on their relationship. According to the mainstream view, when the "insiders" on permanent contracts cannot raise their wage claims, because they are not strongly protected, lower differences in rewards occur between regular and temporary workers (Bentolila and Dolado, 1994). This is the case, in our sample, for the low regulated countries falling in the South-West quadrant of Figure 6.2, even though Poland and Sweden are exceptions, due to their larger wage gaps. On the other hand, when extensive protection for workers with open-ended contract coexists with lighter regulation for fixed-term contracts, firms react by substituting temporary for regular workers and differences in rewards between these two categories of employees are boosted by the emergence of strong dual labour markets (OECD, 2013). Empirically, some countries included in the area of the asymmetric protection levels (Slovenia and Germany) and other countries located nearby (Italy and Portugal) show these characteristics. However, the Netherlands and Czech Republic are exceptions that do not seem to corroborate this view. Moreover, the combination of Figures 6.1 and 6.2 also reveals that there are highly regulated countries, such as Belgium and France, in which the high level of wage gap remarkably declined after the outbreak of the crisis, especially within the group of workers with primary education.

Of course, these aggregate features hide most of the existing heterogeneity in the relationship between employment protection and wage inequality. The micro-econometric analysis we provide in the next section aims at studying at an individual level the impact of labour market institutions discussed above. By taking into account all individual, job and production characteristics of workers, we consider two dimensions along which to study the possible effects of employment protection regimes. The first dimension is the different educational attainment of workers: the impact of employment protection on the regular/temporary workers' wage gap will be evaluated within each group of education (primary, secondary and tertiary education). The second dimension is the wage distribution itself: both the status of temporary workers and the impact of regulation on this labour status will be evaluated not only through the conditional mean (OLS regression) but also in different points of the wage distribution by means of the quantile regression methods.

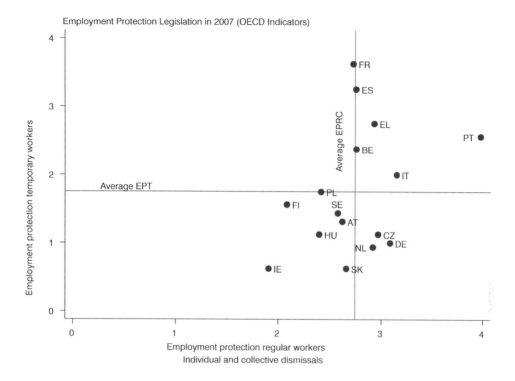

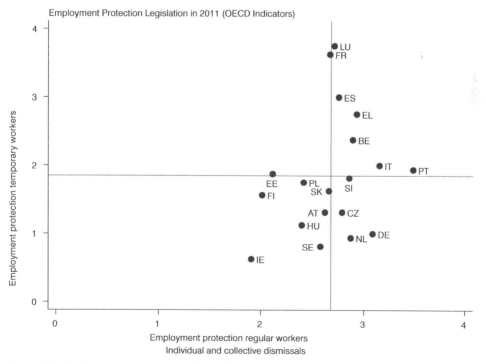

Figure 6.2. Employment protection legislation for temporary and regular workers

Source: Online OECD Employment database

Econometric methods

In order to estimate the baseline empirical model (whole sample) for the drivers of individual wages, expressed as log hourly wages (*lhwage*), we rely on the human capital model as the theoretical basis for the earnings function (Becker, 1964; Mincer, 1958). We, therefore, assume that labour income increases first of all with accumulated formal (education) and informal (experience) skills. The latter is only partially approximated with age, as the work experience measure (PL 200 – number of years spent in paid work) in EU-Silc is not available for all countries and has many missing values. Other explanatory variables, as already mentioned, are gender (*male*), marital status (*married*), health status (*health*); urban/non-urban region of residence (*urb*); second job (*secjob*); part-time job position (*part*); sector of employment (*sec*); occupation (*occ*); size of the firm (*size*). Information about occupations also helps internalizing in the analysis the distinction between routine/not-routine task and their role in shaping relative earnings (Autor et al., 2003). The variable of our main interest here is permanent/temporary employment status (coded as *temp=1* if the contract is temporary and 0 otherwise); the coefficient of this dummy variable can, therefore, be interpreted as the (otherwise) unexplained wage gap (in per cent) due to the employment contract.

The investigation of the impact of institutional factors (of course measured at country level) on the effects of being a temporary worker originates a multilevel structure of data, in which observations at the individual level are nested within the country level. The conservative strategy of simply using clustered standard errors (where the clusters are the countries) (Angrist and Pischke, 2009) allows accounting for the fact that individuals within a country share unobserved characteristics and, therefore, preventing the underestimation of standard errors of the estimated coefficients at individual level. However, this approach is not functional to the aim of the analysis since the within country correlation is controlled for but not explicitly modelled. An alternative approach would be a multilevel (hierarchical) regression modelling techniques, also known as random effects (RE) or mixed models (see, among others, Hox, 2010, or Peugh, 2010), in which country-level regressors can be used as model predictors, besides deriving country-specific intercepts and country-specific slopes of individual variables. Unfortunately, as shown by Bryan and Jenkins (2013), in the presence of a small number of countries the multilevel modelling is likely to produce unreliable estimates of parameters for the country effects (country random variances being biased downwards). In particular, through Monte-Carlo simulations, the authors show that, in order to produce reliable estimates, the number of countries should at least be around 25 (for linear models), which is not the case here. The alternative is to rely on a fixed effect (FE) model, i.e., pooling the country surveys and including distinct country intercepts. In the simplest, baseline case the individual effects are constrained to be equal across countries, but they can be allowed to differ between countries by interacting subsets of individual-level characteristics with the country dummies. The use of country fixed effects prevents the inclusion of additional country-level predictors in the empirical model, since the country intercepts already fully encapsulate cross-country differences (Snijders and Bosker, 1999). However, additional country level variables can be interacted with individual level variables, so to obtain the additional effect that a country level factor produces on the main (individual level) effect. This is what is needed for the purposes of our analysis, i.e., estimating the effects of country-level institutional settings on the temporary/permanent workers pay gap, by simply interacting the (country-level) institutional indicator and the employment status (individual-level dummy variable).

With this approach, we estimate our empirical model for the 19 EU countries, pooling together the 2007 and the 2011 data (total number of observation is 253,835). This pooling allows estimating the effect of the crisis on the condition of being temporary by means of interaction terms between *temp* and the dummy variables for the two years (2007 and 2011) and to statistically test their difference. The inclusion of both interactions (instead of the main effect – *temp* – plus one interaction) has the advantage of directly providing the estimates of *temp* in the two years.

Our baseline (all education levels) pooled (by country and by year) empirical model takes, therefore, the following form:

$$
\begin{aligned}
lhwage_{ic} = {} & cons_{ic} + \omega_1 temp_{ic} \cdot Year07 + \omega_2 temp_{ic} \cdot Year11 \\
& + \vartheta_1 temp_{ic} \cdot INST_c \cdot Year07 + \vartheta_2 temp_{ic} \cdot INST_c \cdot Year11 + \alpha_1 male_{ic} \\
& + \alpha_2 married_{ic} + \alpha_3 age_{ic} + \alpha_4 age_{ic}^2 + \alpha_5 health_{ic} + \alpha_6 urb_{ic} \\
& + \sum_{e=1}^{2} \beta_e educ_{ic,e} + \varphi_1 \sec job_{ic} + \varphi_2 part_{ic} + \sum_{s=1}^{2} \vartheta_s size_{ic,s} + \sum_{n=1}^{7} \upsilon_n \sec_{ic,n} \\
& + \sum_{r=1}^{5} \xi_r occ_{ic,r} + \tau west_c + u_c + u_c \cdot Year11 + \varepsilon_{ic}
\end{aligned}
\tag{6.1}
$$

where subscripts i and c stand for individuals and countries, respectively and the acronyms indicate the explanatory variables described above. In particular, *educ* is the set of dummy variables describing the level of education; *size, sec* and *occ* are the dummies for firms' size, sector and the workers occupation; $west_c$ is a dummy variable which is one for Western Eu members and zero otherwhise; u_c represent unobservable country-specific effects and ε_{ic} is the individual error term. The country specific effects are also interacted with the year 2011 dummy in order to model the country-specific effects of the crisis on individuals' pays.

As customary in the literature (Bassanini et al., 2009; Bourlès et al., 2012), the two institutional variables (EPL_t and EPL_r) are lagged one period in order to alleviate endogeneity issues and to account for the fact that *de jure* institutional reforms take time to become effective.

The baseline empirical model described in equation 6.1 is then estimated for each subsample of workers with primary, secondary and tertiary education (composed of 45,026, 131,725 and 77,084 obeservations, respectively).

The empirical model following from Equation (6.1) allows estimating only average effects of explanatory variables on log hourly wage and, in particular, average temporary/permanent wage gaps. However, such an approach would oversimplify the phenomenon under scrutiny if the gap is not constant across the wage distribution. In addition, a model limited to average effects only would prevent us from identifying the possible heterogeneity of the effects of institutional variables on temporary/regular wage gaps at various points of the wage distribution.

The investigation of the variety of temporary/permanent gap and institutional setting effects across the wage distribution is possible with quantile regression (QR) approaches. Following Koenker and Basset (1978), the model of QR can be simply described in terms of conditional θth quantile (instead of conditional mean as in the standard regression) distribution of y_i conditional on a vector of covariates x_i under the assumption of linear specification:

$$
Q_\theta(y_i | x_i) = x_i \beta_\theta
\tag{6.2}
$$

implying $y_i = x_i\beta_\theta + \varepsilon_{\theta,i}$. The semiparametric nature of the approach lies in the fact that the distribution of the error term $\varepsilon_{\theta,i}$, $F_{\varepsilon,\theta}(\cdot)$, is left unspecified, and $\varepsilon_{\theta,i}$ satisfies $Q_\theta(\varepsilon_{\theta,i}|x_i) = 0$

The θth QR estimator $\hat{\beta}_\theta$ minimizes over β_θ the following objective function:

$$Q(\beta_\theta) = \sum_{ty_i \geq x_i\beta}^{n} \theta|y_i - x_i\beta_\theta| + \sum_{ty_i < x_i\beta}^{n} (1-\theta)|y_i - x_i\beta_\theta| \tag{6.3}$$

The estimated vector of QR coefficients $\hat{\beta}_\theta$ measures the marginal change in the conditional quantile θ due to a marginal change in the corresponding element of the vector of coefficients on x, and is obtained via the optimization techniques described in Cameron and Trivedi (2010), as the usual gradient optimization method cannot be applied since the objective function (6.3) is not differentiable. QR estimations are run using the simultaneous quantile regression (sqreg) routine available in STATA, which allows specifying simultaneously different values of θ and testing whether regression coefficients of interest for various θ do differ (by means of a Wald test). This option provides bootstrap standard errors, which are robust and assume independence over i but do not require errors to be identically distributed.

A last important empirical aspect that needs to be carefully addressed refers to a possible estimation bias due to sample selection. If selection of individuals into employment is non-random the direction in which it may affect the level of earnings is a concern (De la Rica et al., 2008; Heckman, 1979; Buchinsky, 1998). In order to correct for possible bias rooted in self-selection into employment, we follow here the approach by Buchinsky (1998) – see also Albrecht et al. (2009) and Nicodemo (2009) for more details – and include into the specification a term $h_\theta(z\lambda)$, where z is the set of observable characteristics that influence the probability that an individual is employed (see also Perugini and Selezneva, 2015, for further details on the method). The term plays the role that the Mills ratio plays in Heckman (1979) procedure, but is quantile-specific and hence corrects for selection into employment at each θth quantile. Following Arumpalan et al. (2006) and Mendez Errico (2013) we therefore control for the selectivity bias in QR earning equation expanding $h_\theta(z\lambda)$ as a power series in the inverse Mill's ratio, derived from a participation equation dependent on the vector of the z explanatory variables.[3] In order to estimate the first stage participation equation, in addition to the personal characteristics used in equation 6.1, we add variables related to household structure that we were able to build considering the information available in EU-Silc. They refer to the number of household components, of children (less than 3, 4–6 and 7–15 years old) and of elderly (65–74 and over 75 years old).

Results

The results for the baseline specification are reported in Figure 6.3, where the adjusted wage gap between temporary and regular workers has been reported as estimated by both OLS and quantile regressions (complete results of the quantile estimations are available in Tables A2–A5 in the Appendix; OLS results are available upon request). It is worth noting that, once all other observable wage drivers are controlled for, a temporary worker is always penalized in terms of wages with respect to a regular worker. This holds for all groups of workers classified by educational attainment. In addition, the burden of the downward wage adjustment is placed on temporary workers independently on the part of the wage distribution on which they are located. Indeed, the graphics show that for every quantile the estimated coefficient is negative, even though a huge heterogeneity emerges, related to the size of the gap along the wage distribution.

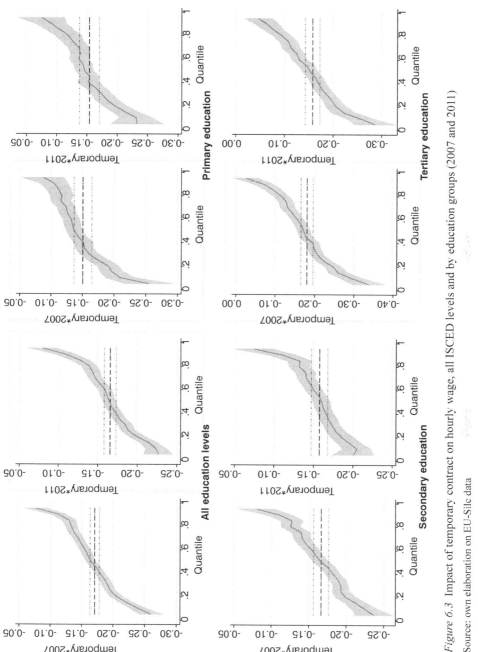

Figure 6.3 Impact of temporary contract on hourly wage, all ISCED levels and by education groups (2007 and 2011)

Source: own elaboration on EU-Silc data

Overall, according to the OLS coefficient (horizontal dashed line[4]) temporary workers earned wages from 18 per cent to 17 per cent lower than regular workers in 2007 and 2011. These adjusted negative gaps, estimated by means of conditional means, are slightly lower for workers with primary education (around -15per cent), increase to -17per cent and -16per cent for workers with intermediate education and peak to -19% and -18% for the highly educated employees. Of course, the overall and systematic negative differential between the temporary and regular workers' rewards is well documented in the empirical studies (Brown and Sessions, 2005; Booth et al., 2002; Picchio, 2008, Bosio, 2014). One reason explaining this wage penalty relies on the efficiency wage theory (Rebitzer and Taylor, 1991; Guell, 2000). The possibility for a contract renewal may be used as an effort-incentive device instead of wages. Thus, fixed-term workers accept lower wages because firms link their performance to the promise of a contract renewal or their hiring on a permanent position. Another explanation for this negative wage gap addresses to investments in a lower amount of firm-specific training (Booth et al., 2002; Bosio, 2014). Due to their high turnover, temporary workers have less incentive to accumulate firm-specific skills that boost productivity: the lower the productivity and the lower the wages they get with respect to the permanent workers. This last explanation allows us to underpin the additional evidence we find in this study, i.e., the larger average negative wage gap associated to higher education levels. If there are complementarities between unobservable firm-specific human capital and formal education, it is plausible to hypothesize major accumulation of this informal knowledge in workers with tertiary education (Arulampalam et al., 2004). Thus, if temporary workers with higher formal education are not allowed to accumulate this firm-specific human capital, the wage gap with respect to regular workers increases relatively more than for lower educated employees.

However, the focus of this study is on temporary/regular workers' wage differences over the whole wage distribution, and Figure 6.3 clearly shows that a strong heterogeneity exists in the magnitude of this wage gap for each group of workers stratified by the education level. Similarly to results obtained for all ISCED levels (upper left-side panel), within each education group the negative coefficients for the dummy "temporary worker" are larger at the bottom of the distribution, whereas they gradually reduce for higher quantiles. This evidence is coherent with the findings of other studies and supports the idea of a *sticky floor effect* for temporary workers, in which the highest wage penalty is charged to lowest-paid jobs (Bosio, 2014; Comi and Grasseni, 2009, Mertens et al., 2007). Despite their similar patterns and the overall reduction of the *sticky floor effect* in 2011 (after the outbreak of the crisis), the magnitude of the wage gaps at the tails of the distribution remarkably varies across education levels. Within the group of workers with tertiary education the 10th percentile wage gap was -25.4% and the 90th percentile wage gap was -6.5% in 2011. The correspondent values for workers with secondary education were -20.5% and -10%, respectively. Workers with primary education show in the same year a wage gap that ranges from -23.1% to -9.1%, respectively. Therefore, a particluarly strong *sticky floor* effect and a large wage gap variability seem characteristics specific to the group of the highly educated workers.

In order to explain this evidence, we have to consider that there are a number of economic variables that are not typically available in micro datasets, as that one we are using here, but that can affect wages. Examples are unobserved ability and unmeasured components of human capital formation such as informal training giving rise to productivity differences. They can explain why there is still a wide dispersion of wages even after conditioning on formal education and on a range of other observable individual, social and productive characteristics. In addition, the wage distribution might reflect heterogeneity in the mix of specific-general skills that workers accumulate through their informal training (Stevens, 1994; Lazear, 2003). Again, if there are complementarities between this skills mix and formal education (Arulampalam et al., 2004), we can hypothesize that high-paid jobs graduate temporary workers are more able to arrange a skill mix where general competences become more important compared to the specific skills. If this is the case, the high job turnover is no longer strongly harmful to the graduate temporary worker, who is now better able to exploit his bargaining power and his outside option by anticipating the contract renewal and by exerting a choice among better-paid jobs. Hence, the wage gap might significantly drop. In contrast, for low-paid jobs the low levels of experience and informal training hinder a skill mix formation with significant general competences. In this case graduate permanent workers are largely advantaged in the firm-specific skills formation and the wage gap with respect to their peers temporarily employed enlarges. If the complementarity assumption between formal education and informal training holds, it is plausible to hypothesize that the phenomena explained above are attenuated for lower levels of education. For secondary and primary educated workers the ability to build skills mix with significant level of general knowledge is lower, hence the *sticky floor* effect remains important and the 90th percentile wage gap is larger than that found for graduate fixed-term employees.

The next step, as anticipated in previous sections, is dedicated to investigate the effects of employment protection regimes on the temporary/permanent jobs wage gap. Again, the analysis takes into account both different groups of workers according to the education levels and the wage distribution within these groups. Figure 6.4 reports the coefficients (OLS – dashed line and quantile regression – solid line) of the interaction between the dummy "Temporary worker" and employment protection of temporary workers (EPL_t), as formalized in equation 6.1. Overall, it seems that higher protection levels for temporary workers plays a positive role in reducing wage inequality, especially within groups of workers with primary and secondary education and after the outbreak of the crisis.

Especially for primary workers, Figure 6.4 describes an important reduction in the *sticky floor* effect (the coefficient for the 10th quantile is significantly higher than the median coefficient) that can be attributed to higher EPL_t. As explained above, temporary employees with low education levels are less able to develop general skills that reduce the negative effects of high job turnover; therefore, lower firm-specific skills negatively reverberate on labour productivity and wages. In addition, according to the efficiency wage theory, the wage paid might be lower even with a high productivity temporary employee, because in this case the employer substitutes the incentive-pay with an incentive based on the possibility for a contract renewal (Guell, 2000). Restrictions on the number of renewals, cumulated duration of fixed-term contracts and motivations on which these contracts are possible, force employers to re-consider the incentive-pay as a driver to extract more effort from the fixed-term employees. This might especially have occurred after the outbreak of the crisis, when the labour reallocation processes from declining to the emerging firms/sectors has been extensive and entrepreneurs had to devote particular attention to the productivity and efficiency improvements of firm organization and its labour force. In contrast, the comparative advantage of highly educated temporary workers in terms of major bargaining power and better outside options explain the poorly significant effect of EPL_t in reducing the wage gap for this category of workers.

Studies on employment protection legislation always recommend that analyses on the restrictions for temporary workers should be paired by investigations upon the effects of

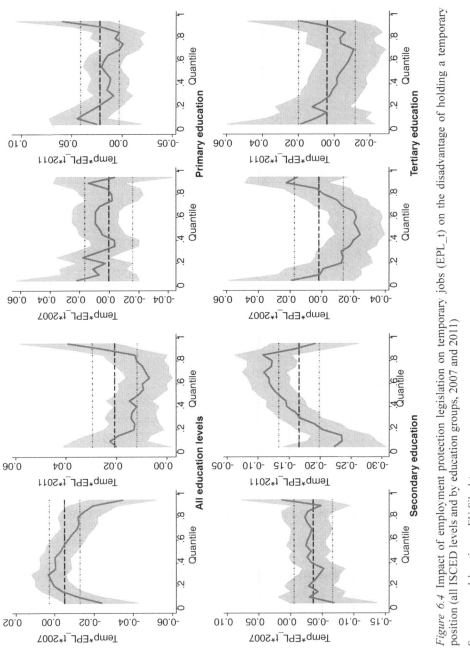

Figure 6.4 Impact of employment protection legislation on temporary jobs (EPL_t) on the disadvantage of holding a temporary position (all ISCED levels and by education groups, 2007 and 2011)

Source: own elaboration on EU-Silc data

protection levels for regular workers (OECD, 2013). Lax rules for fixed-term contracts very often reflect excessive protection for open-ended arrangements. As explained above, higher protection fosters the accumulation of firm-specific skills; as a consequence, higher wage claims from these protected workers also originate from their higher productivity performances. In any case, the final result should be an increase in wage inequality between permanent and temporary employees. Figure 6.5 depicts the impact of restrictions on individual and collective dismissals, i.e. higher EPL_r, on the wage gap under scrutiny. Overall (all ISCED levels) and within each education group, the higher the EPL_r, the higher the negative wage gap of temporary workers with respect to that of the permanent ones. Moreover, in all groups, excessive restrictions exacerbate the *sticky floor* effect, i.e., the wage gap for the low-paid jobs. Therefore, the interpretations provided above receive significant support.

It is worth noting that the opposite results obtained for EPL_t (more regulation reduces inequality) and EPL_r (more regulation worsens inequality) suggest that asymmetries in protection levels are at work and boost dual labour markets and inequality. The country-level descriptive evidence discussed in the previous section supported this line of reasoning by showing that especially Western EU countries mainly fall into the area of the strongest employment protection asymmetries.

Final remarks

This study investigated the extent of hourly wage gap between the temporary and regular workers pay, providing new evidence upon the effect exerted on the gap by employment protection provisions. The cross-country empirical analysis covered 19 European Union members for the years 2007 and 2011, characterized by different regimes of employment protection against individual and collective dismissals and by different restrictions in hiring fixed-term workers. Despite the increasing number of studies focusing on this subject, our investigation adds new knowledge by considering the temporary/permanent hourly wage gap both within different eduction groups (primary, secondary and tertiary) and along the wage distribution of each group. By so doing, we are able to provide a more comprehensive picture of the variability of this gap and to show the heterogenous effects of employment protection provisions, especially on the side of temporary workers hiring regulations.

Coherently with the *sticky floor* hypothesis that dominates the literature on temporary workers, the temporary/regular wage gap is larger for low-paid jobs (bottom of the wage distribution) and gradually reduces with higher quantiles (median and top of the wage distribution), for all education levels. However, we also find that this *sticky floor* is remarkably higher for graduate temporary workers (tertiary level of education) and only for this category of workers more quickly narrows at the top of the wage distribution. Our interpretation is that this specific outcome is due to the strong complementarities between the highest level of formal education and informal (on the job) training; the latter, in turn, shapes the mix of specific-general skills. For low-paid jobs (bottom of the wage distribution) this skills mix is skewed towards firm-specific knowledge. If we compare the conditions between graduate employees with open-ended and fixed-term contracts, what emerges is that the higher turnover makes it difficult for temporary workers to build firm-specific skills. As a consequence, the wage gap is larger at the bottom of the distribution. In contrast, for better paid jobs, general informal knowledge gains importance in the skills mix; hence, job turnover is less harmful and the higher bargaining power of graduate temporary workers allows them choosing new fixed-term contracts by claiming higher wages. Therefore, the

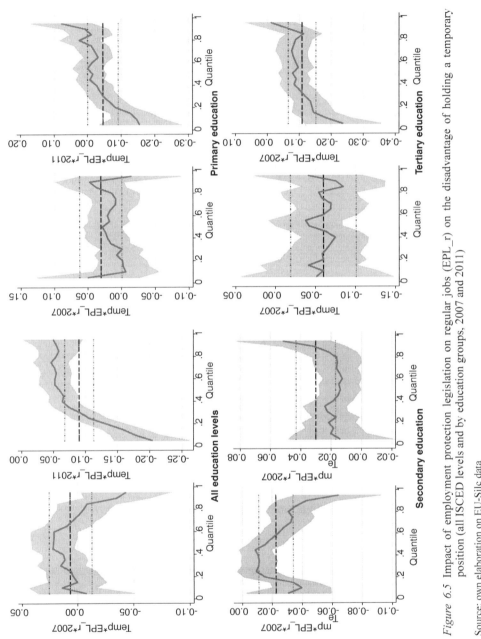

Figure 6.5 Impact of employment protection legislation on regular jobs (EPL_r) on the disadvantage of holding a temporary position (all ISCED levels and by education groups, 2007 and 2011)

Source: own elaboration on EU-Silc data

wage gap decreases. This phenomenon attenuates with lower levels of formal education. This explains why weaker *sticky floors* at the bottom and higher wage gaps at the top of the wage distribution have been found for temporary workers with primary and secondary levels of education.

Generally speaking, the complex picture of the impact of employment protection legislation on the wage penalty for temporary workers can be summarized with the opposite evidence found for protection of temporary and regular workers. Increasing restrictions on temporary contracts improve the conditions of temporary workers by reducing the wage gap; on the contrary, more restrictions on individual and collective dismissals for regual workers enhance the disparity. This result is coherent with the findings from other studies and corroborates the idea of a detrimental effect of the asymmetries existing between the excessive restrictions on the side of regular employment and the strong deregulation for temporary contracts. In our comparative perspective, we were able to show that strong asymmetries are particularly at work in some Mediterranean countries, such as Portugal and Italy, and in Germany.

However, the value added of the study relies on the detailed picture that we offer by depicting the effects of protection for temporary workers within the different workers education groups. The wage gap reducing effect played by more severe restrictions on the recruiting of temporary workers is significant only for individuals with primary and secondary education. For graduate temporary workers at the bottom of the wage distribution where, supposedly, the construction of skills mix with important complementarieties between formal education and general informal knowledge is more difficult, the wage gap remains remarkably high. This indicates that these educated workers are at risk of poor labour income mobility and of falling/staying into low productivity-low wage traps; and in this case reducing asymmetries between protection for regular and temporary workers as they are, would bring little change. More research is needed for a better understanding of the real causes underlying this impressive *sticky floor* effect for educated temporary workers in order to develop adequate policies able to complement current employment protection legislations.

Notes

1 Occupations are classified into six categories: 1. Managers and senior officials, 2. Professional and technicians, 3. Clerks, 4. Skilled agricultural and craft workers, 5. Machine operators, 6. Elementary occupations. Industry breakdown has been limited to eight sectors: 1. Agriculture, 2. Industry, 3. Constructions, 4. Trade, 5. Transport, 6. Hotels and restaurants, 7. Business services, 8. Other services. Lastly, we consider three firm size classes: 0–10, 11–49, 50 and over employees.
2 http://www.oecd.org/els/emp/oecdindicatorsofemploymentprotection.htm, last accessed 27 July 2015.
3 The participation equation is estimated by both: (i) a standard probit approach, and (ii) a single index model (Ichimura, 1993), using the semiparametric ML estimator of Klein and Spady (1993).
4 The dotted lines indicate the 95% confidence intervals. Solid line and the shadowed area are the coefficients of the estimated conditional quantiles and the 95% confidence interval, respectively.

References

Acemoglu, D. and Autor, D. (2012) What does human capital do? A review of Goldin and Katz's *The Race between Education and Technology*. *Journal of Economic Literature*. 50(2): 426–463.

Albrecht, J., Van Vuuren, A. and Vroman, S. (2009). Counterfactual distributions with sample selection adjustments: Econometric theory and an application to the Netherlands. *Labour Economics*, 16(4): 383–396.

Angrist, J.D. and Pischke, J.-S. (2009) *Mostly Harmless Econometrics: An Empiricist's Companion.* Princeton, NJ: Princeton University Press.

Antonczyk, D., Fitzenberger, B. and Sommerfeld, K. (2010) Rising wage inequality, the decline of collective bargaining, and the gender wage gap. *Labour Economics,* 17(5): 835–847.

Arulampalam, W., Booth, A.L., Bryan, M.L. (2004), *Are There Asymmetries in the Effects of Training on the Conditional Male Wage Distribution?* IZA Working Papers 984.

Arulampalam, W., Booth, A.L., Bryan, M.L. (2007) Is there a glass ceiling over Europe? Exploring the gender pay gap across the wage distribution. *Industrial and Labor Relations Review*, 60(2): 163–186.

Arulampalam, W., Manquilef, A. and Smith, J. (2006) Quantile regression analysis of union wage premia in the United Kingdom, 1991–2003, unpublished mimeo.

Atkinson, A., Piketty, T. and Saez, E. (2011). Top incomes in the long run of history. *Journal of Economic Literature*, 49(1): 3–71.

Atkinson, A.B. (2007) The distribution of earnings in OECD countries. *International Labour Review*, 146(1–2): 41–60.

Autor, D. and Katz, L.F. (1999) Changes in the wage structure and earnings inequality. In Ashenfelter, O. and Card, D. (eds). *Handbook of Labor Economics, vol 3A*. Amsterdam: Elsevier Science.

Autor, D., Levy, F. and Murnane, R. (2003) The skill content of recent technological change: An empirical investigation. *Quarterly Journal of Economics*, 118: 1279–1333.

Bassanini, A., Nunziata, L. and Venn, D. (2009). Job protection legislation and productivity growth in OECD countries. *Economic Policy*, 2(58): 349–402.

Becker, G.J. (1964) *Human Capital: A Theoretical and Empirical Analysis, with Special Reference to Education*. Chicago, IL: University of Chicago Press.

Belot, M., Boone, J. and van Ours, J.C. (2007) Welfare-improving employment protection. *Economica*, 74(8): 381–396.

Bentolila, S. and Dolado, J. (1994) Labour flexibility and wages: lessons from Spain, *Economic Policy*, 18: 55–99.

Boeri, T. and Garibaldi, P. (2007) Two tier reforms of employment protection: A honeymoon effect? *Economic Journal*, 117: 357–385.

Booth, A., Francesconi, M. and Frank, J. (2002), Temporary jobs: Stepping stones or dead ends?, *The Economic Journal,* 112 (480): 189–213

Bosio, G. (2014), The implications of temporary jobs on the distribution of wages in Italy: An unconditional IVQTE approach, *Labour*, 28 (1): 64–86.

Bourlès, R., Cette, G., Lopez, J., Mairesse, J. and Nicoletti, G. (2012) *Do Product Market Regulations in Upstream Sectors Curb Productivity Growth? Panel data Evidence for OECD Countries*. NBER Working Paper 16520.

Brandolini, A., Rosolia, A. and Torrini, R. (2010) *The Distribution of Employees' Labour Earnings in the EU: Data, Concepts and First Results*. Eurostat Methodologies and Working Papers, Eurostat.

Brown, S. and Sessions, J. (2005) Employee attitudes, earnings and fixed-term contracts: International evidence, *Review of World Economics*, 141(2): 296–317.

Bryan, M.L. and Jenkins, S.P. (2013) *Regression Analysis of Country Effects Using Multilevel Data: A Cautionary Tale*. IZA Discussion Paper 7583. Bonn: IZA.

Buchinsky, M. (1998) Recent advances in quantile regression models: A practical guideline for empirical research. *Journal of Human Resources*, 23(1): 88–126.

Cameron, A.C. and Trivedi, P.K. (2010) *Microeconometrics Using Stata,* Revised Edition. College Station, TX: Stata Press.

Card, D. (1992) *The Effects of Unions on the Distribution of Wages: Redistribution or Labeling?* NBER Working paper No. 4195.

Checchi, D. and García-Peñalosa, C. (2008) Labour market institutions and income inequality. *Economic Policy*, 23(56): 601–649.

Chusseau, N., Dumont, M. and Hellier, J. (2008) Explaining rising inequality: skill-biased technical change and North–South trade. *Journal of Economic Surveys*, 22(3): 409–557.

Comi, S. and Grasseni, M. (2009) A*re Temporary Workers Discriminated Against? Evidence from Europe*, CHILD Working Paper 17.

De la Rica, S., Dolado, J.J. and Llorens, V. (2008) Ceilings or floors? gender wage gaps by education in Spain. *Journal of Population Economics*, 21(3): 751–776.

Dustmann, C., Ludsteck, J. and Schonberg, U. (2009) Revisiting the German wage structure. *Quarterly Journal of Economics*, 124(2): 843–881.

Firpo, S., Fortin, N.M. and Lemieux, T. (2010) Occupational tasks and changes in the wage structure. UBC unpublished manuscript.

Fortin, N.M. and Lemieux, T. (1997) Institutional changes and rising wage inequality: Is there a linkage? *Journal of Economic Perspectives*, 11(2): 75–96.

Freeman, R.B. (1993) How much has de-unionisation contributed to the rise of male earnings inequality? In Danzinger, S. and Gottschalk, P. (eds). *Uneven Tides: Rising Income Inequality in America*. New York: Russel Sage Foundation.

Goldin, C. and Katz, L. (2008) *The Race between Education and Technology*. Cambridge, MA: Belknap Press for Harvard University Press.

Goos, M. and Manning, A. (2007) Lousy and lovely jobs: The rising polarization of work in Britain. *Review of Economics and Statistics*, 89(1): 118–133.

Goos, M., Manning, A. and Salomons, A. (2009) Job polarization in Europe. *American Economic Review*, 99(2): 58–63.

Guell M. (2000) *Fixed-Term Contracts and Unemployment: An Efficiency Wage Analysis*, CEP Discussion Papers 461, Centre for Economic Performance, LSE.

Heckman, J.J. (1979) Sample selection bias as a specification error. *Econometrica*, 47(1): 153–161.

Hox, J. (2010) *Multilevel Analysis: Techniques and Applications*. London: Routledge Academic.

Lazear, E.P. (2003) *Firm-specific Human Capital: A Skill-Weights Approach*, IZA Discussion Paper 813.

Lehmann, H. and Muravyev, A. (2012) Labor market institutions and labor market performance: What can we learn from transition countries? *Economics of Transition*, 20(2): 235–269.

Levy, F. and Murnane, R.J. (1992) U.S. earnings levels and earnings inequality: A review of recent trends and proposed explanations. *Journal of Economic Literature*, 30(3): 1333–1381.

Koenker, R., and Bassett, G. (1978) Regression quantiles. *Econometrica*, 46(1): 33–50.

Machin, S. (2008) An appraisal of economic research on changes in wage inequality. *Labour*, 22: 7–26.

Mendez Errico, L. (2013) The impacts of social networks on immigrants' employment prospects: The Spanish case 1997–2007, Document de Treball No. 13.1, Universitat Autonoma de Barcelona. http://www.ecap.uab.es (last accessed 27 March 2015).

Mertens A., Gash V. and McGinnity, F. (2007) The cost of flexibility at the margin. Comparing the wage penalty for fixed-term contracts in Germany and Spain using quantile regression, *Labour*, 21(4/5): 637–666.

Mincer, J. (1958) Investment in human capital and personal income distribution. *The Journal of Political Economy*, 66(4): 281–302.

Nickell, S. and Layard, R. (1999) Labour market institutions and economic performance. In Ashenfelter, O. and Card, D. (eds.). *Handbook of Labor Economics*. Amsterdam: North Holland Press.

Nicodemo, C. (2009) *Gender Pay Gap and Quantile Regression in European Families*, IZA Working Paper 3978, Bonn: Institute for the Study of Labor (IZA). http://www.iza.org/en/webcontent/publications/papers (last accessed 27 March 2015).

OECD (2011) *Divided We Stand: Why Inequality Keeps Rising*. Paris: OECD Publishing.

OECD (2013), *OECD Employment Outlook*, 2013, Paris: OECD Publishing.

OECD (2014), *OECD Employment Outlook*, 2014, Paris: OECD Publishing.

Perugini, C. and Selezneva, E. (2015) Labour market institutions, crisis and gender earnings gap in Eastern Europe, *The Economics of Transition*. DOI: 10.1111/ecot.12072.

Peugh, J.L. (2010) A practical guide to multilevel modeling. *Journal of School Psychology*, 48(1): 85–112.

Picchio M. (2008) Temporary contracts and transitions to stable jobs in Italy, *Labour*, 22(1): 147–174.

Ponzellini, A.M., Aumayr, C. and Wolf, F. (2010) *Addressing the Gender Wage Gap: Government and Social Partner Actions*. Dublin: Eurofound.

Rebitzer, J. B and Taylor, L.J. (1991) A model of dual labor markets when product demand is uncertain, *The Quarterly Journal of Economics*, 106(4): 1373–1383.

Stevens, M. (1994) A theoretical model of on-the-job training with imperfect competition, *Oxford Economic Papers*, 46: 537–62.

Snijders, T.A.B. and Bosker, R. (1999) *Multilevel Analysis: An Introduction to Basic and Advanced Multilevel Modeling*. Thousand Oaks, CA: Sage Publications.

Van Reenen, J. (2011) Wage inequality, technology and trade: 21st century evidence. *Labour Economics*, 18(6): 730–741.

Appendix

Table 6.A1 Raw hourly wage gap between permanent and temporary workers

	All ISCED levels		Primary		Secondary		Tertiary	
	2007	2011	2007	2011	2007	2011	2007	2011
AT	1.16	1.23	1.33	1.42	1.19	1.20	1.10	1.22
BE	1.37	1.28	1.37	1.13	1.35	1.31	1.38	1.29
CZ	1.15	1.2	1.07	1.05	1.14	1.2	1.09	1.22
DE	1.49	1.49	1.54	1.29	1.48	1.52	1.41	1.38
EE	0.92	1.00	1.68	1.02	0.95	1.02	0.93	0.96
EL	1.54	1.38	1.32	1.13	1.38	1.24	1.57	1.44
ES	1.38	1.37	1.22	1.23	1.35	1.28	1.40	1.40
FI	1.33	1.23	1.41	1.23	1.32	1.22	1.30	1.24
FR	1.38	1.25	1.3	1.11	1.36	1.20	1.30	1.31
HU	1.22	1.36	1.20	1.20	1.18	1.22	1.15	1.19
IE	1.23	1.22	1.18	1.2	1.43	1.12	1.21	1.25
IT	1.40	1.47	1.33	1.34	1.39	1.52	1.40	1.45
LU	1.39	1.49	1.29	1.37	1.53	1.49	1.25	1.44
NL	1.22	1.26	1.10	1.15	1.16	1.25	1.33	1.29
PL	1.45	1.40	1.24	1.22	1.33	1.28	1.43	1.38
PT	1.28	1.30	1.16	1.26	1.74	1.51	1.64	1.5
SE	1.37	1.43	1.03	1.29	1.42	1.51	1.42	1.33
SI	1.35	1.37	1.07	1.21	1.28	1.25	1.57	1.50
SK	1.16	1.14	1.06	1.08	1.14	1.12	1.06	1.16
Total	1.50	1.52	1.39	1.42	1.51	1.51	1.43	1.42

Source: own elaboration on EU-Silc data

Table 6.A2 The drivers of hourly wage and the role of employment protection legislation (All education levels, quantile regressions on the pooled 2007 and 2011 sample)

	(1)	(2)	(3)	(4)	(5)	(6)	(7)	(8)	(9)
Temporary*2007	−0.239***	−0.165***	−0.113***	−0.213***	−0.159***	−0.074***	−0.277***	−0.226***	−0.017
	(0.006)	(0.004)	(0.006)	(0.014)	(0.009)	(0.014)	(0.042)	(0.028)	(0.042)
Temporary*2011	−0.224***	−0.165***	−0.109***	−0.267***	−0.189***	−0.156***	0.253***	−0.002	0.037
	(0.006)	(0.004)	(0.006)	(0.016)	(0.010)	(0.015)	(0.054)	(0.032)	(0.049)
Temp*EPL_t*2007				−0.012*	−0.003	−0.019***	0.014	0.022**	−0.035**
				(0.006)	(0.004)	(0.006)	(0.015)	(0.010)	(0.015)
Temp*EPL_t*2011				0.023***	0.012**	0.025***	−0.177***	−0.060***	−0.055***
				(0.007)	(0.005)	(0.007)	(0.020)	(0.012)	(0.018)
Temp*EPL_r*2007							0.014	0.022**	−0.035**
							(0.015)	(0.010)	(0.015)
Temp*EPL_r*2011							−0.177***	−0.060***	−0.055***
							(0.020)	(0.012)	(0.018)
Male	0.137***	0.167***	0.199***	0.136***	0.167***	0.199***	0.137***	0.167***	0.199***
	(0.004)	(0.002)	(0.003)	(0.004)	(0.002)	(0.004)	(0.004)	(0.002)	(0.003)
Married	0.026***	0.032***	0.040***	0.027***	0.032***	0.040***	0.026***	0.032***	0.040***
	(0.003)	(0.002)	(0.003)	(0.003)	(0.002)	(0.003)	(0.003)	(0.002)	(0.003)
Age	0.208***	0.158***	0.181***	0.208***	0.159***	0.182***	0.200***	0.159***	0.178***
	(0.026)	(0.016)	(0.025)	(0.026)	(0.016)	(0.024)	(0.026)	(0.016)	(0.025)
Age2	−0.015***	−0.009***	−0.012***	−0.015***	−0.010***	−0.012***	−0.014***	−0.010***	−0.011***
	(0.003)	(0.002)	(0.003)	(0.003)	(0.002)	(0.003)	(0.003)	(0.002)	(0.003)
Health status	−0.022***	−0.021***	−0.022***	−0.022***	−0.021***	−0.022***	−0.022***	−0.021***	−0.022***
	(0.002)	(0.001)	(0.002)	(0.002)	(0.001)	(0.002)	(0.002)	(0.001)	(0.002)

Secondary educ.	0.067***	0.103***	0.131***	0.067***	0.103***	0.131***	0.067***	0.103***	0.131***
	(0.005)	(0.003)	(0.005)	(0.005)	(0.003)	(0.005)	(0.005)	(0.003)	(0.005)
Tertiary educ.	0.203***	0.285***	0.379***	0.203***	0.286***	0.379***	0.202***	0.286***	0.379***
	(0.007)	(0.004)	(0.007)	(0.007)	(0.004)	(0.007)	(0.007)	(0.004)	(0.007)
Part-time	−0.077***	−0.000	0.106***	−0.077***	−0.001	0.106***	−0.077***	−0.001	0.107***
	(0.004)	(0.003)	(0.004)	(0.004)	(0.003)	(0.004)	(0.004)	(0.003)	(0.004)
Second Job	−0.182***	−0.027***	0.009*	−0.181***	−0.027***	0.008	−0.183***	−0.028***	0.009
	(0.006)	(0.004)	(0.006)	(0.006)	(0.004)	(0.006)	(0.006)	(0.004)	(0.006)
Firm size (11–49)	0.131***	0.068***	0.037***	0.131***	0.068***	0.037***	0.131***	0.068***	0.036***
	(0.004)	(0.002)	(0.003)	(0.003)	(0.002)	(0.003)	(0.004)	(0.002)	(0.003)
Firm size (over 50)	0.228***	0.155***	0.113***	0.228***	0.154***	0.113***	0.229***	0.154***	0.112***
	(0.003)	(0.002)	(0.003)	(0.003)	(0.002)	(0.003)	(0.004)	(0.002)	(0.003)
Urban	0.017***	0.041***	0.057***	0.017***	0.041***	0.057***	0.017***	0.041***	0.057***
	(0.003)	(0.002)	(0.003)	(0.003)	(0.002)	(0.003)	(0.003)	(0.002)	(0.003)
West	1.463***	1.359***	1.183***	1.048***	0.942***	0.805***	1.050***	0.944***	0.803***
	(0.013)	(0.008)	(0.013)	(0.016)	(0.010)	(0.015)	(0.016)	(0.010)	(0.016)
Constant	−1.648***	−0.901***	−0.165***	−1.020***	−0.143***	0.566***	−1.218***	−0.491***	0.223***
	(0.065)	(0.040)	(0.062)	(0.061)	(0.038)	(0.057)	(0.062)	(0.038)	(0.059)
Sector/occup/country/country*2011 dummies	yes	yes	yes	yes	yes	yes	yes	yes	yes
Sample–selection correction	yes	yes	yes	yes	yes	yes	yes	yes	yes
Obs	253835	253835	253835	253835	253835	253835	253835	253835	253835
Pseudo R–sq.	0.414	0.462	0.385	0.414	0.462	0.385	0.414	0.462	0.385

Notes: Standard errors in parentheses. ***, ** and * denote significance at the 1, 5 and 10 per cent level, respectively.

Table 6.A3 The drivers of hourly wage and the role of employment protection legislation (Primary educated, quantile regressions on the pooled 2007 and 2011 sample)

	(1)	(2)	(3)	(4)	(5)	(6)	(7)	(8)	(9)
Temporary*2007	-0.209***	-0.137***	-0.105***	-0.226***	-0.152***	-0.139***	-0.192***	-0.220***	-0.242***
	(0.011)	(0.006)	(0.011)	(0.033)	(0.019)	(0.031)	(0.073)	(0.041)	(0.076)
Temporary*2011	-0.231***	-0.146***	-0.091***	-0.328***	-0.182***	-0.138***	0.175	-0.098*	-0.108
	(0.013)	(0.007)	(0.013)	(0.035)	(0.021)	(0.034)	(0.110)	(0.058)	(0.099)
Temp*EPL_t*2007				0.007	0.007	0.014			
				(0.013)	(0.007)	(0.012)			
Temp*EPL_t*2011				0.044***	0.016*	0.021			
				(0.015)	(0.009)	(0.014)			
Temp*EPL_r*2007							-0.006	0.029**	0.047*
							(0.025)	(0.014)	(0.026)
Temp*EPL_r*2011							-0.145***	-0.016	0.006
							(0.038)	(0.020)	(0.034)
Male	0.137***	0.168***	0.228***	0.135***	0.169***	0.230***	0.136***	0.168***	0.228***
	(0.009)	(0.005)	(0.008)	(0.009)	(0.005)	(0.008)	(0.009)	(0.005)	(0.009)
Married	0.031***	0.022***	0.036***	0.029***	0.023***	0.037***	0.031***	0.023***	0.038***
	(0.007)	(0.004)	(0.007)	(0.007)	(0.004)	(0.006)	(0.007)	(0.004)	(0.007)
Age	0.041	0.032	0.069	0.032	0.039	0.075	0.031	0.036	0.056
	(0.061)	(0.034)	(0.060)	(0.062)	(0.035)	(0.056)	(0.064)	(0.034)	(0.062)
Age2	0.003	0.003	-0.001	0.004	0.002	-0.002	0.004	0.003	0.000
	(0.007)	(0.004)	(0.007)	(0.007)	(0.004)	(0.007)	(0.007)	(0.004)	(0.007)
Health status	-0.020***	-0.017***	-0.016***	-0.020***	-0.018***	-0.016***	-0.020***	-0.017***	-0.016***
	(0.005)	(0.003)	(0.005)	(0.005)	(0.003)	(0.005)	(0.005)	(0.003)	(0.005)

	(1)	(2)	(3)	(4)	(5)	(6)	(7)	(8)	(9)
Part–time	-0.048***	0.014***	0.159***	-0.048***	0.014***	0.160***	-0.048***	0.014***	0.159***
	(0.009)	(0.005)	(0.009)	(0.009)	(0.005)	(0.008)	(0.009)	(0.005)	(0.009)
Second Job	-0.167***	-0.019***	0.002	-0.168***	-0.019***	0.004	-0.167***	-0.019***	0.001
	(0.013)	(0.007)	(0.013)	(0.013)	(0.007)	(0.012)	(0.013)	(0.007)	(0.013)
Firm size (11–49)	0.148***	0.076***	0.052***	0.149***	0.076***	0.052***	0.149***	0.075***	0.052***
	(0.007)	(0.004)	(0.007)	(0.008)	(0.004)	(0.007)	(0.007)	(0.004)	(0.008)
Firm size (over 50)	0.231***	0.158***	0.138***	0.230***	0.157***	0.138***	0.230***	0.157***	0.138***
	(0.007)	(0.004)	(0.008)	(0.008)	(0.004)	(0.007)	(0.007)	(0.004)	(0.008)
Urban	0.007	0.020***	0.048***	0.009	0.020***	0.048***	0.007	0.020***	0.049***
	(0.007)	(0.004)	(0.007)	(0.007)	(0.004)	(0.007)	(0.007)	(0.004)	(0.008)
West	0.918***	1.089***	1.056***	0.893***	1.110***	1.128***	0.920***	1.084***	1.059***
	(0.050)	(0.029)	(0.051)	(0.050)	(0.029)	(0.048)	(0.053)	(0.029)	(0.053)
Constant	-0.423**	-0.066	0.390**	-0.468***	-0.082	0.390**	-0.402**	-0.065	0.416**
	(0.177)	(0.099)	(0.178)	(0.181)	(0.103)	(0.171)	(0.186)	(0.099)	(0.184)
Sector/occup/country/country*2011 dummies	yes	yes	yes	yes	yes	yes	yes	yes	yes
Sample–selection correction	yes	yes	yes	yes	yes	yes	yes	yes	yes
Obs	45026	45026	45026	45026	45026	45026	45026	45026	45026
Pseudo R–sq.	0.390	0.408	0.310	0.390	0.409	0.310	0.390	0.409	0.310

Notes: Standard errors in parentheses. ***, ** and * denote significance at the 1, 5 and 10 per cent level, respectively.

Table 6.A4 The drivers of hourly wage and the role of employment protection legislation (Secondary educated, quantile regressions on the pooled 2007 and 2011 sample)

	(1)	(2)	(3)	(4)	(5)	(6)	(7)	(8)	(9)
Temporary*2007	-0.225***	-0.167***	-0.111***	-0.157***	-0.139***	-0.035*	-0.143**	-0.080*	0.020
	(0.009)	(0.005)	(0.008)	(0.020)	(0.012)	(0.019)	(0.069)	(0.042)	(0.064)
Temporary*2011	-0.205***	-0.160***	-0.111***	-0.242***	-0.185***	-0.171***	0.425***	0.201***	0.312***
	(0.009)	(0.005)	(0.009)	(0.024)	(0.014)	(0.021)	(0.077)	(0.045)	(0.071)
Temp*EPL_t*2007				-0.040***	-0.015**	-0.043***			
				(0.010)	(0.006)	(0.010)			
Temp*EPL_t*2011				0.020*	0.014**	0.031***			
				(0.012)	(0.007)	(0.011)			
Temp*EPL_r*2007							-0.030	-0.032**	-0.048**
							(0.025)	(0.015)	(0.023)
Temp*EPL_r*2011							-0.235***	-0.133***	-0.157***
							(0.029)	(0.017)	(0.026)
Male	0.151***	0.183***	0.236***	0.151***	0.183***	0.235***	0.151***	0.183***	0.236***
	(0.005)	(0.003)	(0.005)	(0.005)	(0.003)	(0.005)	(0.005)	(0.003)	(0.005)
Married	0.019***	0.028***	0.038***	0.019***	0.028***	0.038***	0.019***	0.028***	0.038***
	(0.004)	(0.003)	(0.004)	(0.004)	(0.003)	(0.004)	(0.004)	(0.003)	(0.004)
Age	0.312***	0.253***	0.255***	0.316***	0.250***	0.246***	0.318***	0.253***	0.264***
	(0.041)	(0.025)	(0.038)	(0.041)	(0.025)	(0.037)	(0.040)	(0.024)	(0.038)
Age2	-0.028***	-0.022***	-0.022***	-0.028***	-0.022***	-0.021***	-0.029***	-0.022***	-0.023***
	(0.005)	(0.003)	(0.004)	(0.005)	(0.003)	(0.004)	(0.005)	(0.003)	(0.004)
Health status	-0.034***	-0.029***	-0.029***	-0.034***	-0.029***	-0.029***	-0.034***	-0.029***	-0.030***
	(0.003)	(0.002)	(0.003)	(0.003)	(0.002)	(0.003)	(0.003)	(0.002)	(0.003)

	(1)	(2)	(3)	(4)	(5)	(6)	(7)	(8)	(9)
Part–time	-0.080***	-0.000	0.125***	-0.080***	0.000	0.124***	-0.080***	-0.000	0.124***
	(0.006)	(0.004)	(0.006)	(0.006)	(0.004)	(0.006)	(0.006)	(0.004)	(0.006)
Second Job	-0.128***	-0.019***	0.006	-0.128***	-0.018***	0.004	-0.128***	-0.018***	0.006
	(0.008)	(0.005)	(0.008)	(0.008)	(0.005)	(0.008)	(0.008)	(0.005)	(0.008)
Firm size (11–49)	0.127***	0.067***	0.039***	0.126***	0.067***	0.040***	0.126***	0.066***	0.040***
	(0.005)	(0.003)	(0.005)	(0.005)	(0.003)	(0.005)	(0.005)	(0.003)	(0.005)
Firm size (over 50)	0.224***	0.155***	0.118***	0.223***	0.155***	0.118***	0.224***	0.155***	0.119***
	(0.005)	(0.003)	(0.005)	(0.005)	(0.003)	(0.005)	(0.005)	(0.003)	(0.005)
Urban	0.020***	0.045***	0.063***	0.019***	0.045***	0.062***	0.021***	0.045***	0.062***
	(0.004)	(0.003)	(0.004)	(0.004)	(0.003)	(0.004)	(0.004)	(0.003)	(0.004)
West	0.441***	0.456***	0.543***	1.324***	1.169***	0.982***	-0.137***	-0.085***	0.228***
	(0.022)	(0.014)	(0.022)	(0.025)	(0.015)	(0.024)	(0.031)	(0.019)	(0.031)
Constant	0.110	0.630***	0.862***	-1.669***	-0.789***	0.010	0.705***	1.167***	1.187***
	(0.102)	(0.062)	(0.096)	(0.096)	(0.057)	(0.087)	(0.105)	(0.062)	(0.102)
Sector/occup/country/ country*2011 dummies	yes	yes	yes	yes	yes	yes	yes	yes	yes
Sample–selection correction	yes	yes	yes	yes	yes	yes	yes	yes	yes
Obs	131725	131725	131725	131725	131725	131725	131725	131725	131725
Pseudo R–sq.	0.397	0.478	0.384	0.397	0.478	0.384	0.398	0.479	0.384

Notes: Standard errors in parentheses. ***, ** and * denote significance at the 1, 5 and 10 per cent level, respectively.

Table 6.A5 The drivers of hourly wage and the role of employment protection legislation (Teretiary educated, quantile regressions on the pooled 2007 and 2011 sample)

	(1)	(2)	(3)	(4)	(5)	(6)	(7)	(8)	(9)
Temporary*2007	-0.295***	-0.172***	-0.071***	-0.298***	-0.126***	-0.115***	-0.131	-0.055	0.134
	(0.014)	(0.008)	(0.012)	(0.031)	(0.018)	(0.030)	(0.097)	(0.058)	(0.087)
Temporary*2011	-0.254***	-0.152***	-0.065***	-0.272***	-0.146***	-0.069**	0.248**	0.065	0.096
	(0.014)	(0.008)	(0.012)	(0.031)	(0.018)	(0.029)	(0.108)	(0.060)	(0.090)
Temp*EPL_t*2007				0.001	-0.022***	0.022*			
				(0.013)	(0.008)	(0.013)			
Temp*EPL_t*2011				0.010	-0.003	0.002			
				(0.014)	(0.008)	(0.013)			
Temp*EPL_r*2007							-0.059*	-0.042**	-0.076**
							(0.035)	(0.021)	(0.031)
Temp*EPL_r*2011							-0.184***	-0.080***	-0.063*
							(0.039)	(0.022)	(0.033)
Male	0.109***	0.152***	0.163***	0.108***	0.151***	0.163***	0.109***	0.152***	0.164***
	(0.007)	(0.004)	(0.006)	(0.007)	(0.004)	(0.007)	(0.007)	(0.004)	(0.006)
Married	0.045***	0.045***	0.048***	0.045***	0.045***	0.048***	0.045***	0.045***	0.048***
	(0.006)	(0.003)	(0.005)	(0.006)	(0.003)	(0.005)	(0.006)	(0.003)	(0.005)
Age	0.430***	0.611***	0.721***	0.428***	0.608***	0.728***	0.435***	0.609***	0.728***
	(0.056)	(0.032)	(0.050)	(0.056)	(0.032)	(0.051)	(0.057)	(0.032)	(0.050)
Age2	-0.038***	-0.057***	-0.069***	-0.037***	-0.057***	-0.070***	-0.038***	-0.057***	-0.070***
	(0.006)	(0.004)	(0.006)	(0.006)	(0.004)	(0.006)	(0.007)	(0.004)	(0.006)
Health status	-0.006	-0.018***	-0.026***	-0.006	-0.018***	-0.026***	-0.006	-0.019***	-0.026***
	(0.005)	(0.003)	(0.004)	(0.005)	(0.003)	(0.004)	(0.005)	(0.003)	(0.004)

Part–time	-0.110***	-0.015***	0.059***	-0.110***	-0.015***	0.059***	-0.111***	-0.015***	0.059***
	(0.008)	(0.005)	(0.008)	(0.008)	(0.005)	(0.008)	(0.009)	(0.005)	(0.008)
Second Job	-0.298***	-0.050***	0.007	-0.298***	-0.050***	0.007	-0.296***	-0.049***	0.006
	(0.012)	(0.007)	(0.011)	(0.012)	(0.007)	(0.011)	(0.012)	(0.007)	(0.011)
Firm size (11–49)	0.143***	0.058***	0.004	0.143***	0.058***	0.004	0.143***	0.059***	0.003
	(0.008)	(0.004)	(0.007)	(0.008)	(0.004)	(0.007)	(0.008)	(0.004)	(0.007)
Firm size (over 50)	0.244***	0.146***	0.076***	0.245***	0.146***	0.076***	0.244***	0.146***	0.076***
	(0.007)	(0.004)	(0.006)	(0.007)	(0.004)	(0.006)	(0.007)	(0.004)	(0.006)
Urban	0.017***	0.047***	0.054***	0.017***	0.048***	0.055***	0.018***	0.047***	0.054***
	(0.006)	(0.003)	(0.005)	(0.006)	(0.003)	(0.005)	(0.006)	(0.003)	(0.005)
West	1.595***	1.522***	1.319***	1.147***	1.101***	0.889***	1.154***	1.115***	0.895***
	(0.026)	(0.016)	(0.024)	(0.038)	(0.022)	(0.036)	(0.041)	(0.023)	(0.036)
Constant	-2.564***	-2.215***	-1.421***	-2.019***	-1.661***	-0.940***	-2.043***	-1.678***	-0.955***
	(0.128)	(0.075)	(0.113)	(0.132)	(0.076)	(0.121)	(0.134)	(0.076)	(0.119)
Sector/occup/country/2011 country*2011 dummies	yes		yes	yes		yes	yes		yes
Sample-selection correction	yes		yes	yes		yes	yes		yes
Obs	77084	77084	77084	77084	77084	77084	77084	77084	77084
Pseudo R–sq.	0.375	0.386	0.318	0.375	0.386	0.318	0.376	0.386	0.318

Notes: Standard errors in parentheses. ***, ** and * denote significance at the 1, 5 and 10 per cent level, respectively.

7 Do rights matter?

Comparing inequalities in the governance of the EU

Charles Dannreuther

Everything economic science posits as given, that is, the range of dispositions of the economic agent which ground the illusion of the ahistorical universality of categories and concepts employed by that science, is, in fact, the paradoxical product of a long collective history, endlessly reproduced by individual histories which can be fully accounted for only by historical analysis.

(Bourdieu 2005: 5)

An implicit ontology of the people and the relation between the people and the state often shapes how we think in normative terms about politics

(Petit 2005).

Introduction: Representing inequalities in the EU

Inequality has been a constant thread of debate within the European Union. Established as a system for mediating differences between nation states with unequal access to raw materials, the study of the EU has typically focused on inequalities between large and small states within the EU, between states in and out of the EU, between the member state institutions and the supranational institutions, and between these supranational institutions of the Commission, the European Parliament and ECJ Commission and the Parliament. Each of these has taken the focus of inequality to concern the exercise of power between rational actors, be they the national interests of states, the bureaucratic interests of the Commission, the democratic rights of the EP or the constitutional aspirations of the ECJ. These debates reflected normative agendas: balancing the relationship between the intergovernmental and supranational institutions would help to secure peace in Europe; decisionmaking effectiveness would result from qualified majority voting in Council; greater democratic credentials would accompany equal powers for the Parliament in the legislative process.

These inequalities were of the utmost relevance to the "village" of Brussels and the intellectual community that sought to develop the EU as a polity. Essentially the inequalities under discussion concerned power and so were informed by notions of national interest, legislative procedure and accountability. These institutionalised relations would manifest themselves in the outcomes of policy negotiations such as the CAP, ERDF, Cohesion Fund and most recently the Global Adjustment Fund. But the characteristics and needs of the society of the European Union have been poorly represented. Inequality in the economies and societies of the EU, and the policies and processes designed to address them have and remain predominantly national concerns in both analysis and practice even as the EU evolves into something new[1].

Debates over how Europe should balance the impact of global economic change with the wishes and needs of European society had become increasingly vocal even before the current financial crisis set in. The EU's Lisbon Agenda specifically addressed this tension in 2000 by explicitly linking its response to globalisation to social inclusion. The strategy of pursing competitiveness that had been introduced and formalised in the 1990s now became the method for delivering social inclusion and economic sustainability within a global economy. For the first time the EU explicitly linked its strategic goals and policies directly with those of the member states and their populations.

So ambitious was this scheme that some of the EU's institutions began to debate the EU's Social Question.[2] In 2007 and 2008, for example, the Commission held a consultation over what the social reality of the EU was for its citizens and prepared a series of proposals for the European Council meeting based around the idea of a renewed social agenda.[3] The significance of the Social Question was that it refers directly to the late C19th and early C20th when the main social compromises in European nation states were forged between the state, trade unions, business and the middle classes. These were central and not always happy periods in which the role of the nation state was cemented in social institutions.

Like the Lisbon Agenda this social reality stocktaking placed special emphasis on a solid evidence base with which to assess the progressive realisation of rights of groups to social inclusion and equality. This evidence has contributed to further debates concerning the EU's role in societal issues and specifically a recent proposal for an EU wide measure for poverty. This was proposed on the basis that people related to other groups across the EU in terms of their real and subjective notions of poverty.[4] The question of how to measure and address inequality across the EU has therefore become one of practical concern. A renewed Lisbon Agenda called "EUROPE 2020 – A European strategy for smart, sustainable and inclusive growth" has confirmed the method and approach of its predecessor.[5] The proposal confirms the integration of economic environmental and social goals and on the use of performance targets as the main instrument for realizing these ambitious goals.[6]

The question that this chapter seeks to address is how the EU justifies its interventions in relation to inequalities and what the implications are for these approaches in the realisation of its objectives, such as those outlined in the EUROPE 2020 vision. So far, it appears that the inequalities of power between the member states of the EU have been transmuted into inequalities between social groups within the member states of the EU. We begin with justifications for intervention that draw on utilitarian, Pareto then welfare economics to highlight the role that fact value distinctions play in the study of inequality. We then examine how deontological accounts, with their emphasis on universal outcomes and rights are difficult to operationalise within a multi-level governance system like that of the EU. Next we explore the role of organisational bias, and specifically the importance of categorical distinction in maintaining hierarchies of opportunity drawing on Tilly's notion of "durable inequalities". The redefinition of European society as individuals has dramatically altered the representation of inequality in the EU but without addressing the main sources of these inequalities. We shall briefly demonstrate this through social indicators such as those used in the Lisbon Agenda and European Employment Strategy as an explanation for the transmutation of durable forms of inequality within the EU. Finally we examine how the greater participation of civil society organisations may assist in addressing these failures.

Equality and the Union

Deciding which inequalities matter and how to address them presents a range of problems for policy makers and analysts.[7] The identification and representation of inequality reveals assumptions of power and often objectivity, points that reflect competing political ontologies of the European Union.[8] The following section begins from the normative arguments that used to justify interventions by the EU to address inequality in order to introduce the link between fact and value and in order to demonstrate some of the challenges facing the EU in addressing the inequalities that it contributes to.

Utilitarians and social choice

The clearest and most cited justification for European integration, if more often implicit than explicit, is still usually presented in utilitarian terms: by avoiding further war European integration has helped "to prevent the happening of mischief, pain, evil, or unhappiness to the party whose interest is considered".[9] Fifty years of European integration have indeed benefitted the European community of individuals (and communities) with peace and prosperity, not least through the promotion of individual interest through its four freedoms. For utilitarians, the fact that the consequence of European integration has been greater happiness and fewer fears for the many is enough. The problems arise in deciding what it is that makes people happy and so which inequalities need to be addressed before others.

Social choice explores how peoples satisfy their preferences through their choices in conditions of ideal information and without imposing harm (or taxation) on others. The pursuit of such "ideal" conditions has been a central policy standpoint for the Single market programme in its focus on the removal of market distortions. In a classic liberal pursuit of common goals the negotiation and harmonisation of regulations to realise the Single Market programme and more recently in Service Directive explicitly advocated positive sum benefits to the member states.[10]

Arrow observed that it was logically impossible for individual preferences to produce a social choice without some authoritarian or non-participatory input. If there are many preferences they cannot be ordered in a linear fashion to inform effective policy choices, a conclusion he demonstrates across a range of different social choices. His observation that this may only be possible through methods that are "imposed or dictatorial"[11] has played out more keenly than he could have imagined in the Euro-scepticism that followed Delors' proposal for a redistributive agenda to accompany the Single Market.

Welfare economists and social choice theorists have therefore argued that the best way to make such judgements is through developing indices for making comparisons between individual well-being, or better still "type to type" well-being. This also allows individuals to take responsibility for their outcomes within their type.[12] This asserts the agency of the individual so that the choice that they make is not conflated with the situation they find themselves in. In Dowding's words:

> Any measure that tries to include the choice that people make given their situations, as well as the actual outcomes they gain, will fail to adequately address that freedom of choice without a theory that specifies what rational choices are. Inevitably such analyses will be both moralized and controversial. The alternative is to accept choices made without criticism. Public policy can thus be developed at an institutional or structural level (specifying principles of distribution) using rough global comparisons across types of people.[13]

Recent Commission discussions of cohesion policy have drawn attention to the importance of different methodologies in measuring convergence across the EU.[14] The discussion demonstrates how methodologies infer different mechanisms and possibilities for the removal of inequalities. Beta convergence draws on neo-classical growth theory to focus on the rate of catch up[15] while Sigma convergence focuses on the reduction of regional disparity accommodating the possibility of structural regional inequalities. Both of these approaches indicate impediments to the operation of the free market. The Gini coefficient describes degrees of economic inequality within a population. The Atkinson index the movement within a population and the Thiel index explores average inequality within and among subgroups, making it useful for exploring the impact of inter member state convergence with intra member state regional divergence.[16] Each provides a measure of inequality that presents type to type comparisons according to the inequality being explored and to a lesser degree the effectiveness of the likely intervention. Beta convergence indicates the efficiency of the market in resolving inequality, while Sigma convergence implies the possibility of additional intervention while Gini, Atkinson and Thiel all assert the likelihood of inequality but focus on different measures of it. Central to their significance are the objectivity claims that accompany these measures derived from their rigorous methodologies and substantial datasets. But there is less of a discussion of what the political implications of such surveys are for the EU and the implications that they have for both relations within the EU and specifically the amelioration of inequality across its society.

By following Pareto and rejecting redistribution as a mechanism, welfare economics also rejects the utilitarian moral justification for the greatest happiness to the greatest number. This cost may seem worth paying given the interest of member states in limiting their contributions to the EU's budgets. But the problem emerges that without the utilitarian morality the actions of the EU as a political system are severely constrained. The EU is, for example, unconvincing on the need for Germany to help Greece in order to save the Euro because it cannot make arguments on the basis that the richer member state must suffer for the benefit of all. Germany must make the decision herself.

Deontological approaches

The best that the EU can do is to refer to the rules (e.g., Broad Economic Policy Guidelines) and institutions (e.g., ECB) of the Eurozone which enshrine clear moral rules that ought to be followed. Such deontological approaches play far more to Kant's Categorical Imperative to "act only according to the maxim by which you can at the same time will that it should become a universal law".[17] Germany's support for the Greek economy will help to sustain the universal monetary orthodoxy that the Eurozone has linked itself to. Deontological approaches place limits on the choice of individuals to assert specific rights, like property rights, or norms, such as welfare and social justice because they are right regardless of their consequences. In some cases the choices may be starker. In the pursuit of economic integrity, the BEPG propose a serious limitation on the range of choices that elected governments can make in relation to the size of the public deficit and the possibility of public sector led growth.

The problem for the EU in much of its history has been that the "universe" of application has not been represented consistently across different policy areas or competencies. Property rights have enjoyed far greater universal application across the history of European integration than social rights have.[18] In large part this is because the compromises that evolved to support the liberal international trading system in the post-1945 period had been reached at the national level. For social policy, among others, the national level retained its significance as the initial site for the practical realisation of goals that were and had been universal to those communities. The national capitalisms seen as contrary to a supranational social agenda, are so because they were practiced at the national level rather than because the values of universal provision were given an explicitly German, or French flavour (for example). The institutionalist methodologies that prevail in the VoC debate tend to downplay this distinction between fact and value, displaying values as norms and the facts in the repetitive habits of these organisations. Notions of universalism or consequentialism are rejected in favour of endogenous order and path dependent change.[19] Hence the varieties of capitalism come with fact and value integrated into a package of national social and economic relations. Without a macro-level theorisation of what makes these institutions similar, explaining how they all contribute to a stable period of accumulation for example, it is unclear which social relation is worthy of comparison across countries or what universal beliefs these national capitalisms share.[20]

The VoC literature demonstrates that institutional configurations endure over time. This is in part because of institutional inertia.[21] But it is also because the institutions reflect compromises that unified cleavages of class during periods of nation building. These cleavages are especially evident in the transformation of welfare provision across the EU. Ferrera demonstrates how the changing of boundaries was central to the changing nature of welfare in Europe.[22] The strength of the social compromises was made possible through their ability to institutionalise social rights that was in turn made possible by enabling dissent to be expressed through effective voice functions. Location and voice were bounded by notions of solidarity to form enduring social compromises that sustained universal values. The expansion of supranational competencies and the subversive influences that this has had on notions of solidarity and community has eroded much of the substance of these compromises.[23] In its place, the Lisbon Agendas approach shows a promise that was too early for Ferrera to evaluate.[24]

Durable inequalities

Sociological approaches to European integration studies have increasingly argued for engagement with traditional notions of power in understanding social institutions.[25] Tilly's *Durable Inequalities* placed special significance on these institutional characteristics in the maintenance of inequality. The key mechanism was the persistence of "categorical pairs" that define unequal value producing resources societies: men and women, black and white, young and old. These are classifications of groups that have been formalised within organisations to have real meaning because of the fact that they are related to each other: women earn less than men because there is a hierarchical distinction in labour markets and organisational prejudices that favours men. Such inequalities are significant as they reproduce themselves in new times and environments in order to maintain the privileges of the hierarchy. So "stereotype threat" describes how less equal groups perform according to how they feel they ought to perform, rather than to their best ability (boys in schools, caste groups in India).[26]

Despite his association with historical sociology, Tilly's conceptualisation of inequalities has been criticised as overly ahistorical. In addition and in part because of the relational perspective he pursues, the durable inequalities approach has also been seen as overly dependent on cost benefit calculations at the expense of an analysis of the individual's experiences.[27] Yet this is to understate the motives of Tilly in exploring the importance of relational factors contributing to inequality. As Olin Wright argues, "durable inequalities" draws extensively on functionalist arguments in establishing that the opportunity hoarding that explains why inequalities endure is sustained through categories that are given real meaning through organisational bias.[28] Such purposeful agenda setting power is a clear characteristic of organisational functionalism, while the interest in explaining deep inequality through the exploitation of organisational bias rather than the means of production specifically.[29]

These categorical distinctions may well be important in explaining the fact of inequalities in society and in part the immediate mechanisms that sustain them. As we have seen above the identification of type for type groups for comparison is an important consideration for welfare economists. The use of categories is also essential in the development of the social indicators that enable comparison. These categories are central to the strategic interventions of the UN's Millennium Development Goals (MDGs) and the EU's Lisbon Strategy. These were both landmark political initiatives intended to demonstrate the ability of the EU to address the challenges of globalisation and of the international community to address global poverty. Both of these programmes have raised the profile of inequality for policy makers in identifying performance criteria and convergence towards shared benchmarks.[30] Both have also used the language of rights to legitimate their interventions and to define the categories in which improvements in performance would be evaluated. The next section explores how the rights based approach of the Lisbon Agenda avoids many of the problems of universal, social choice and deontological approaches. But we then go on to assess how effectively it has been in addressing the challenge of "durable inequalities" that Tilly has described.

Rights-Based Approaches and the European political economy

Rights-Based Approaches (RBA) begin from the assertion that "all peoples have the right of self-determination".[31] The main innovation is that this places the individual holder of rights before the constitutional, social, economic and political context in which she finds herself and empowers her to assert her needs in her self-determination. Interventions can then be justified and channelled to the individual through a multitude of organisations and in the pursuit of a multitude of goals. Through this focus on empowering the individual and their contingent needs, traditional human rights (the right to not be tortured, the right to freedom of expression, the right to be and the right to love) have been supplemented over time by an array of other rights, elevating rights once pursued through national institutions (such as social or health rights) to new global ones and asserting a new generations of economic rights as equivalent in value to more traditional ones.

In asserting the *a priori* right of individuals to particular conditions of life, rights-Based Approaches focus interventions not on the redistribution of material assets found in the traditional welfare relation but on the redistribution of opportunity according to different needs.[32] The normative dimension of building on capabilities to realise rights coincided with the greater policy awareness and value attributed to the role of society in economic development. Economists have long argued the relationship between property rights for economic development[33], and others have demonstrated the relationship between civil, political social rights.[34] But now economic and social rights were bound together linking social capital and competitiveness in the in the transnational policy community.[35]

The EU's Lisbon agenda has become a prime example of the integration of these two pursuits of social justice and economic prosperity.[36] In 2000 the EU's Heads of Governments met in Lisbon as the European Council to propose a new strategic goal for the EU...

Box 7.1 Lisbon agenda employment benchmarks [para 30]:

- employment rate from an average 61% today to as close as possible to 70% by 2010
- women in employment from an average of 51% today to more than 60% by 2010

... to become the most competitive and dynamic knowledge-based economy in the world capable of sustainable economic growth with more and better jobs and greater social cohesion[37]

Central to the effective achievement of these goals was the deployment of evaluation methodologies as a policy tool that would enable actors, including member states, to be assessed in relation to a clear set of stated benchmarks [see Box 7.1]. These benchmarks would enable progress to be measured and reviewed in annual reports under the scrutiny of the EU Commission to produce collective recommendations supported by the Member States at the Spring European Council.

Social indicators have become increasingly important in the governance of the EU specifically drawing on evidence based policies to exhort member state to improve their performances through the declaration of the March European Councils as well as for making international comparisons.[38] A number of authors have used these social indicators to demonstrate trends in pan-European inequality. Heidenreich and Wunder argue that convergence between the member states economies has lowered inequality levels across the EU, but that this has been accompanied by greater intra state inequality, notably in newly acceded member states.[39] The question then becomes whether it matters to people or not that they are poorer or richer than people within their national societies or whether their frame of reference extends across the EU. Fahey identifies real and subjective notions of poverty that are shared across national boundaries and uses this to argue for a pan-European understanding of poverty. Whelan and Maitre, however, differentiate between weak and strong versions of this. In the former a standard of participation within societies that defines it is informed by greater awareness and knowledge of other member states. From this "weak" perspective the national normative redistributive agenda remains unchallenged. In the latter the overemphasis on national systems is seen to have obfuscated pan-European inequalities so that European-level conflicts and redistributions are seen as necessary. The stronger notion, therefore, describes how "norms shift from the national to the transnational level, as does the responsibility for meeting the associated claim".[40]

Measuring achievements through outputs helped to demonstrate the realisation of inclusion objectives that were informed by economic rights. Improvements were indicated through convergence towards a benchmark, rather than absolute achievements that would have disadvantaged certain states. This allowed a more consensual and mutually supportive political environment to characterise the project that would be supported through explicit engagements with civil society through an Open Method of Coordination. The Lisbon Agenda has demonstrated how all rights – political, social, economic and cultural – could be realised through collective endeavour.

Progress was initially slow and a halfway review in 2005 criticised the member states for their poor implementation records. The report of the high-level group of experts criticised member states that had "not taken the execution and delivery of the agreed measures seriously enough".[41] Macroeconomic conditions had not been conducive so that "many Member States have been caught in a conundrum. Because of structural weaknesses and low demand, national economic performance has been poor. As national economic performance has been poor, it has been more difficult to implement the Lisbon strategy".[42] Even in the EU the rights provided through the Lisbon Agenda were by no means guaranteed but were conditional on the macroeconomic conditions and the inclination of governments to invest in and realize these goals. Millennium Development Goals also place an emphasis on a rights based approach but "in practice claiming and establishing rights is a political process, mediated by the presence of power".[43] Rights-Based Approaches need to be coherent too, coordinating a variety of different claims if they are to succeed in their implementation.[44]

Durable inequalities and the Rights-Based Approach

Despite the promises of the Lisbon agenda and its rights based approach, the EU has not delivered on the reduced inequalities that the agenda promised. Beneath we shall discuss three examples of how RBA fail to address durable inequalities concerning property rights, policy influence and gender.

The economic rights approach has not been uncontroversial. One of the main criticisms of it as an approach has been that it means different things in different places and is inevitably vulnerable to local political whims and administrative capacity. But this belies a more central problem with the concept which makes economic rights hard to describe, difficult to enforce and subject to interpretation.[45] At the heart of the economic rights agenda is a lack of acknowledgement of the judiciability of rights, and this is based upon a misunderstanding of the legal meaning of property. Terence Daintith explains:

> The rights of [individually held] property and freedom of contract are widely viewed as "economic rights." Yet they can be as personal as any "personal right" one can imagine the right of several property includes the right to control one's body, including one's sexual behavior. The right of freedom of contract includes the right to purchase books, birth control devices, or intoxicating substances from willing sellers.
>
> If, on the other hand, "property" is given a meaning more familiar to lawyers, limiting its application to our relations with various categories of things, whether physical or incorporeal, then the definition does not appear broad enough to encompass all forms of economic activity. Work as such is thus not a subject of rights and enjoys a protection inferior to that of capital.[46]

Economic rights cannot be described as particular things so they are difficult to enforce and remain subject to interpretation. The vacuum left by the lack of legal certainty of economic rights leaves the rights agenda open to exploitation for ends other than the provision of need. Indeed a proliferation of actors now seek to attribute rights to recipients through the transferring of specific things. An example might include skills, provided through training service companies to unemployed people, which are central to active labour market policies. Another in the European Employment Strategy, is the formation of new businesses, which embody economic rights to trade. Governments pursue this agenda by driving down the start-up costs and times before an unemployed person can describe themselves as self-employed. The Commission claims that:

For example, the average time and cost to start-up a private limited company is now 8 days (compared to 9 days in 2008) and the cost is € 417 (compared to € 463 in 2008).[47]

These initiatives may improve the opportunity of individuals to generate future property for themselves but more SMEs does not mean greater wealth or equality. Rather the "crowded platform" effect in which one start-up small firm forces another to close in a crowded market has been well-documented. Indeed one of the central characteristics of a successful SME economy is often seen to be the "churn effect", in which a slightly higher number of companies are started up each year than those that fail. The social costs of high numbers of business failure can be very high especially to those who are already in low income areas or do not have additional career opportunities. Schemes to support entrepreneurship may also require participants to sign off of employment benefits reducing their access to other rights. There is therefore an inherent bias in Right Based Approaches to address inequality through the same mechanism as through property rights. In other words the market still prevails as an ideology in the evaluation of EU policies despite the rights agenda.[48] Like market base approaches those with property are better able to access the resources required to sustain or improve their accumulation of property which results in greater inequality in property again.

The extension of some economic rights, such as the opportunity to trade across the EU, may directly infringe on other rights like political rights, such as the right to express dissent on the negotiation of certain EU legislation.[49] The case has been made for separating the link between rights agendas and democracy for both political and moral clarity.[50] This lack of clarity reflects a theoretical tension between Sen and Nussbaum, the two main theorists of the Rights-Based Approach.[51] The Central Human Capabilities (CHCs) is a list of basic human needs such as life, bodily integrity and health, designed by Martha Nussbaum and intended to enable the measurement of rights and their availability so that international organizations and states can hold elites to account.[52] The more abstract notion of capabilities, associated with Sen, is intended to inform an interactive process of public reasoning. Sen's more deliberative approach might see success in "... the extent to which a political system possesses structures to host deliberation that is authentic, inclusive, and consequential".[53] Governments may embrace the importance of participation in the Open Method of Coordination but in doing so reduce it to a "top down technocratic prescription" or even a "tyranny of participation.[54]

The Open Method of Coordination has not always delivered the open and meaningful deliberations of the governance approach under the Lisbon Agenda.[55] But what has in fact occurred has been the redefinition and privatisation of representative processes. The act of representation can take the form of a principal representing an individual (as a barrister in a court or an elected official) or it can be a graphical representation of an objective truth (as in a photograph or a statistical chart).[56] The former provides accountability through vote of severance of contract but the latter is accountable not to the individual in the survey but to the master paying for it. Social indicators are a less reliable mechanism for achieving political outcomes because they deny the opportunity of exit and voice, both of which help to sustain political community.

Social indicators have been used since the 1960s in the USA to promote community development.[57] Their greatest impact has been that they help to maintain momentum of social groups in initiatives to address inequality by the building of social knowledge. This means that the effective use of indicators requires the involvement of more not less communities in the validation and evaluation of indicator systems to be inclusive.[58] Others have been far more critical of the role of social indicators demonstrating how they have been used to strengthen central government control over communities or even to provide post hoc evidence to support to government policy ambitions.[59] Social indicators also often do not represent how people live as they provide only snap shots of historically contingent events or series of repeated behaviours. Life-cycle approaches, for example explore how needs and resources change over the working life and into retirement by exploring cohorts and generations. These approaches have the additional benefit that they can integrate national variations into comparative data to demonstrate how variations in national regime may influence, for example, the fairly universal common interests shared by employer and employee for early retirement.[60]

The key difficulty in the use of social indicators in the pursuit of rights outlined in the new Lisbon Agenda is that they present a data set constructed of individuals. As Dowding points out this enables individual choice and hence responsibility to be integrated into intervention decisions by locating those choices within types that can be compared cross nationally. But such assumptions also strip the moral and historical compromises that have integrated those communities and framed the delivery of other rights, such as political end social rights. By replacing socially embedded actors with rational self-maximising individuals parts of the compromise are lost.

Conclusions

In this chapter we have explored the reasons why the EU intervenes to address inequalities and the consequences of the methods that it uses. The traditional justifications for intervention have demonstrated some of the shortcomings of the EU for addressing inequalities. Utilitarian approaches have placed special emphasis on the consequences of interventions but are unable to easily define the ideal policy choice from a plural set of interests without imposing authoritarian decisions. The social choice arguments propose measures for defining levels of inequality and so the potential for their resolution, but in doing so blur the fact and value distinction upon which they rely. Deontological approaches, which in many ways have also worked well to promote universal values at the European level, are at some point compromised by competing values at different levels of government. These are not simple procedural issues but may represent challenges to fundamental social compromises that inform the identity of European nation states.

The Rights-Based Approach has in many ways synthesised the key characteristics of these approaches. The individual responsibilities of utilitarian social choice have been combined with the assertion of universal rights norms that we might associate with a deontological approach to social justice. The accompanying growth in the use of social indicators enables type to type measures that demonstrate to communities their convergence with European norms in both subjective and objective measures of inequality. But the categories that the Rights Based Approaches employ as instruments of change may tend to sustain inequalities rather than addressing them. Labour market reforms may embrace women into the workforce but on terms that are less favourable than men's, and individuals may start up their own businesses but still be less able to access finance from credit markets. Rights-based approaches may also compromise one set of rights in order to achieve another.

The central difference to the Lisbon Agenda and one that has not been sufficiently addressed relates to how the EU will be able to justify significant redistributions should the market driven approaches of the new Lisbon Agenda fail. It resolved the inability to reflect social choices through the concept of subsidiarity, but this impedes rather than enhances its abilities to redistribute. The EU has proposed ideas of common values and institutions but been unable to sustain commitments to them without significant economic interests. The Rights-Based Approach may well have had its best opportunity to work when the economy was growing and there high levels of confidence in the market. But without such supportive conditions the inequalities that characterise the EU's society may seem insurmountable and the circumstances for credible activity undermined. In such circumstances the project to integration requires far bolder claims and political leadership to deliver the equalities that its people deserve.

Notes

1   Adrian Favell and Virginie Guiraudon 2009 "The Sociology of the European Union: An Agenda" *European Union Politics* 2009 10: 550–576; Richard Münch 2008 "Constructing a European Society by Jurisdiction" *European Law Journal* 14, 5, pp. 519–541.

2   Thomas Faist 2009 "The Transnational Social Question: Social Rights and Citizenship in a Global Context" *International Sociology* 24; 7, pp.7–35.

3   Commission Staff Working Paper 2007 *Report On The Public Consultation On Europe's Social Reality And On A New Social Vision For 21st Century Europe*; Commission 2007 "Social Reality Stocktaking: Interim report to the 2007 Spring European Council" COM(2007) 63 final Brussels, 26.2.2007; Commission "Opportunities, access and solidarity: towards a new social vision for 21st century Europe", COM(2007) 726, 20.11.2007; Commission Renewed social agenda: Opportunities, access and solidarity in 21st century Europe COM(2008) 412 final Brussels, 2.7.2008.

4   People from poorer states with higher incomes relative to their societies but poorer incomes relative to European norms both experienced greater hardship and perceived it to be so too. See Tony Fahey 2007 "The Case for an EU-wide Measure of Poverty" *European Sociological Review* 23, 1, pp. 35–47.

5   COMMISSION 2010 "EUROPE 2020 A strategy for smart, sustainable and inclusive growth" *COM* (2010) 2020 Brussels, 3.3.2010.

6   The specific themes are "Smart growth: developing an economy based on knowledge and innovation. Sustainable growth: promoting a more resource efficient, greener and more competitive economy. Inclusive growth: fostering a high-employment economy delivering social and territorial cohesion" ibid: 3.

7   This section draws on the argument presented by of Irene van Staveren 2007 "Beyond Utilitarianism and Deontology: Ethics in Economics" *Review of Political Economy* 19, 1, 21–35. For a critical response to this see Mark White 2009 'In Defense of Deontology and Kant: A Reply to van Staveren' *Review of Political Economy*, 21, 2, 299–307.

8   Niilo Kauppi 2010 "The political ontology of European integration" *Comparative European Politics* 8, 19–36.

9   See paragraph III of Chapter I: Of The Principle of Utility by Jeremy Bentham 1781 *An Introduction to the Principles of Morals and Legislation.*

10   Andrew Moravcsik 1991 "Negotiating the Single European Act: National Interests and Conventional Statecraft in the European Community" *International Organization*; A.Moravcsik 1993 "Preferences and Power a liberal intergovernmentalism" *Journal of Common Market Studies* 231, 4, pp.473–525; Commission 2002 "Report from the Commission to the Council and the European Parliament on the State of the Internal Market for Services presented under the First Stage of the Internal Market Strategy for Services" COM(2002) 441 final, Brussels, 30.07.2002; Line Vogt 2005 "The EU's Single Market: At Your Service?" *OECD Economics Department Working Papers* #449 Paris Cedex 16, France.CPB (Netherlands Bureau for Economic Policy Analysis) 2005 "A quantitative assessment of the EU proposals for the Internal Market for Services".

11   See page 342 Kenneth J. Arrow 1950 "A Difficulty in the Concept of Social Welfare" *The Journal of Political Economy*, 58, 4, pp. 328–346.

12   Keith Dowding 2008 "What is Welfare and How Can We Measure it?" in Harold Kincaid and Don Ross 2008 *Handbook of Philosophy and Economics* Oxford University Press.

13   Ibid page 24. For an illustration see Kalapana Wilson 2008 "Reclaiming 'Agency', Reasserting Resistance" *IDS Bulletin* 39, 6, pp. 83–91.

14   Philippe Monfort 2008 "Convergence of EU regions Measures and evolution" *Working papers A series of short papers on regional research and indicators produced by the Directorate-General for Regional Policy* n° 01/2008

15   Evangelia Desli 2009 "Convergence and efficiency: evidence from the EU-15" *Journal of Post Keynesian Economics* 31, 3, 403–430.

16 Martin Heidenreich and Christoph Wunder 2008 "Patterns of Regional Inequality in the Enlarged Europe" *European Sociological Review* 24, 1, pp. 19–36.

17 Quoted from I.Kant 1785 *Groundwork of the Metaphysics of Morals* NY: Cambridge UP quoted page 23 of Irene van Staveren 2007 "Beyond Utilitarianism and Deontology: Ethics in Economics" *Review of Political Economy* 19, 1, 21–35.

18 C.Dannreuther 2006 "Regulation Theory and the EU" *Competition and Change* 10, 2 pp.180–199.

19 James March and Johan Olsen. 1984. "The new institutionalism: organizational factors in political life" *American Political Science Review*, 78, pp.734–49.

20 Bob Hanke, Martin Rhodes and Mark Thatcher 2007 *Beyond Varieties of Capitalism – conflict contradictions and complementarities in the European economy*Oxford University Press.

21 Kathleen Thelen 2003 *How Institutions Evolve: The Political Economy of Skills in Germany, Britain, The United States and Japan* Cambridge University Press.

22 Maurizio Ferrera 2005 *The Boundaries of Welfare: European Integration and the New Spatial Politics of Social Protection* Oxford University Press.

23 See Ferrera op cit; Martin Rhodes 1995 "'Subversive liberalism': market integration, globalization and the European welfare state" *Journal of European Public Policy*, 2, 3, pp. 384–406. For another view see Patricia Frericks, Robert Maier and Willibrord de Graaf 2009 "Toward a Neoliberal Europe? Pension Reforms and Transformed Citizenship" *Administration & Society* 41, 2 pp. 135–157.

24 See chapter 6 of Ferrera op. cit.

25 Jane Jenson and Frederic Merand 2010 "Sociology, institutionalism and the European Union" *Comparative European Politics* 8, 74–92.

26 Karla Hoff and Priyanka Pandey "Economic Consequences Of Social Identity: Discrimination, Social Identity, and Durable Inequalities" *American Economic Review* 96 , 2 pp. 206–211.

27 Barbara Laslett 2000 "The Poverty of (Monocausal) Theory: A Comment on Charles Tilly's Durable Inequality" *Comparative Studies in Society and History* 42, 2, pp. 475–481.

28 Erik Olin Wright 2000 "Metatheoretical Foundations of Charles Tilly's Durable Inequality" *Comparative Studies in Society and History* 42, 2 pp. 458–474.

29 Ibid 462.

30 A.B. Atkinson "Social Indicators, Policy and Measuring Progress" chapter 4 in Stefan Svallfors ed 2005 *Analysing inequality: life Chances and Social Mobility in Comparative Perspective* Stanford, CA: Stanford University Press.

31 Article 1.1 International Covenant on Economic, Social and Cultural Rights http://www2.ohchr.org/english/law/cescr.htm [viewed 09/10/09].

32 See A. Sen "Equality of What?" THE TANNER LECTURE ON HUMAN VALUES Delivered at Stanford University May 22, 1979.

33 For example, see H.de Soto 2000 *The Mystery of Capital: Why Capitalism Triumphs in the West and Fails Everywhere Else* New York: Basic Books.

34 See T. Marshall, 1964 *Class, Citizenship and Social Development* Westwood: Greenwood Press.

35 See R.D. Putnam, 2000 *Bowling Alone: The Collapse and Revival of American Community* New York: Simon & Schuster. World Bank 2002 "Building Institutions for Markets" *World Development Report*, T. Faist 2009 "The Transnational Social Question: Social Rights and Citizenship in a Global Context" *International Sociology*, 24, 7, pp. 7–35; D. Whelan and J. Donnelly 2007 "The West, Economic and Social Rights, and the Global Human Rights Regime: Setting the Record Straight" *Human Rights Quarterly* 29, pp. 908–949; A. Kirkup and T. Evans 2009 "The Myth of Western Opposition to Economic, Social, and Cultural Rights? A Reply to Whelan and Donnelly" *Human Rights Quarterly* 31, pp. 221–238.

36 C. Dannreuther 2006 "Regulation Theory and the EU" *Competition and Change* 10, 2 pp.180–199.

37 Lisbon European Council 23 And 24 March 2000 *Presidency Conclusions* http://www.europarl.europa.eu/summits/lis1_en.htm#a [viewed 09/10/09].

38 Almas Heshmati and Jong Eun Oh 2006 "Alternative Composite Lisbon Development Strategy Indicators: a comparison of EU, USA, Japan and Korea" *The European Journal of Comparative Economics* 3, 2, pp.133–170.

39 Martin Heidenreich and Christoph Wunder 2008 "Patterns of Regional Inequality in the Enlarged Europe" *European Sociological Review* 24, 1 pp. 19–36.

40 See page 118 Christopher Whelan and Bertrand Maître 2009 "Europeanization of inequality and European reference groups" *Journal of European Social Policy* 19, pp. 117–130.

41   Page 10 of *Facing the challenge The Lisbon strategy for growth and employment* Report from the High Level Group chaired by Wim Kok http://ec.europa.eu/growthandjobs/pdf/kok_report_en.pdf [viewed 09/10/09].

42   Ibid.

43   See 74, S. Shetty2004 "Can Rights Base Approach Help in Achieving the Millennium Development Goals?" *IDS Bulletin* 36, 1 pp.73–76.

44   See E. Dominguez Redondo 2009 "The Millennium Development Goals and the human rights based approach: reflecting on structural chasms with the United Nations System" *International Journal of Human Right* 13, 1 pp. 29–43.

45   See J. Mapulanga-Hulston 2002 "Examining the Justiciability of Economic, Social and Cultural Rights" *International Journal of Human Rights* 6, 4, pp. 9–48; See 58–59; T. Daintith 2004 "The constitutional protection of economic rights" *International Journal of Constitutional Law* 2, 1 pp. 56–90.

46   See 58–59 T. Daintith 2004 "The constitutional protection of economic rights" *International Journal of Constitutional Law* 2, 1 pp. 56–90.

47   See page 3 of COMMISSION 2009 "Report on the implementation of the SBA" *COM*(2009) 680 Brussels [emphasis in original].

48   Kurt Rothschild 2009 "Neoliberalism, EU and the evaluation of policies" *Review of political economy* 4, 21 , 2 pp. 213–216.

49   See page 135 ibid.

50   See L. Chun 2001 "Human Rights and Democracy: the case for decoupling" *International Journal of Human Rights* 5, 3 pp. 19–44.

51   See S. Feldman and P. Gellert 2006 "The seductive quality of central human capabilities: sociological insights into Nussbaum and Sen's disagreement" *Economy and Society* 35, 3 pp. 423–452.

52   See J. Welling 2008 "International Indicators and Economic, Social, and Cultural Rights" *Human Rights Quarterly* 30 , pp. 933–958.

53   See page 1382 of J. Dryzek 2009 "Democratization as Deliberative Capacity Building" *Comparative Political Studies* 42, 11, pp. 1379–1402.

54   See page 183 of T. Davis, 2009 "The Politics of Human Rights and Development: The Challenge for Official Donors" *Australian Journal of Political Science*, 44, 1 pp. 173–192; B.Cooke and U.Kothari (eds) *Participation: The New Tyranny?*, Zed Books, London.

55   Stijn Smismans 2008 "'New Modes of Governance and the Participatory Myth" *West European Politics* 31, 5 pp. 874–895.

56   Ian Mclean 1991 "Forms of Representation and Systems of Voting" in D. Held (ed.) 1991 *Political theory Today* Polity Press, Oxford.

57   Milan Dluhy and Nicholas Swartz 2006 "Connecting Knowledge and Policy: the Promise of Community Indicators in the United States" *Social Indicators Research* 79, pp. 1–23.

58   R. Gahin, V. Veleva and M. Hart 2003 "Do Indicators Help Create Sustainable Communities" *Local Environment* 8, 6 pp. 661–666; Meg Holden 2009 Community Interest and Indicator System Success" *Social Indicators Research* 92, pp. 429–448.

59   Yvonne Rydin 2007 "Indicators as a governmental technology? The lessons of community- based sustainability projects" *Environment and Planning D: Society and Space* 25, pp. 610–624; Lee Stapleton and G. Garrod 2008 "Policy Preceding Possibility? Examining Headline Composite Sustainability Indicators in the United Kingdom" *Social Indicators Research* 87, pp. 495–502.

60   K.Meyer 2005 "Life courses and Life Chances in a Comparative Perspective" chapter two in Stefan Svallfors ed. 2005 *Analysing inequality: life Chances and Social Mobility in Comparative Perspective* Stanford, CA: Stanford University Press.

8 Modern technologies, modern disparities

Regional inequalities in innovations in the EU countries

Jacek Wallusch and Beata Woźniak-Jęchorek

Introduction

Recent developments in macroeconomics indicate changes in technology as the singular most important factor driving long-term GDP growth. Innovative economies enjoy a high level of human capital and, therefore, achieve the fastest growth rate of GDP per capita. Since the seminal papers of Romer (1986) and Lucas (1993), the literature on technological background of economic development has flourished. When dealing with technology, mainstream economics almost exclusively operates on aggregate variables. Hence, it is not surprising that some factors influencing R&D remain unnoticed. An important aspect of possible slowdown is the regional disparities. Within the European Union, this problem is rooted in centralistic inclinations of governments and historical events observed for centuries. If we bring the aggregates and regions together, a vital question arises: can the regional disparities compromise the sustainable growth?

In this chapter we present the modern, mostly not even recognized, inequalities in terms of regional perspective. We try to elucidate the regional disparities in selected R&D variables and confront them with regional inequalities in GDP and unemployment rate. Our intuitions were stimulated by the results obtained by Barro (1991) and Sala-i-Martin (2013). Barro found a positive correlation between baseline level of human capital per capita and the GDP. The former has determined the pace at which GDP has grown in poor countries. Sala-i-Martin, on the other hand, was more skeptical towards the impact of technology. According to his powerful statement regarding the innovations and institutions, Sala-i-Martin (2013) argued that 'an economy with bad institutions is inefficient in the sense that it takes more inputs to produce the same amount of output'.

Switching the perspective from country-level to regional, one should obtain findings relating technology to institutional limitations. Our study was performed at the NUTS 2 level. We substituted the school enrollment rates used by Barro with total intramural R&D expenditure (251 regions), total R&D personnel and researchers (227 regions), and patent applications (208 regions). The intramural expenditure on R&D defines innovative potential of an economy. The expenditure constitutes the sum of current expenditure and investment overlays designed for creative work. To approximate the innovative potential, we also applied the number of pending patent applications. This variable specifies the number of patent applications filed by residents and non-residents in national patent offices and applications in other places around the world using the international PCT application. The sample was discontinuous and covered the time span between the year 2002 and 2011, but the majority of estimations were performed for the year 2011 due to the availability of data published by the Eurostat. Country-wise, the sample consisted of Austria, Bulgaria, Czech Republic, France, Germany, Greece, Hungary, Italy, the Netherlands, Poland, Portugal, Romania, Slovak Republic, Spain, Sweden, and the UK. The group of countries selected for the analysis is extremely heterogeneous and composed of economies with different institutional background regarding centralization, history, the impact of government sector on R&D expenditure, or the structure of GDP by the type of activity.

Following the standard routine, we first calculated the Gini coefficients for selected variables. The second part of the study dealt with the deviations from the national averages.[1] Most of our results indeed show a strong relationship between technological and GDP disparities. Interestingly, the former are more persistent and their magnitude (measured by Gini coefficient) is much larger. Less obvious are the links between the labour market and employment in R&D. Even if the correlation is weaker, the relationship is statistically significant.

The remainder of this paper is as follows. The next section presents the European Union policy towards innovations. The third section focuses on the statistical properties of the time series employed in our empirical investigations and the next section reports the estimations' results regarding the relationship between regional inequalities in innovations. The last section concludes.

Technological disparities in European regions: EU Policy

In its strategic documents, the EU uses two types of innovation ranking: the Innovation Union Scoreboard and its regional counterpart, the Regional Innovation Scoreboard. The annual Innovation Union Scoreboard provides a comparative assessment of the research and innovation performance of the EU Member States and the relative strengths and weaknesses of their research and innovation systems. It helps Member States assess areas in which they need to concentrate their efforts in order to boost their innovation performance. The Regional Innovation Scoreboard presented every two years (the last for 2014) provides a comparative assessment of innovation performance across 190 regions of the European Union, Norway and Switzerland using a limited number of research and innovation indicators.

Similarly to the Innovation Union Scoreboard, in which countries are classified into four different innovation performance groups, European regions have been classified into Regional Innovation leaders (34 regions), Regional Innovation followers (57 regions), Regional Moderate innovators (68 regions) and Regional Modest innovators (31 regions). The most innovative regions are usually to be found within the most innovative countries. All the EU regional innovation leaders (27 regions) are located in only eight EU Member States: Denmark, Germany, Finland, France, Ireland, the Netherlands, Sweden and the UK. This indicates that innovation excellence is concentrated in relatively few areas in Europe. In addition, 14 countries have regions in two performance groups and four Member states, France, Portugal, Slovakia and Spain, have regions in three different regional performance groups, which indicate more pronounced innovation performance differences within countries. Only Austria, Belgium, Bulgaria, Czech Republic, Greece and Switzerland show a relatively homogenous innovation performance as all regions in those countries are in the same performance group.

Each year, Europe spends on R&D 0.8 per cent of GDP less than the US and 1.5 per cent less than Japan (Gouardères, 2015). Moreover, the effect of brain drain can be witnessed because the best researchers and innovators move to countries that offer them better working conditions. Although the EU market is the largest in the world, it remains fragmented, which is particularly noticeable at the regional level and insufficiently conducive to innovation.

Innovation Union is one of the seven flagship initiatives designed under the strategy "Europe 2020" to create a smart, sustainable and inclusive economy. The aim of the Innovation Union is therefore to create a genuine homogenous European market for innovation that will attract innovative companies and enterprises. To achieve this goal, it was proposed to implement different measures in the field of patent protection, standardization, public procurement and smart regulation.

In order to finance this initiative, the project Horizon 2020, which has a budget for 2014–2020 funds in the amount of EUR 77 billion (in prices of 2013) for the funding of research and innovation in Europe. The objective is to allow a transfer of innovative ideas to real products and services, so that it will increase economic growth and the number of jobs in Europe. The programme "Horizon 2020" is designed to facilitate access to innovation, to engage SME sector procurement to support innovation, to facilitate cooperation between the worlds of science, business and to support social innovation research.

At the regional level, the Structural Funds (SFs) are instruments of the EU's cohesion policy aiming at counterbalancing the research and innovation capacity by investing especially in those regions that lag behind in performance. For this reason, the EU cohesion policy introduced two types of regional funding objectives. The SF Convergence objective (CON) covers the regions that have GDP per capita below 75 per cent of the EU average and aims to accelerate the economic development in these regions. The Regional Competitiveness and Employment objective (RCE) comprises all other regions above this threshold and seek to reinforce competitiveness, employment and attractiveness of these regions (RIS, 2014, p. 24). The Framework Programme for Research and Technological Development (FP) is another EU intervention that provides significant funding for research and innovation, but differs in its nature. If SFs favour the emergence of the knowledge economy and aim to foster socio-economic cohesion, the FP is based on organizations bidding for competitive funding based on criteria of excellence. For this reason, it is usually the case that innovation leaders are also the best performers in attracting FP funds (RIS, 2014, p. 27).

According to new EU projects for subsequent years, the European Fund for Strategic Investments will be crucial for research and innovation, in particular to restore venture financing to its pre-crisis levels. In addition, through the Capital Markets Union, the Commission aims to further improve access to finance for businesses, and in particular, SMEs. Strengthening the synergies between the EU's research funding programme Horizon 2020 and Structural Funds will also play an important role in stimulating investment levels. Through the new Policy Support Facility, the Commission will assist Member States in reforming their national research and innovation systems and in leveraging business innovation. The Single Market Strategy will result in presenting further steps towards creating a more innovation-friendly business environment. In addition, efforts will be made to make the unitary patent work and for standards to be more conducive to innovation. In parallel, the Commission is taking action to speed up the digital transformation of industry and to create a business environment where innovative companies can flourish and obtain easier and affordable intellectual property protection for their innovations (European Commission, 2015).

Technological disparities in European regions: An illustration

Although the regional income disparities attract much more attention, the inequalities in R&D variables are much stronger. Figure 8.1 depicts the values of Gini coefficients calculated for GDP (upper panel) and R&D expenditure in the year 2011. With the average of 0.387, the magnitude of technological inequalities is more than two times larger. Not surprisingly, so is the dispersion.

Gini coefficient offers a generalised and aggregate measure of disparities and is therefore particularly helpful in tracing down the dynamics of inequalities. Not surprisingly, different patterns were observed across Europe. The first decade of the 21st century marked an increase of regional income inequalities, particularly in the New EU countries.[2] Only four countries managed to reduce the disparities, and on average the inequalities had increased by almost 13 per cent (or 8.4 per cent after excluding the Bulgarian case, which clearly is an outlier). For the same years, the technological regional inequalities had been reduced by 5.5 per cent. Seven countries had obtained impressive figures exceeding a 10 per cent decrease. Even more impressive is the fact that this group of countries is highly differentiated and encompasses countries with strong centralistic tradition (the Czech Republic, Hungary,

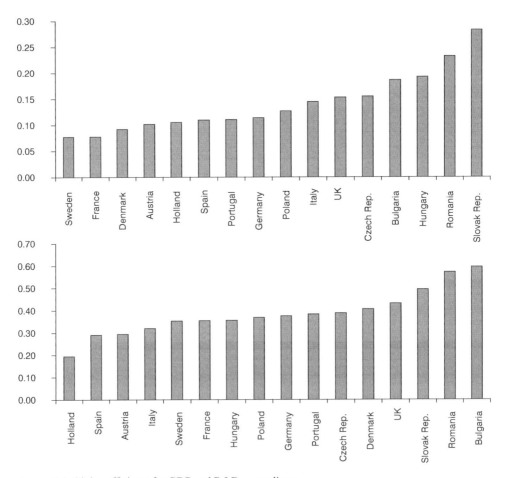

Figure 8.1 Gini coefficients for GDP and R&D expenditure

Source: Own estimations based on Eurostat data.

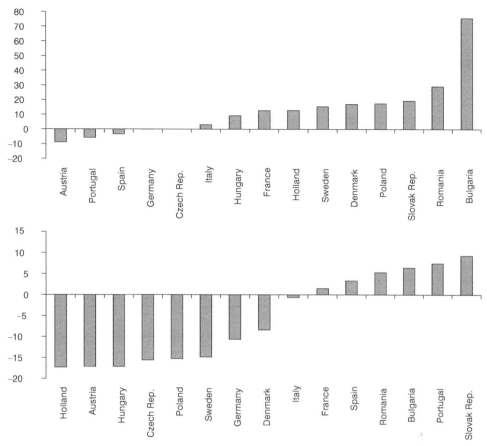

Figure 8.2 Percentage change in regional disparities in GDP and R&D expenditure (2003–2011)
Source: Own estimations based on Eurostat data.

Poland) or historically-determined regional inequalities (Germany, Poland). Assuming that the economic growth is highly sensitive to technological changes, closing the technological gap between regions is essential for the further reduction of the regional disparities in capital formation and GDP. The changes in Gini coefficients are depicted in Figure 8.2.

Figure 8.3 provides an additional insight into the dynamic features of technological inequalities. The upper panel shows the series following a negative trend. (Notice that Denmark has been excluded due to the smaller number of observations). The other series behave in a rather stationary manner. On the one hand, no particular increase in disparities has been noted. Hikes, like those observed in Bulgaria in 2005 or Portugal in 2010, were offset within the next few years. Even the increase of the largest magnitude, which according to Figure 8.2 was observed in the Slovak Republic, was due to the level shift in 2003. On the other hand, however, the stationary-like behaviour of Gini coefficient indicates no long-run decrease in inequalities. Closing the gap between regions is therefore very unlikely.

An additional insight is offered by the disaggregated data. To focus on disparities, for every region we simply calculated the percentage of national average[3], assuming that the national average = 1. Table 8.1 and Figure 8.4 illustrate the results. The distribution of deviations from the national averages are highly right-skewed and leptokurtic for all variables. Not

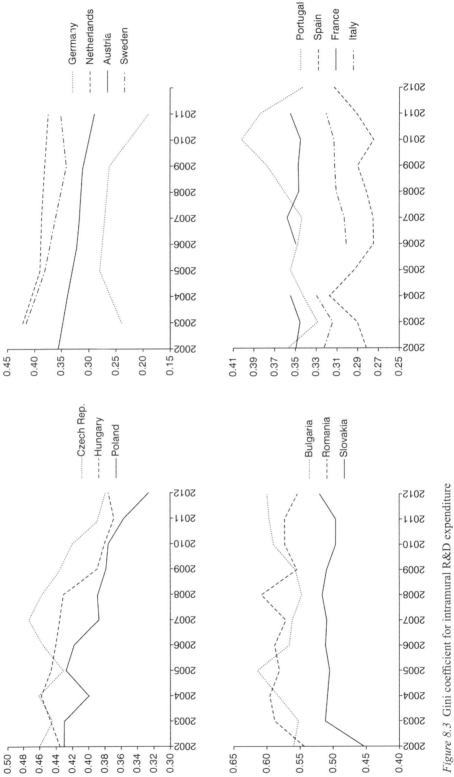

Figure 8.3 Gini coefficient for intramural R&D expenditure

Source: Own estimations based on Eurostat data.

Table 8.1 Descriptive statistics of regional disparities

Variable	Median	Std. dev.	Skewness	Kurtosis
GDP	0.902	0.310	3.013	18.287
R&D Expenditure	0.737	0.788	2.040	8.184
Patents	0.663	1.105	2.394	10.160
Unemployment	0.954	0.308	0.975	4.634
R&D personnel	0.913	0.575	1.658	8.233

Source: Own estimations based on Eurostat data.

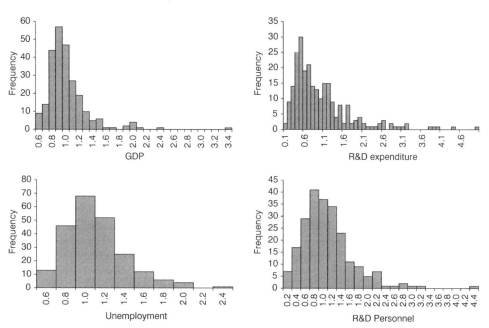

Figure 8.4 Distribution of regional disparities

Source: Own estimations based on Eurostat data.

surprisingly, the medians for GDP and unemployment rate are closer to 1 than the median for R&D variables. Combined with the higher value of standard deviations for the latter group of variables, a similar pattern emerges for the disaggregated data: technological disparities are larger than the inequalities observed in income or in the labour market.

The relationships between disparities

What type of interdependencies between regional disparities in income, unemployment, and R&D variables should we expect? Contemporary macroeconomics suggests a positive correlation between GDP and R&D expenditure. Similar results should be found for the disparities. Some recent empirical studies performed at the regional level not only support this supposition, but also claim a causal relationship driven by innovations. Paas and Vahi (2012) showed that a large portion of GDP variability in EU regions is explained by the

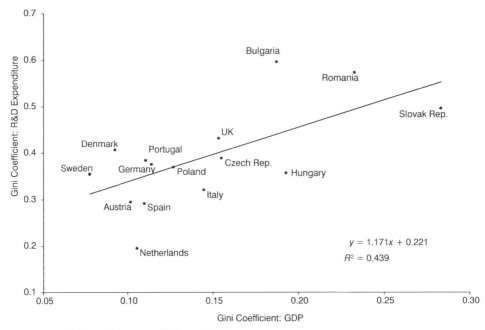

Figure 8.5 Gini coefficients for GDP and R&D
Source: Own estimations based on Eurostat data.

composite indicators of regional innovation performance. Fan et al. (2012) found R&D to be the major factor driving the regional inequalities in China.

Our findings for the aggregate measure of disparities are ambiguous. We found a positive relationship between Gini coefficients calculated for GDP and R&D expenditure, but the relationship between unemployment and R&D personnel turned out to be positive as well. A positive correlation (0.4) observed in the labour market is surprising, and might be explained by the job destruction caused by technological changes. A very poor fit, however, requires a necessary caution in interpreting this finding. Figures 8.5 and 8.6 depict the results.

Less controversial are the results obtained for the variables expressed as the percentage deviations from national average. Our estimations, summarized in Table 8.2, show a positive relationship between GDP and R&D expenditure and personnel, and a negative one between unemployment rate and the R&D-related variables. More interesting is the magnitude of the estimated coefficients. The correlation analysis shows a much closer relationship between the GDP and the R&D personnel than between the unemployment rate and R&D personnel. The latter is about three times smaller (in absolute terms) than the former. One should not, however, jump into conclusions too eagerly. It appears that the relationship between intramural R&D expenditure and unemployment is slightly stronger than between unemployment and GDP. Moreover, after extracting the new EU countries from the sample we found a strong, negative, and possibly non-linear relationship between unemployment and R&D personnel.[4]

Figure 8.7 graphs the relationship between GDP and R&D Expenditure. An interesting pattern emerges once the largest R&D disparities are inspected. In our sample, 8 out of 10 regions with the largest positive deviation from national average include the capital cities. The R&D expenditure are highly centralised in Romania, Bulgaria, Poland, France, Spain, Hungary, the Slovak Republic, and the Czech Republic. In five other countries (Denmark, Greece, Austria, Portugal, and Sweden) the largest deviation from national average is

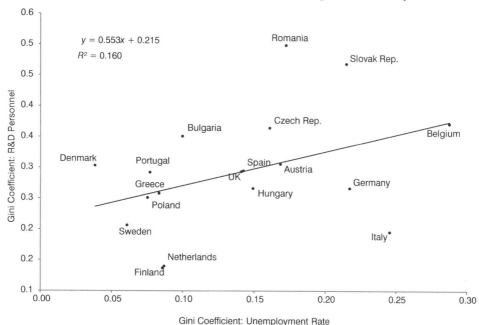

Figure 8.6 Gini coefficients for unemployment rate and R&D personnel

Source: Own estimations based on Eurostat data.

Table 8.2 Correlation and significance analysis: deviations from average

Relationship	Correlation coefficient	Testing for significance	
		Test statistic	*p-value*
R&D personnel and GDP	0.717	15.427	0.000
R&D personnel and unemployment	−0.200	−3.059	0.026
Unemployment and GDP	−0.267	−4.158	0.012
R&D expenditure and GDP*	0.680	14.571	0.000
R&D expenditures and unemployment	−0.282	−4.402	0.010
Patents applications and GDP	0.482	7.887	0.002

* both series expressed in natural logarithms

Source: Own estimations based on Eurostat data.

observed in regions encompassing the capital cities. As the salaries govern the labour market, the regional disparities in R&D personnel follow the disparities in R&D expenditure: 8 out of 10 regions with the largest positive deviation from the national average include the capital cities (Bucurest-Ilfov, Praha, Bratislavsky Kraj, Inner London, Yugozapaden, Közep-Magyarorszag, Wien, and Mazowsze). Centralism appears to be a serious institutional factor influencing the allocation of R&D resources. It is also a limitation that could be easily overcome. Martin (1999) noted that 'policies that lead to a decrease in the cost of innovation, through subsidies for example, can lead to higher growth, lower monopolistic profits for capital owners and more even spatial distribution of incomes and economic activities'. Central government across Europe, however, are not particularly keen to actively fight the centralization and its monopolistic profits.

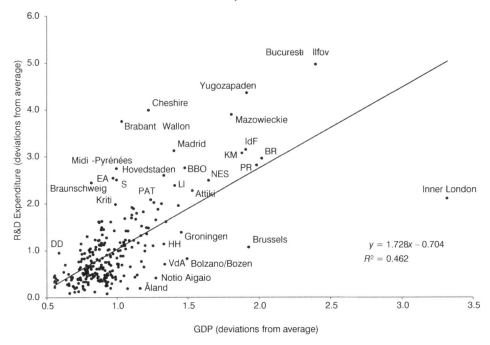

Figure 8.7 Regional disparities in GDP and R&D expenditure

Source: Own estimations based on Eurostat data

Note: BBO – Berkshire, Buckinghamshire and Oxfordshire, BR – Bratislava, DD – Dresden, EA – East Anglia, IdF – Île de France, KM - Közép-Magyarország, LI – Lisbon, NES – North Eastern Scotland, PAT – Provincia Autonoma di Trento, PR – Praha, S – Stuttgart, VdA – Vallée d'Aoste.

Slightly different picture emerges when patenting activity is considered. The results regarding the sign (positive), power (0.482) and significance of the relationship match our expectations. The leading regions, however, are not necessarily those including the capital cities. Among ten regions with the largest deviation from national averages we found Lombardia, Noord-Brabant, Cataluña, Rhône-Alpes, Oberbayern, and Stuttgart. The patenting activity is perhaps much more historically determined and, therefore, less dependent on the centralistic inclinations. For instance, the south-western German regions have remained the technological leaders for the last 140 years.[5] The same remark applies to Italy, the Netherlands, and Spain.

Concluding remarks

There is little doubt that regional disparities may effectively diminish the economic growth. In the European Union, the inequalities go far deeper than the division between old and new EU members. Regional disparities are generated by variety of institutional factors, among which the centralistic inclinations of governments and historical background are particularly important. If the changes in R&D variables are also subject to regional disparities, the sustainable economic growth customarily attributed to changes in technology may be compromise.

The main goal of this paper was to provide an additional insight into regional disparities in R&D variables within the European Union. Unlike the EU documents, we focused on inequalities in total intramural R&D expenditure, total R&D personnel and researchers as

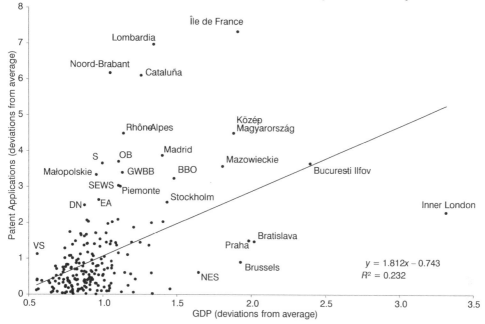

Figure 8.8 Patents over GDP

well as in the patent applications, and confronted them with the inequalities in GDP and unemployment rate. The empirical exercise was performed for two types of indicators: the Gini coefficient and the percentage of national average. Due to the very limited availability of data, the cross-regional estimations were performed for the year 2011. The magnitude of technological inequalities turned out to be more than two times larger than the magnitude of income disparities. Not surprisingly, so was the dispersion of technological inequalities.

The Gini coefficients were mostly employed to trace down the dynamic features of technological inequalities. Despite the larger magnitude, between 2002 and 2011 the technological inequalities had been reduced by 5.5 per cent, whilst the income inequalities had increase by almost 13 per cent. Seven countries obtained impressive figures exceeding a 10 per cent decrease.

Our results from correlation analysis matched the expectations and confirmed a relatively strong relationship between the regional disparities in R&D variables and GDP. The correlations between the former and the unemployment was weaker, yet significant. Moreover, the inequalities in R&D personnel were much closely related to the income disparities than to the inequalities in unemployment rate. The analysis also revealed a very strong centralisation of the R&D expenditure. In 13 countries (out of 19) the largest deviation from national average has been found in regions encompassing the capital cities.

In the short run, the regional technological disparities may deepen the income inequalities and result in compromising the sustainable long-run growth. Can the gap between regions be bridged? Our study showed that closing the gap is very unlikely. Despite some positive tendencies observed in many countries throughout the last decade, the technological inequalities are very persistent. The problem is well-recognized by the European Commission, but the proper diagnosis requires more detailed, time-series oriented studies. Moreover, an active policy, but not necessarily based on income re-distribution, should be recommended.

Notes

1 Throughout this paper the deviation from national average is meant as the percentage of the national average calculated for specific region.
2 Boosker (2009) presents a similar conclusion regarding the Eastern Europe.
3 Due to the availability of data the calculations were performed for the year 2011.
4 The estimations were performed for the deviations from average. The correlations coefficient was equal to -0.519 and was highly statistically significant (p value = 0.001).
5 German regions that had increased the innovativeness in the 19th century revealed their strength in technological clusters of the primary importance (Streb et al. 2006). Obviously, centralistic inclinations are also historically determined. In the mid-1920s almost 40 per cent of the registered patents in Poland were granted to companies and inventors residing in the capital city of Warsaw (Wallusch 2015).

References

Barro, R. (1990), Government spending in a simple model of endogenous growth, *The Journal of Political Economy*, Vol. 98, No. 5, Part 2, S103–S125.

Barro, R. (1991), Economic growth in a cross-section of countries, *The Quarterly Journal of Economics*, Vol. 106, No. 2, 407–443.

Durlauf, S., Johnson, P. and Temple, J. (2005), Growth econometrics. In Aghion, P. and Durlauf, S. (eds) *Handbook of Economic Growth*, Amsterdam: Elsevier.

European Commission (2014), Innovation performance: EU member states, international competitors and European regions compared, Memo, 4 March, http://europa.eu/rapid/press-release_MEMO-14-140_pl.htm

European Commission (2015), Unleash innovation to spur growth in Europe, Press release, 7 May, http://europa.eu/rapid/press-release_IP-15-4927_en.htm

Fan, P., Wan, G. and Lu, M (2012), China's regional inequality in innovation capability, 1995–2006, *China & the World Economy*, Vol. 20, No. 3, 16–36.

Gouardères, F. (2015), *Innovation policy*, European Parliament, http://www.europarl.europa.eu/atyourservice/en/displayFtu.html?ftuId=FTU_5.9.7.html

Grossman, G. and Helpman, E. (1990), Trade, innovation, and growth, *The American Economic Review*, Vol. 80, No. 2, 86–91.

Innovation Union Scoreboard (2015), Report: European Commission http://ec.europa.eu/growth/industry/innovation/facts-figures/scoreboards/files/ius-2015_en.pdf

Kuznets, S. (1971), *Economic Growth of Nations: Total Output and Production Structure*, Cambridge, MA: Harvard University Press.

Lucas, R.E. (1993), Making a Miracle, *Econometrica*, Vol. 61, No. 2, 251–272.

McGrattan, E. and Schmitz, J. (1998), *Explaining Cross-Country Income Differences*, Minneapolis, MN: Federal Reserve Bank of Minneapolis.

Mankiw, N. G., Romer, D. and Weil, D. N. (1992), A contribution to the empirics of economic growth, *The Quarterly Journal of Economics*, May: 407–437.

Paas, Tiiu, and Vahi, Triin, (2012) Economic growth, convergence and innovation in the EU regions. *Discussions on Estonian Economic Policy: Theory and Practice of Economic Policy*. Vol 20, No 1, 105–121.

Martin, P. (1999) Public policies, regional inequalities and growth, *Journal of Public Economics* Vol. 73, 85–105.

Regional Innovation Scoreboard (2014), Report, European Commission, http://ec.europa.eu/news/pdf/2014_regional_union_scoreboard_en.pdf

Romer, P. (1986), Increasing returns and long-run growth, *The Journal of Political Economy*, Vol. 94, No. 5, 1002–1037.

Sala-i-Martin, X. (2013), Some lessons from 10 years of empirical growth literature, http://www. clmeconomia.jccm.es/pdfclm/xavier_i.pdf

Streb, J., Baten, J. and Yin, S. (2006), Technological and geographical knowledge spillover in the German Empire 1877–1918, *Economic History Review* Vol. 59, No. 2, 347–373.

Wallusch, J. (2015), (Un)finished transition: Stock of knowledge in Poland, 1924–2012, *Economics and Business Review* Vol. 15, No. 1, 89–102.

9   A classification of school-to-work transition regimes

Francesco Pastore

Introduction

The aim of this chapter is three-fold. First, it aims to provide an up-to-date overview of the evidence on the youth labour market problem in a cross-country perspective and of the relevant literature.[1] Second, it aims to offer a frame of mind which should allow the reader understanding of the roots of the youth labour market problem, its causes and consequences. Third, it aims to catch some important shifts in the recent evolution of the debate on the causes and remedies of youth unemployment across countries.

The empirical evidence on youth unemployment across countries suggests the existence of a number of stylised facts that the economic literature has struggled to explain. They can be summarised as follows:

1   the youth disadvantage, proxied, for instance, by the youth unemployment rate exhibits strong cyclicality;
2   nevertheless, with few exceptions, it is almost in every country about twice, or more times, as big as the unemployment rate of adults;
3   there is large variation across countries in youth unemployment rates and in the ratio of youth to adult unemployment rates;
4   this variability tends not to follow a continuous line, but rather to generate clusters of countries with similar indices of youth absolute and relative disadvantage.

While trying to explain the above stylized facts, first of all, it is important to spell out that despite the strong cyclicality of youth unemployment, macroeconomic factors alone fail to explain the permanent nature of the youth unemployment problem. This does not mean that macroeconomic factors are not important. They are indeed able to reduce the absolute youth disadvantage, say their specific unemployment rate, but are not necessarily able to cancel out their relative disadvantage, say the ratio of theirs to the adult's unemployment rate. Moreover, macroeconomic trends tend to generate different results in different countries.

The permanent nature of the youth disadvantage at the labour market can be better understood by looking also at the specific weakness of young people's participation to the labour market in every country, namely what I call the "youth experience gap", and the way different education, training and welfare systems are organized and are able to affect and reduce it. Indeed, the main difference between young and adult workers is to be found in the lower degree of work experience of the former, also in a period of increasing levels of education attainment. In other words, young people miss two of the three components that Becker (1962) considers as constituting human capital, namely generic and job-specific work experience.

Moreover, while everywhere the youth unemployment gap depends on the youth experience gap, which is a constant across countries, instead, cross-country differences in youth disadvantage depend on the way different welfare system mixes seek to address the youth experience gap.

In the early 1990s (OECD, 1994), labour market flexibility in sclerotic EU countries was seen as a tool able to abate also youth unemployment. A higher job-finding rate, also by means of temporary work, also introduced through reforms at the margin, namely reforms affecting especially the new entrants, were expected to reduce the length of unemployment spells and also the youth experience gap. Temporary work, more than pro-active policy tools were expected to effectively increase the chances of young people to get the wor experience they need to compete with the adults.

The unsatisfactory experience of implementation of two-tier reforms inspired by this mainstream approach has made the emphasis of the theoretical debate shift away from the early 1990s emphasis on labour market flexibility as the key, if not the only policy tool to fight youth unemployment (OECD, 1994). In other words, the past emphasis of the debate on labour market flexibility alone is considered nowadays more and more ill posed. This implies also a re-consideration of the virtues of two-tier reforms of the labour market like the ones implemented in South-European countries (see, among others, Blanchard and Landier, 2002; Dolado, Garcìa-Serrano and Jimeno, 2002; Bentolila, Dolado and Jimeno, 2012). A first stream of the literature has moved in the direction of reconciling theory and facts by arguing that the failure of flexibilization policies is to be attributed to the way reforms were implemented and the insufficient mix of flexibility and flexicurity that was introduced. This means that the reforms failed, on the one hand, because they did not affect the job security of the insiders and, on the other hand, because they did not provide legal arrangement to substitute job with employment protection. The keyword of flexicurity, as based on the Danish experience, has inspired this literature.

Another stream of the literature has instead argued that the countries that are more successful in reducing the youth unemployment problem are not those countries with the most flexible labour market, but rather those who have a better developed educational and training system. This stream of the literature supports the hypothesis that more important to reduce the youth disadvantage is the way the school-to-work transition is organized within a country. An education-to-work regime is identified by the set of institutions that affect the ability of new entrants to smoothly move from education to the world of work, namely the education system itself and its links to the labour market, the legal arrangements existing in the labour market, the availability of effective placement services, as well as of passive income support and pro-active schemes (for a detailed definition of the concept of transition system, see Raffe, 2008).

To sum up, when attempting to reduce the youth experience gap, which is the main long-term cause of the youth disadvantage in the labour market, one should consider different sets of policy interventions, namely: a) the degree of labour market flexibility and of job security, but also: b) the effectiveness of the educational system in smoothing the transition to work; b) all the factors able to affect the intensity and effectiveness of a job search, such as the intensity and length of passive income support schemes, the effectiveness of public and private placement services and training programmes; c) the spells and length of unemployment; d) the quality of employment.

Based on these criteria, this chapter proposes to group countries into five different school-to-work transition regimes. Such classification tends to largely overlap the Esping-Andersen

(1990) classification of welfare systems into: a) liberal; b) conservative; and c) social-democratic. It includes also the Latin Rim, theorized by Ferrera (1996) and Rhodes (2009), and the former socialist world, theorized, among others, in Fenger (2007) and Burlacu (2007).

The outline of this chapter is as follows. We begin by laying down some stylized facts about the youth experience gap. We then set the theoretical framework of the analysis starting from what we call the mainstream approach to filling the youth experience gap. In what follows we raise a number of critiques to the mainstream approach, concluding that every EU country addresses, in fact, the youth unemployment problem with some form of state intervention. The next section brings to the fore our classification of European school-to-work transition regimes and discusses differences among them. Some final remarks conclude the discussion.

Some stylized facts

Before starting the analysis, it may be useful to make a number of clarifications. First, when analysing young people's behaviour in the labour market, it is misleading to think of it only in terms of employment/unemployment rates especially if focusing on teenagers (aged 14–19 years), because education and/or training are a better option for them than employment. Looking at employment rates is more meaningful when considering young adults (aged 20–24 years) and further age groups (25–34 years). In recent years, also for young adults there is often a trade-off between employment, which is a short-term objective, and increasing their investment in education and work experience, which are the most important long-term objectives.

$$AD_Y = u_Y = \frac{U_Y}{E_Y + U_Y} = \frac{U_Y}{LF_Y}$$

We should keep in mind this caveat when looking at the youth unemployment rate (YUR), the most common indicator of the absolute disadvantage (AD_y):
where E, U and LF represent respectively the number of employed, unemployed and job seekers. As usual, the lower case letter indicates the unemployment rate. Other indicators of absolute disadvantage could be the employment and inactivity rate, the not-in-education-employment-training and the like.

AD indicators do not allow understanding whether the disadvantage is due to the same macroeconomic factors that affect also other groups. To understand the specificity of the disadvantage of young people, relative measures are more important. The most common measure of relative disadvantage (RD) is:

$$RD_{Y,A} = \frac{u_Y}{u_A}$$

$RD<1$ if young people' disadvantage is lower than that of adults; the opposite is true if $RD<1$, in which case specific measures are necessary to support young people. Macroeconomic measures might not be able to reduce the RD to the same extent to which it reduces AD.

Figure 9.1 has the merit to show both measures at the same time. the adults' (25–64 years) unemployment rate (AUR) is on the horizontal axis, whereas the horizontal axis reports the YUR (15–24 years). Each dot coordinates represent the AUR and YUR of a given country

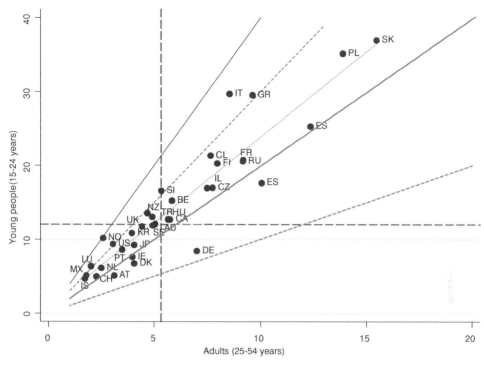

Figure 9.1 Youth and adult unemployment rate in OECD countries (2000)

Source: own processing of OECD data.

Note: Data on Estonia and Slovenia refer to 2002.

in 2000. The horizontal dotted line represents the OECD average youth unemployment rate, whereas the vertical dotted line represents the OECD average adult unemployment rate. The diagonal lines represent different ratios of the youth to the adults' unemployment rate, starting from a ratio of one down to the right to a ratio of four up to the left. The green line is the regression line, which lies just below the diagonal corresponding to a ratio of two.

The year 2000 has been taken to represent a situation of expansion of the business cycle, before September 11 attacks, when the average unemployment rate is relatively low for both groups. A number of facts emerges:

1   nowhere RD>1 or RD>4;
2   RD tends to 1 only in a few countries, namely Germany and Austria. In Denmark and Ireland RD<2;
3   in most countries, RD is in between 2 and 3;
4   some Eastern and South European countries – Spain, the Slovak republic and Poland – exhibit particularly high youth unemployment rates, while others – Italy, Greece and Slovenia – also exhibit an RD>3;
5   almost all former socialist countries are in the upper right rectangle, with a high YUR and AUR;
6   Germany and other central European countries, such as Austria and Denmark, have the lowest RD, lower than 2, despite the hardship of reunification and the difficult economic condition of the Eastern *landers*;

7   Anglo-Saxon countries – United Kingdom, United States, Australia, Ireland, New
     Zeeland – lie in the first rectangle down to the left or exhibit relatively low YUR and
     AUR;
8   several Scandinavian countries, such as Norway, report high values of the RD, but low
     YUR values.

How did the situation change after the crisis? Overall, the analysis confirms the strong
variability of the YUR, but not always also of the RD, to the business cycle. Two main factors
should be considered under this respect. First, the LIFO (last-in-first-out) principle is always
implemented by managers during mild downturns: they prefer to fire first the last hired workers,
who are generally younger. Within the context of panel data econometrics based on 70 countries
observed over the years from 1980 to 2005, Choudhry, Marelli and Signorelli (2012) confirm
that financial crises have an impact on the YUR that goes beyond the impact resulting from
GDP changes; and the effect on the YUR is greater than the effect on overall unemployment.
Moreover, their results suggest that financial crises affect the YUR for five years after the onset
of the crises, although the most adverse effects are found in the second and third year.
     Second, Newell and Pastore (1999) argue that one of the main features of episodes of
dramatic structural change as opposed to cyclical downturns is the large share of mass-
layoffs which, by their very nature, tend to involve also prime-aged workers, beyond the
LIFO principle. The share of mass-layoffs and the extent to which the downturn is affecting
also the adults should be taken as one of the most specific indicators of the depth of economic
crises.
     Figure 9.2 reproduces the previous figure with data relative to 2011, when the great
depression hit the labour market of all OECD countries. Both the average YUR and AUR
have increased. Several observations are in order:

1   with few exceptions, cross-country differences are rather persistent, but with some
     interesting switches;
2   despite the financial crisis, Germany, Denmark and Austria lie still below the RD=2
     diagonal, together with Japan and few other countries;
3   South-European countries worsen their position, overcoming also Eastern European
     countries, both in terms of YUR and RD;
4   Ireland and other Anglo-Saxon countries have been among the most hit countries in
     terms of YUR, but not of RD.

Figure 9.3 shows the evolution of RD relative to a selection of OECD countries over a long
period of time. Germany has been stubbornly close to a value of 1, except for the mid- to
late-1970s. Japan has been the second closest to the like of parity between young and adult
people. The United Kingdom and United States exhibit a strong cyclicality. In Sweden the
ratio has recently escalated. Italy has always been the worst performer. The convergence of
the mid-1980s is due to the increasing unemployment rate of the adult segment of the labour
force.
     Figure 9.4 compares the YURs by gender. It shows that nowadays, in general, men fare
worse than women, since most dots lie below the bisector, although in no OECD country the
relative disadvantage of women is twice that of men. Only in a few cases women fare worse
than men: Chile, Greece, France, Italy, Mexico, Poland, Portugal, Turkey.
     The relative advantage of women is due to: a) their increasing educational levels; b) the
tendency of women to delay maternity decisions to avoid discrimination (Figure 9.4).

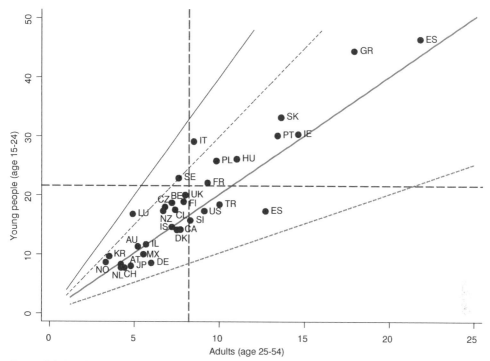

Figure 9.2 Youth and adult unemployment rate in OECD countries (2011)

Source: own processing of OECD data.

Note: Real time data. Data for Brasil refer to 2011 and data for China and India refer to 2010.

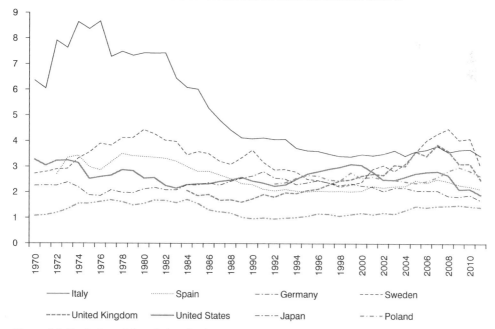

| —— Italy | ·········· Spain | —·—· Germany | – – – Sweden |
| –––– United Kingdom | —— United States | –··–·· Japan | –·–·– Poland |

Figure 9.3 Evolution of the relative disadvantage across countries

Source: own processing of OECD data.

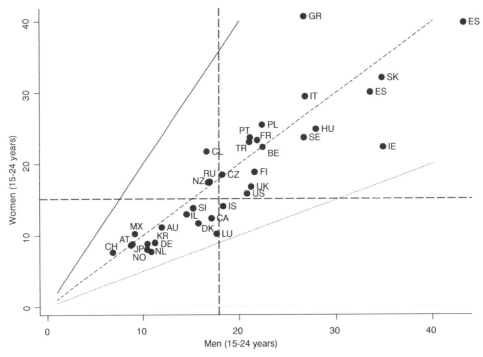

Figure 9.4 Gender differences in YURs by country (2010)
Source: own processing of OECD data.

Another underlying process is the strong convergence in the degree of strictness of the labour market regulation of EU countries around a value of 2 on the index. Two exceptions are notable: the United Kingdom, which maintains a position of greater flexibility than elsewhere and Spain, where the convergence has stopped in the early 1990s at around a value of 3 on the index (Figure 9.5).

The youth experience gap

This section provides a general theoretical framework useful when thinking of cross-country differences in the youth unemployment problem and the role of different policy instruments to help young people have a smooth school-to-work transition. The main reason for young people moving between different labour market statuses is their lower level of human capital and, therefore, productivity compared to adults, which *ceteris paribus* makes employers prefer adults. As also Becker (1962) noted, human capital has three general components: education, generic work experience and job-specific work experience. Generic work experience includes the ability to cope with the functional distribution of tasks within an organization, to respect deadlines and the internal hierarchy of an organization. All these skills can be learned in any type of job and are easily transferred from one job to another. Job-specific work experience comprises specific skills that can only be gained and used in a given type of job. They include the ability to carry out specific types of task, such as, in rural areas, harvesting, feeding livestock.

This type of reasoning helps solve a typical puzzle of youth labour markets. With ever increasing educational attainment worldwide, the educational level of the younger generation

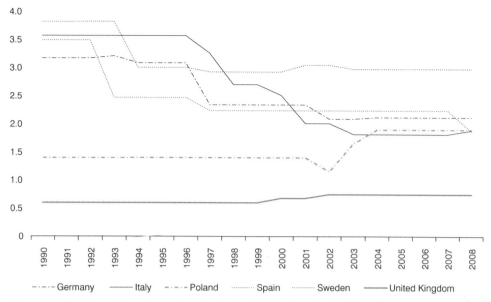

Figure 9.5 Strictness of employment protection legislation (version 1, 1985–2008)

is almost always greater than the older generation. Despite this, young people still have lower chances of finding employment. Why is that? The likely explanation is their lack of the other two components of human capital, generic and job-specific work experience. That is, that behind the youth unemployment problem, there is a "youth-experience gap".

Aiming to fill this gap, young people move in and out of employment in search of a best job–worker match, but if not found quickly, they tend to become unemployed or inactive while searching for a better job. During employment, some young people become aware of their gaps in education or training and, consequently, return to school (Clark and Summers, 1982 and the entire NBER volume edited by Freeman and Wise, 1982).

Youth unemployment is clearly related to the hardship involved in accumulating work experience. In the neo-liberalist view (see, for instance, OECD, 1994), causes of youth unemployment, especially the long spells experienced by many young people, can be found in past unemployment experiences, reducing their chances of finding gainful employment. In this stream of economic thought (Blanchard and Diamond, 1994), unemployment causes a process of deskilling from the supply side: since the unemployed cannot use their skills because they are unemployed, they have lower productivity. On the demand side, employers see unemployment as a stigma: a sign of lack of skills and motivation. Lowering the share of long-term unemployment and reducing the average period would be an important policy target for neo-liberalists.

The OECD (1994) and Krugman (1994), among others, suggested that by rendering the labour market more flexible through legalizing and encouraging part-time and fixed-term contracts, the policy-makers will provide a simple and effective solution to young people's problem of work experience, enabling them to find the job they desire. There are two ways this might happen. First, easily accessible fixed-term contracts would provide young people with more opportunities to gain the work experience they need and learn different working methods and tasks through short periods of employment. Second, increasing the degree of turnover in the labour market shortens the average duration of unemployment.

It should now be clear why, within this framework, labour market flexibility and low entry wages are the best solution to ease school-to-work transition. These solutions to the youth experience gap also have the merit of being low cost, since they automatically exist in the labour market. This is an important aspect of such a policy and helps understand its appeal in a time of increasingly stringent budget constrains for many governments worldwide.

Two arguments cast doubt on this solution to youth unemployment, suggesting that it is too simplistic and in need of amendments. The first is based on the empirical finding that only the least skilled and least motivated fall into long-term unemployment, therefore, there would be no lower job finding rate for them; instead the causal link would go in the opposite direction. Less skilled individuals would experience greater difficulty in finding gainful employment and, as a consequence, also longer unemployment spells (Heckman and Borjas, 1980; Heckman and Singer, 1984).

The policy implications of this reasoning are important. Training programmes finely tuned to the least skilled and motivated groups would be the best policy option to reduce youth unemployment. They would be more effective than increasing labour market flexibility. There is no guarantee that labour market flexibility would help the least skilled and least motivated and it is more likely it would only help those who are better educated and more motivated.

The second argument, for which Becker (1962) provides the theoretical basis, criticizes the effectiveness of labour market flexibility to actually help young people increase their human capital to the level of adults with similar education. The reasoning is that fixed-term contracts only generate sufficient incentive to invest in the formation of generic work experience. They do not allow young people to increase other skills specific to a given type of job due to their short time horizon. Why should employers and employees invest in the accumulation of skills specific only to a given type of job if the contract is temporary?

It is a common occurrence in countries with increased flexibility in youth labour markets that short-term contracts fail to provide young people with specific work experience. This type of market failure should be addressed by providing incentives to prolong short-term contracts or, specific programs of on-the-job training aimed at enabling young people to accumulate job specific work experience.

In addition, from a more practical point of view, there is increasing empirical evidence to support the view that fixed-term contracts create precariousness of income for many young people experiencing frequent interruptions to their career. Too many temporary workers end up in dead-end jobs that they hoped would be a stepping stone to decent work (Bentolila and Dolado, 1994; Berton, Devicienti and Pacelli, 2011).

The above arguments help understand why, in many of the countries, increasing flexibility of labour market entry – the so called two-tier reforms – has reduced youth unemployment only to a small extent, while generating work precariousness (Blanchard and Landier, 2002; Bentolila, Dolado and Jimeno, 2012). Fixed-term contracts alone cannot fill the youth experience gap.

Moreover, as ILO (2004) and Cazes and Nesporova (2007), among others, note, the experience of flexibility has shown that what its advocates usually consider its main advantage, namely its supposed universality is, in fact, one of its major shortcomings. Labour market flexibility is not the best solution for every country and confirms the wisdom that there are no such policy interventions that fit any country or economic condition. Labour market flexibility alone proves too often to be ineffective. It is a good instruments in particular types of labour market conditions where, for instance, there is also a high average level of educational attainment, where it goes together with flexibility in the market for goods and financial services.

These arguments also explain why labour market flexibility is only one of the policy instruments adopted in any country to help young people fill in the youth experience gap. Efficient educational and training systems, passive income support schemes on a contractual basis, fiscal incentives for employers who are willing to hire long-term unemployed, prove to be no less important instruments.

It is certainly difficult to find policies concordant with the institutional framework of any country. However, comparison of different countries' outcomes in addressing the problem of school-to-work transition suggests that youth unemployment is lower where:

- educational systems are more flexible;
- educational systems follow a dual (as opposed to a sequential) principle, which means that young people are provided training while at school and not after school;
- where labour market flexibility is coupled with high educational attainment;
- where ALMP is fine-tuned to the needs of the weakest groups and targeting and evaluation of training programs are implemented in a systematic way to discard the least effective and develop the most effective;
- where households do not bear all the cost of youth unemployment.

The educational system is more flexible if it foresees few or no obstacles to young people moving from one curriculum to another, does not impose constraints to access a given type of education and requires a reasonable number of years to attain a diploma. The educational systems that are more flexible and provide training, together with general education, appear to be more inclusive and feature lower dropout rates.

To sum up, labour market flexibility is not the one-size-fit-all solution to every problem young people encounter during their school-to-work transition. Labour market institutions are also very important. In particular, in the case of young people, the educational and training systems play a no less important role than the degree of labour market flexibility.

A classification of school-to-work transition regimes

Another stream of the literature has argued that the policy to fight youth unemployment should be a mix of different instruments, which, in turn, depend not only on the degree of labour market flexibility or of flexicurity, but also on efficient educational, training and, more generally, welfare systems and the system of fiscal incentives to hire the weakest groups of youth unemployed (Hennan, Raffe and Smyth, 1996; Ryan, 2001; O'Higgins, 2001; Raffe, 2008). Transition systems differ according to:

1   the overall amount of resources allocated to employment policy;
2   the relative share of pro-active versus passive income support schemes;
3   targeting, scale and evaluation of expenditure in employment policy;
4   state- versus family-based welfare systems;
5   size and type of fiscal incentives to hire young people.

Different types of transition regimes are able to importantly affect the size of the youth experience gap and hence the smoothness of school-to-work transitions, contributing this way to reduce or to increase youth unemployment. A stylized fact of the first section, was that countries tend to cluster around similar values of the YUR, AUR and RD. Also the evolution of the AD and RD are similar within given groups of countries.

Following, among others, Vogel (2002), at least five different transition regimes can be identified: a) the North-European or Scandinavian; b) the Continental European; c) the Anglo-Saxon; d) the South-European; e) that of former socialist countries, which include the new EU member states. These transition regimes overlap very well with those identified by Esping-Andersen (1990) with reference to welfare state regimes – social democratic, conservative, liberal – with the addition of the so-called Latin Rim (identified for the first time in Ferrera, 1996; see, also, for a recent appraisal, Rhodes, 2009) and the former socialist world (identified, among others, in Fenger, 2007; and Burlacu, 2007). At this stage, it is still hard to say whether (some or all of) the transition system of New Member States belong to a specific new group or rather to one of the existing groups. The common socialist heritage would suggest considering them as an autonomous group, but a number of cross-country differences do not allow disentangling clearly the specificity of such group. Moreover, many legislative changes are still on-going and the final outcome is not clear as yet.

The study of divergences among countries may help find the systemic causes of youth unemployment. The attention is not paid so much to macro-economic, rather micro-economic and institutional aspects. This does not mean that *aggregate demand management* policies are ineffective or are of no importance. They are absolutely necessary to abate the YUR in all countries, but would not probably change much of cross-country differences, which are the main focus of this chapter. Moreover, macroeconomic policy is dealt with in any macroeconomics handbooks.

The rest of the chapter shortly describes the main features of these transition regimes, with the aim of listing advantages and disadvantages of each in smoothing school-to-work transitions.

North-European system: Active Labour Market Policy

The North-European group was originally inspired to the lesson of Lord William Beveridge more than Bismarck. It includes the Scandinavian countries (Finland, Norway, Sweden and, according to some observers, also Denmark and the Netherlands). The flagship of Scandinavian Social Democracies, the welfare state, is characterized by its universal scope of coverage and citizenship, a non-contributory tax funding, envisaged flat rate, high levels of expenditure and supplied services, a substitutive rather than complementary role of the state (Leibfried and Mau, 2008).

In this regime, the state undertakes the aim of full employment and each citizen is guaranteed the "right to be employed". The state is the employer of last resort. Employment is key to access citizenship and social rights. Accordingly, the welfare state is very well developed, while labour markets are far from flexible. Job search through public and private employment agencies is frequent.

The labour force has a high level of unionisation. The strength of the unions depends heavily on the so-called Ghent system, namely the role of unions in the management of income support schemes and active labour market policy, together with the public employment services (Skans, 2007).

The main feature of this system is perhaps the fact that it relies on a very well developed welfare state system. In fact, passive income support schemes are available for the unemployed. Recently unemployment benefits are given on a contractual basis and, namely, provided based on the obligation to attend training courses. Active labour market policy (ALMP) is implemented on a large scale. There is large evidence of a gross impact of ALMP on youth employment opportunities for those individuals who attended training programmes, though the net impact is a matter of discussion. By net impact of ALMP we mean the gross impact minus the number of those who would have obtained a job anyway, independent of attendance of training schemes (see, for an assessment, Sianesi, 2004).

The European Employment Strategy (EES) is already largely in place in as much as education, training or job opportunities are offered to each unemployed young people within 6 months of the unemployment spell. Overall, young people experience a high degree of employment protection, based on a long tradition of welfare state. The European Youth Guarantee a scheme that the EU has promoted in 2013 to fight youth unemployment in all member states is inspired to the Scandinavian model.

The disadvantages of this system include low social mobility and the high cost for the State budget of the overall transition. Especially the expenditure in ALMP is very high.

Different from Germany, the Swedish labour market – especially the youth labour market – has been experiencing severe hardship for over two decades. Until the 1980s, Sweden has been one of the countries with the lowest unemployment rate (1.5–2 per cent) and the highest employment rate (83 per cent) in the world. In the early nineties, the unemployment rate grew up to 8 per cent and employment was reduced down to 73%. The recovery of the mid-nineties was interrupted again in the 2000s, when both the youth unemployment rate and the ratio to the adult unemployment rate were high (Figures 9.1 and 9.2). By contrast, the long-term unemployment incidence is among the lowest (less than 10per cent) among OECD countries (Quintini, Martin and Martin, 2007, page 30).

This last figure, which would abstractly suggest that a high *turnover* rate exists, is apparently in contrast with the extremely low figure – among the lowest in the world – concerning the job destruction rate (Quintini, Martin and Martin, 2007, page 32). The most obvious explanation is to be searched for in the broad utilisation in Sweden of temporary work (concerning at present over 50 per cent of young unemployed; Quintini, Martin and Martin, 2007, page 38) as well as of vocational training schemes provided, together with unemployment insurance, to all persons out of a job after a certain length of time since unemployment occurred. This suggests that vocational training conceived in the framework of active employment policies produces effects of precarious work similar to those generated by temporary work.

By considering the similarities between the two welfare systems, the factor that, at first sight, could explain the difference between the performance of Sweden and Germany is the educational system. The German *dual system* is not only a youth social integration instrument, but also a wonderful tool to simplify school-to-work transitions. The education system is flexible and sequential.

A comparison of the effectiveness of employment services suggests the higher level of effectiveness of the Swedish system of employment services as compared to both the liberal and continental European ones. The proportion of workers who find a job through public employment agencies equalled 12.4% in 2007, a bit lower than Germany (13 per cent), but nearly double than in the United Kingdom (7.7%) and about four times bigger than in Italy (3.7 per cent) (Cicciomessere and Sorcioni, 2007, Table 9.3; Giubileo, 2011; Pastore, 2013).

Against this very high outcome, in terms of mediated work, PES expenditure in Sweden is much lower than in other countries. The share of GDP equals 0.8% and is, hence, closer to the United Kingdom (0.6%) rather than Germany (1.3%). Also the number of staff in employed in the PES (10,250) is much lower than in Germany (about 74 thousand) and Britain (about 67 thousand).

It is difficult to say what the secret of the Swedish system of PES is. Maybe, it is the continuous attention paid to the unemployed, also due to the small number of unemployed per employee of the PES, which equals nearly 28.9 units – one of the lowest – together with the United Kingdom and Denmark. This indicator depends on both the low density of population and the effectiveness of PES action. An important contribution is no doubt to be attributed to the attention towards businesses and their occupational needs, other than to the continuous monitoring and evaluation activities.

Continental-European: The dual educational system

The Bismarckian regime is also named continental European (Flora and Heidenheimer, 2003; Bertola, Boeri and Nicoletti, 2001), wage payment system or industrial achievement performance (Titmuss, 1958), corporate-conservative (Esping-Andersen, 1990), or still occupational pure (Ferrera, 1996). This is a model of welfare state (and school-to-work transition) in the middle between the liberal and residual typical of Anglo-Saxon countries and the Social Democratic and universalistic model typical of Scandinavian countries. It is ruled by a wage payment or social insurance system aimed at workers and not at all citizens; it provides average performances and pre-figures a state intervention which can be defined complementary.

The Bismarckian regime is typical of Germany, Austria, as well as – in someone's opinion – of Belgium and Denmark's traditions. After Belgium, the continental European regime surely takes after – at least partially – the so-called Ghent model of trade unions relationships (Weishaupt, 2011).

The countries belonging to this regime have always featured the lowest youth-to-adult unemployment ratio worldwide at around 1 and, in any case, always below 2 in the case of Germany (see again Figure 9.3) and slightly more than 1.5 in Denmark (unreported). In other words, in Germany the risk of unemployment for young people is roughly the same as that of the adults. Despite the German reunification and the high unemployment rate of the Eastern länders, still the German youth-to-adult unemployment ratio has remained astonishingly low in the last decade.

As Steedman (1993), Ryan (2001, pp. 55$_{ss}$; 2008) and O'Higgins (2001) argue, the main candidate to explain the success of the Continental-European, and especially the German model, is the specific nature of the dual educational system, which is adopted also in Austria, Denmark, the Netherlands and Switzerland[2]. Apprenticeship is perhaps the most important tile of the mosaic.

Dietrich (2007) and Büchel (2002) report that at the end of primary school (*Grundschule*), at the age of 10, children are offered the opportunity either to attend the gymnasium, which gives access later on to the university, or to attend vocational school and go into apprenticeship programmes (*Realschule*) or to the general high secondary school (*Hauptschule*). This dramatically reduces the youth unemployment rate, by offering to workers not wishing to attend the University a high degree of integration in the educational system and, in the meantime, an important training opportunity to become skilled manual workers.

The degree of labour market flexibility is low in Germany, but high in Denmark (so-called "flexicurity system"). Job search happens through employment agencies. There is a high level of unionisation of the labour force. Apprenticeship is provided on a large scale for many high school students. Active labour market policy is provided for the weakest groups. Passive income support schemes are available for the unemployed.

The identikit of youth unemployment in Germany is as follows: a) Men with low education attainment; b) Little work experience; c) Long unemployment spells; d) Low social capital:

no active participation in social life; e) Having children increases the risk of unemployment; f) Training programmes have no gross impact (Caroleo and Pastore, 2003).

The advantages of this system are: a) Low youth unemployment; b) Smooth school-to-work transitions; c) High degree of social integration; d) High degree of protection for young people; e) Based on a long tradition.

The main weakness of the Continental-European educational system is its rigidity, especially the obligation for students to choose their future very early (so-called early tracking), when the influence of parents. Those who have chosen to go into vocational education have little chance to change their mind and attain higher levels of education later. As a consequence social mobility is very low. Moreover, in a period of increasing tertiary education, this might represent an important constraint to the development of a skilled workforce. For now, however, Germany still scores one of the highest share of young people with a tertiary diploma worldwide.

Other disadvantages include: a) Difficult to export, as shown by the experience of the Eastern länders, where the dual system is still less effective; b) The few who drop out have big problems to integrate. They are the bulk of unemployment for the rest of their lives; c) Too many are excluded by university education; d) Low social mobility; e) Very costly for schools, firms and young people. There is also some evidence that the employment opportunities offered to several young teenagers through the dual system vanish when they become young adults.

The Anglo-Saxon system: High quality of education and labour market flexibility

The case of the Anglo-Saxon youth labour market, especially the USA and the UK, is the most difficult to summarise in few words, since it is the most studied and, therefore, the literature is very large (see, for instance, Freeman and Wise, 1982; Blanchflower and Freeman, 1990; Ryan, 2001; O'Higgins, 2001; Bell and Blanchflower, 2011).

As already noted in Section three, there is a higher degree of labour market flexibility, but fewer temporary jobs than in Europe. Booth, Francesconi and Frank (2002, page F189) and Ryan (2001, page 66), note that temporary work concerns only about 7 per cent of women and 10 per cent of men who are employed, and that these proportions have been very stable over time. This may impress those who are used to thinking of the United States in particular, and of the Anglo-Saxon countries in general, as characterized by a low degree of labour market regulation. In fact, in Anglo-Saxon countries all work contracts can be easily terminated, and this makes it less useful for firms to turn to temporary work as a substitute.

The high degree of turnover of the United States reported in Table 9.1 is due, instead, to the fact that also the jobs of insiders are intimately more unstable: firms may dismiss activities and workers more easily than in Europe. On the other hand, though, it is much easier to find jobs. As a consequence, not only the length of unemployment spells, but also that of transition to a permanent work is lower than average in these countries. Interestingly, the overall duration of school-to-work transitions is lower than in Scandinavian and South European countries, but higher than in Germany and Austria (Quintini, Martin and Martin, 2007, page 30 and pages 34–35).

The rate of unionisation used to be high several decades ago, but has dramatically shrunk from the 1980s, while there is a relatively high degree of decentralization of wage bargaining. Nonetheless, the minimum wage is common to all Anglo-Saxon countries, although recently with a different value for young people and the adults.

Table 9.1 Comparative evidence across countries of job finding and job loss

Country	Finding job	Losing job
United States, 1992–1993	65.9	2.8
Poland, regions of low unemployment, 1994–2005	36.3	2.5
Poland, regions of high unemployment, 1994–2005	31.5	4.4
Russia, 1994–1995	40.8	3.7
Italy, 1994–1995	13.1	1.6
Italy, 2001–2002	20.3	1.5
Italy, 2007–2008	33.5	1.6
Italy, 2008–2009	28.3	2.3
Italy, 2009–2010	26.9	2.3

Job search happens often through private employment agencies. Apprenticeship is available on a small scale. Passive income support is available for the weakest groups, provided that they attend pro-active schemes. Already from the 1980s, the length of unemployment benefits and the possibility of renewal after an employment spell has dramatically reduced to prevent young people living on the dole for the rest of their lives.

As reported in Weishaupt (2011) and Pastore (2013), distinguishing features of the employment services are:

1   a predominant role of the state in the general management;
2   the exclusively consulting role of social partners;
3   the tendency to contract out to private agencies an increasing part of placement services and training programs, although under the monitoring and evaluation of the public sector.

In Australia, employment services are entirely contracted out to private agencies, even if they are funded by the state, rather than being paid by users (Webster and Harding, 2001). A gradual but progressive privatisation of employment services is happening also in the United Kingdom. This is fully coherent with the Anglo-Saxon tradition according to which intermediation between labour supply and demand must have a mere informational role and be launched as such to both public and private bodies, who freely and autonomously manage it, in competition with each other. The basic idea of the liberal regime is that competition among various bodies is a key condition to ensure greater efficiency, although in the framework of clear rules and correctives of failure that are inexorably generated by the market. Within the liberal system, distortions related to the assignment of employment services to private bodies (so-called creaming or cherry-picking of the best customers; discrimination of the most hardly employable; gaming between private agencies, employers and unemployed and so on) are not denied, but rather are considered as minor bottlenecks as compared to the goal of reaching a greater effectiveness of the system as a whole.

Different from what is generally believed, it is questionable whether the core of the Anglo-Saxon school-to-work regime and of its success in achieving smooth transitions to work is really to be found in the high degree of labour market flexibility. A more convincing candidate to explain this in turn is the educational system, which is sequential, but generally very flexible, of a high quality and with good links to the labour market. An important advantage, often neglected in other countries, is that the competences acquired in education are much oriented to problem-solving, which helps students overcoming more easily the passage from general and abstract notions to skills that can be used on the job. Moreover, the system is flexible in many directions, which have become more and more important with the expansion of the share of people achieving tertiary education:

1   it allows students moving quite easily from one educational track to another;
2   students may complete their educational path with a university diploma already at the age of 21, when they can decide whether to accumulate job-specific work experience or to invest into further more specialized education;
3   the system of university credits allows achieving post-graduate diplomas in fields that are different from that of tertiary education.

Furthermore, both secondary and tertiary educational institutions provide very good placement services, which allow young people to find more easily job vacancies suitable to them. Job placement services are especially good for students enrolled in many graduate programs oriented to produce skills which are on demand in the skilled labour market. It is not by chance that the educational and training system of Anglo-Saxon countries is a model alternative to the German dual system for other countries experiencing longer education-to-work transitions.

In the UK, the YUR is relatively low at slightly more than 10 per cent, but the RD is one of the highest among OECD countries, at about 3 (see Figures 9.1 and 9.2). Again this is the consequence of the very low average YUR and AUR and the strong cyclicality of the YUR. Nonetheless, when the crisis is strong and prolonged, as Newell and Pastore (1999) note with reference to transition from plan to market, like the current one, the RD goes down because the AUR has increased more than the YUR. A similar finding regards also the United Sates.

Ireland has experienced ups and downs in the last decades, with values of the YUR and AUR very low in the late 1990s and the 2000s, but high in 2011, after the financial bubble exploded. The Irish RD has remained relatively low, though (compare Figures 9.1 and 9.2).

The bulk of unemployment in the Anglo-Saxon system is constituted of people with a particularly poor family background. Otherwise youth unemployment is a temporary phenomenon and the market bears the responsibility to facilitate the passage to adulthood.

To sum up, the advantages of this system are: a) low youth unemployment rate, but still high if compared with that of the adults; b) low share of temporary jobs; c) high level and quality of education; d) high social mobility.

The disadvantages of this system are:

1   a bulk of low-skill long-term unemployed for those who drop out early from the educational system;
2   low degree of employment and social protection for young people;
3   extreme segmentation of the youth labour market;
4   very costly for individuals and households who have to bear the cost of long-term unemployment.

The South European System: The family and ... temporary work

The European-Mediterranean regime, typical of France, Greece, Italy, Portugal and Spain[3], is "rudimentary", in as much as rights to public services are fully stated and recognized as universal, but the welfare state is only a semi-institutionalized promise (Ferrera, 1996). The right to health and to education, among others, is universal and granted to all residents, though. There are important aspects of the school-to-work transition that are common to the countries belonging to this group and allow me considering them as belonging to the same education-to-work regime.

The role of the state is less important than in the Central-European and Scandinavian regimes and, with time passing, tends to shrink ever more in different fields. The degree of unionization of the labour force is generally high, though decreasing recently. Passive income support is granted to dismissed workers only and is therefore related to employment as a pre-condition. Subsequently, considerable responsibilities – as well as costs – of unemployment for new entrants and temporary workers who lose their job lie on their family.

Another typical feature of this regime is the persistent reference to an alleged rigidity of the labour market that a number of reforms seem to have been unable to domesticate. In the last decades, the degree of labour market flexibility has dramatically increased for young people though, through the use of fixed-term contracts. These last reduce the hiring and firing costs only for those involved, as it is typical of reforms at the margin. Nonetheless, as noted in a previous section, such reforms have shown many shortcomings.

The expenditure in ALMP is insufficient and also the institutional context for its implementation is poor. Italy's spending in active policies amounts only to 0.37% of GDP, a much lower share than Germany and France (1%), not to say of Denmark (1.48%), the homeland of flexicurity.

Apprenticeship programmes were forbidden until the Single act of 2011, when they were liberalized and allowed also for university graduates (for an appraisal of the novelty introduced, see Tiraboschi, 2011).

Informal networks of family and friends are the most common method of job search for young people (Mandrone, 2011), which proves to be a rumour rather than a channel to reduce informational asymmetries between employers and employees, as proven by the wage penalty experienced by those using this job search method (Pistaferri, 1999; Meliciani and Radicchia, 2011).

As Pastore (2013) argues, the preference of individuals and firms for informal recruitment channels has its roots, on the one hand, in the role attributed to the family as a safety net for those most in need. It is commonly believed that family networks are the best channels to convey true information about the skill level of job candidates. On the other hand, the legislative history of the public employment services, assigned to the state until recently in a regime of monopoly and to private agencies in a regime of competition with the public actor, have contributed to make this channel highly ineffective. After the 2003 reform, still only about 3 per cent of the new employment is channelled through public and private employment services. The low share of financial and human resources assigned to the public employment services is also to be noted.

Besides, among the observers, the suspicion that labour market reforms cannot replace a greater effectiveness of the education system, is more strongly diffused than it used to be in the past. According to many observers, also from different perspectives and approaches (Caroleo and Pastore, 2005; Gelmini and Tiraboschi, 2006; AlmaLaurea, 2008; Pastore, 2009; 2012a), it is in the weaknesses of the educational and training system that may be found the weakest link of the Italian school-to-work transition system.

Howeverm the labour market is designed, the issue of excessively long post-secondary education remains. This, in turn, reduces the incentive to invest in education, and determines a share of dropouts that is the highest in the world (about 55 per cent of those enrolled, according to the OECD) (Pastore, 2012a). The OECD (2013) note that while younger Italians tend to be better educated than their older compatriots, only 15 per cent of 25–64 year-old Italians have a university-level education, compared to the OECD average of 32 per cent. The level of tertiary attainment among 25–34 year-olds is one of the lowest among OECD and G20 countries with available data. (21 per cent, rank 34/36).

There is an intrinsic contradiction in an educational system that enables access to post-secondary education to all students holding a high secondary school diploma and that, at the same time, sees them dropping out after many years of endless studies. In fact, in Italy, despite the very low proportion of graduates, a high number of students enrols at the university.[4] The educational reforms implemented at the end of the 1990s and at the beginning of the 2000s have only slightly affected these problems, which still remain dramatic. As Bratti, Checchi and de Blasio (2008) note, the reforms have led to an increased number of matriculations, but not of graduates.

The reason for this failure may be found in the low democratic nature of the reforming process, which has not allowed teachers, students and parents to assimilate the positive content of the reforms, which were in line with the Lisbon and Bologna processes.

Furthermore, secondary education shows obvious shortcomings, mirroring the low proportion of persons holding a diploma: e.g. still far away is the objective of Europe 2020 according to which 90 per cent of young people between 15 and 22 years old should have completed high secondary education. Despite continuous but low growth over recent years, in 2011 the percentage of persons holding a diploma between 25 and 34 years old was around 79 per cent, with strong differentials between centre-north and south of Italy (OECD average: 83 per cent).

Vocational training concerns only a small minority of the employed workforce. There is broad empirical evidence according to which the reforms of 2001 teaching regulations – the so-called 3+2 reforms – has only slightly contributed towards "democratizing" the post-secondary education system. In recent decades, the proportion of graduates whose parents have low social origins and/or education levels has increased. This is also due to the enlarged training supply (see the AlmaLaurea annual reports).

Yet, as Caroleo and Pastore (2012) document, this improvement has not been able to alter the strongly "classist" features of our post-secondary educational system. The level of education and family social extraction still seems to play a key role in children's university performance. They affect not only the likelihood to pursue a university degree, but also other successful post-secondary education indicators, such as the field of study chosen, the duration of education and the final degree grade.

The share of I level graduates whose parents are both graduated is over the average in the case of degrees that provide a qualification giving access to liberal professions, namely medicine, architecture, pharmacy, engineering. It is clear that for liberal professions the economic value of inter-generational transfers is particularly high. The same proportion of graduates with both graduated parents is lower than average in all other areas.

Very similar conclusions emerge when instead of looking at the inter-generational transfer of educational levels, we consider social welfare. Also in this case, we note a very low level of mobility, to demonstrate the direct linkage existing between the level of education of individuals and their social class of origin. If one wants to encourage social mobility, ensuring equal opportunities of access to higher education to all is important.

Yet, econometric estimates seem to suggest that the effect of the socio-economic condition of families on graduates' performance is rather indirect. The influence of parents' conditions on children seem to emerge above all from the choice of and performance during higher education: the latter, in fact, impacts also on university performance.

Paradoxically, if one considers that since 1969 tertiary education may be accessed with any high school diploma, Italy presents a degree of social immobility higher not only than the United States, but also than most continental European countries. Nevertheless, the direct cost of education is generally much higher in the United States than in Europe, and in particular in Italy (Checchi, Ichino and Rustichini, 1999). This suggests that the direct cost of education is neither the only hindrance, nor the main barrier preventing the three weakest social classes from accessing higher education. Obviously, there are other aspects of the education system that affect the capacity to offer equal opportunities to the beneficiaries of education. The most likely candidate to provide an explanation of the strong degree of the Italian educational and social immobility is the indirect cost of education – above all post-secondary, as measured by the foregone income that the student may have gained by working rather than studying. In the case of Italy, the necessary time to complete school-to-work transitions is particularly long, about 7–8 years on average. In addition, it is clear that educational reforms have been unable to sufficiently reduce either the direct or the indirect cost of education, from which the disadvantage of the weakest social classes originates (Pastore, 2009; and 2012a).

Apart from Poland and the Slovak Republic, that have experienced a dramatic restructuring of the economy due to the transition from plan to market, South-European countries score the highest YUR in Europe. Italy and Greece score also some of the highest RD, due to the extremely high YUR (Figure 9.1). Over the early to mid-2000s, the YUR has slightly reduced, but at the cost of a dramatic explosion of temporary, often precarious or dead-end jobs. This is particularly true for Spain, but also France and Italy. The crisis has caused a further explosion of the YUR in most of the countries belonging to this regime, as Figure 9.2 illustrates. Figure 9.3 shows that the Italian RD is, however, reducing over the decades and converging to the OECD average, because of the increased AUR. The very high AUR of the countries in the area explains why they maintain a relatively low RD.

The identikit of youth unemployed in Spain and in Italy are similar: a) New entrants; b) Women, especially with children; c) And with low education attainment; d) Trapped in precarious temporary employment; e) That causes frequent unemployment spells; f) With poor family background; g) As a positive note, youth unemployment shows negative duration dependence, but this is due to the high share of temporary work (Caroleo and Pastore, 2003; and 2005).

In the case of Italy, ALMP has no impact on the probability to experience unemployment for young people, not even the gross impact. Interestingly, Caroleo and Pastore (2005) find evidence of what they call a "training trap": participation into training programmes does not affect employment chances, but rather the probability to participate into other training programmes. This is similar to the lock-in effect that van Our (2004) has found in the case of subsidized jobs.

The gender dimension is also a peculiarity of youth unemployment in this group of countries. While in other Northern European countries, men have long had lower educational levels and lower job opportunities than their female counterparts, in Southern European countries, women are increasing their educational level only recently and, consequently, young women still represent the bulk of the unemployed. This is due to different attitudes on gender roles and the preference for the one-bread-winner model. In turn, this traditional view is ever more in contrast with the legitimate career ambitions of women and, coupled with little support by the state in favour of conciliation strategies, is causing increasing divorce rate and female age at first child and, hence, decreasing fertility.

The advantages of this model are:

1　low direct (but not indirect) cost of access to the university;
2　mild introduction of flexibility and duality in the educational system;
3　move to the 3+2 university system (Lisbon strategy);
4　increasing labour market flexibility;
5　increasing awareness of the youth unemployment problem;
6　households are good support for young people.

The disadvantages are:

1　very long school-to-work transitions;
2　very high youth unemployment rate;
3　low education attainment, especially at the tertiary level;
4　low quality of education, increasing length of tertiary education and a high share of dropouts;
5　failure of the educational reform;
6　increasing job precariousness; g) lowest social mobility;
7　highest costs of unemployment spells for households.

The new member states: Building a modern welfare system

Due to the ongoing reforms, it is still not clear whether the New EU Member States are a different group or whether they are better understood as part of the previous regimes. In fact, the countries belonging to this group are heterogeneous, although sharing a common heritage. Consequently, also the outcomes in terms of youth unemployment are similar.

The labour market position of young people in the new member states is on average worse than the EU average and close to that in Southern European countries (Figures 9.1 and 9.2). The ratio of the adult to youth unemployment rate fluctuates between 2 and 3 from one country to the other. Beleva et. al. (2001) find a ration of 2.1 for Bulgaria, whereas Domadenik and Pastore (2006) and Pastore (2012b) find a ratio of 2.8 for Slovenia and 3 for Poland. However, almost everywhere the youth unemployment rate is high and the anecdotal evidence suggests that while few particularly skilled young people have been the real winners of transition, most low-skilled young people have been the losers.

During the socialist system, in Central and Eastern European Countries (CEECs), workers were used to a pervasive welfare state. Unemployment was virtually non-existent due to the commitment of socialist regimes to full employment as a way to exploit all the available labour surplus (Kornai, 1992), but this implied also the commitment of state firms to provide jobs for all, though at very low wages. Moreover, the state used to provide also several other benefits to the most in need as well as free social services for all, including childcare facilities, health care, hospices and other services for the elderly. This was possible thanks to very soft budget constraints for state firms, the hidden state budget deficit and strong trade unions.

Only in the late 1990s, when transition seemed to have become irreversible and state budget were suffering dramatic imbalances, the debate has shifted from the gradualism/shock therapy debate to a debate on the optimal design of labour market institutions. Two streams of literature have emerged that this research aims to discuss theoretically and test empirically. Some scholars (Boeri, 2000) started to point to passive income support schemes as the origin not only of threat for the financial and monetary stability of the countries involved, but also as a source of social distress for the actual way of working of the labour market and, consequently, for the speeding up of a transition process which seemed to experience a dramatic slowdown. Boeri (2000) claimed that the right sequence for the implementation of non-employment benefits would have been the opposite of that actually followed: the governments should have started from low passive income support schemes to facilitate the flow from the state sector to non-employment and back to employment in the private sector. Only at a later stage, when unemployment was really involuntary, the governments should have started to provide income support to the losers of transition, namely those who were actually not employable in the private sector.

Other scholars (Micklewright and Nagy, 1999; 2002) advocated that the sequence of reforms was the right one and that income support schemes in the early stages of transition were indeed necessary to help people bear the consequences of dramatic structural and cultural change. Moreover, in the early stages of transition, un When transition began (youth) unemployment started to emerge as a new reality and with it a debate started on the need to introduce some kind of employment protection legislation, state subsidies to the unemployed, early retirement schemes and support to inactive people. This type of new welfare state started under the auspices of the early Optimal Speed of Transition models (Aghion and Blanchard, 1994), which suggested that passive income support schemes might be useful to buy out workers from state owned enterprises and win their resistance to the reform process. At that time, the emphasis on rapid restructuring versus gradualism was dramatically affected by the fear of a return to the past and the need to make the transition process irreversible. This way of thinking found an encouraging consensus in the population as well as in all political parties worried to make the increasing unemployment, inequality and poverty socially acceptable. Also a widespread feeling was that the state, not the households should bear the social cost of reforms. The almost immediate consequence was the explosion of the social public expenditure, the pressure on the pension system, the dramatic increase of the dependency ratio, all factors that led the CEECs state budget to the edge of a dramatic collapse.

employment was essentially involuntary, whereas later, when long-term unemployment started to emerge, unemployment benefits should have been reduced to increase incentives to work for non-employed people. Finally, unemployment benefits have been very low in CEECs also compared to the low average wages and their bite would be minor.

Also in new EU member states, youth unemployment is worrisome, among other reasons, because it contributes to make harder a dilemma that the young people in CEE have to face between continuing to invest in their own education, therefore reducing the household's budget, on the one hand; and accessing immediately the labour market, therefore contributing to the household income, but reducing their own chance to find gainful employment in the future, on the other hand.

Pastore (2012b) focuses on Poland as a typical example of the changes new member states are facing. Poland is the transition economy experiencing the highest degree of structural change and the highest unemployment rate in the area. It adopted a Big Bang approach to the reform process, by introducing simultaneously price and trade liberalisation, together with privatisation and macroeconomic stabilization already in the early 1990s. A massive flow of foreign direct investment has triggered the process of technological change, on the one hand, and generated the need for skill upgrading of the workforce, especially of the youngest segments, on the other hand.

Over the years, similar to other transition countries, the share of individuals with high education attainment has dramatically increased in Poland and other new member states, together with the progressive abatement of the share of people with vocational secondary degrees (Boeri, 2000). Domadenik and Pastore (2006, Tab. 5 and A5) find that from 1997 to 2002 the percentage of young teenagers (15–19) in education increased from about 84 to 88, while that of young adults (20–24) increased from 20 to 31. The corresponding figures for the early 1990s were 45 and 13 per cent respectively. In both cases, Poland seems to be close to the educational targets fixed within the Lisbon strategy for the year 2010.

However, these figures raise an important issue, namely what is the reason of the striking contrast between the excellent (at least quantitative) achievement in educational attainment and the delay in reducing youth unemployment rates, which remain well below the Lisbon objectives.

In recent years, almost all new member states have implemented the 3+2 educational reform. Several former Yugoslavian countries – Bosnia and Herzegovina, Croatia, Macedonia, Montenegro, Serbia, Slovenia – have adopted the dual educational system. Moreover, their ratio of expenditure in pro-active versus passive schemes has dramatically increased.

The educational attainment level is further increasing in all former socialist countries, which is raising concern that over education and over skilling might become more and more important issues (Farčnik and Domadenik, 2012).

The positive sides of the welfare systems in new member states include:

1   the old tradition of high investment in human capital formation;
2   the existence of several forms of protection for young people by the State and also by international organisations, including the EU;
3   deep reforms aimed to modernize the educational and training system.

The disadvantages include:

1   a mismatch between the composition of supply of and demand for skills, which the educational system partly contributes to maintain;
2   an excessive trust in the virtues of market forces;
3   the low average income of household and high state deficit;
4   the need to cope with increasing external constraints due also to EU accession;
5   a massive process of brain drain.

Discussion and summary remarks

This study has attempted to provide a theoretical framework within which to think of the youth unemployment problem. The main conclusion is that youth unemployment depends on the hardship young people find in filling the youth experience gap. In a mainstream approach to the issue, it is typical to think that a flexible labour market is the best solution to the youth experience gap. Through sizeable moves across different labour market statuses, young people achieve the human capital they need to become adult and productive, making it convenient for employers to hire them. Therefore, within this framework, labour market flexibility and low entry wages are the best solution to the youth experience gap.

Two main argument cast doubts on the mainstream approach. First, comes the Heckman and Borjas (1980) and Heckman and Singer (1984) argument that there is no duration dependence from unemployment when controlling for omitted skill heterogeneity. The policy consequence is that training programmes may be in principle more efficient in reducing youth unemployment than increasing labour market flexibility. Becker's work provides a second important argument: it suggests, in fact, that fixed-term contract may generate sufficient incentive to invest only in the formation of generic, but not of job specific work experience. There is therefore a failure in the market for job tenure, which should be addressed by providing some incentives to invest in human capital accumulation or job specific training programmes.

These arguments explain why labour market flexibility is only one of the policy instruments adopted in any country to help young people to fill the youth experience gap. They also let us understand why increasing entry flexibility in traditionally rigid EU countries has reduced youth unemployment only marginally, while generating much work precariousness. An important stream of the literature has attempted to elaborate on flexicurity as an alternative to flexibility alone. Flexicurity necessitates providing employment stability, if not job stability. In turn, this calls for social security rights for temporary workers and passive income support during frequent unemployment spells, also to discourage the abuse of fixed term contracts. It also calls for more developed training and recruitment systems.

Other not less important policy tool than labour market flexibility to fight youth unemployment is the educational system itself. At certain conditions, the latter may in fact be the most effective tool to raise the employability of young people.

It is certainly difficult to find recipes that accord to the institutional framework of any country and it is clear that in each group of countries there are bad and good performers. However, comparison of the outcomes of different European models in addressing the problem of school-to-work transition suggests that youth unemployment is lower:

1   <listing>with flexible, dual educational systems, which are also more inclusive;
2   where labour market flexibility is coupled with high education attainment;
3   where ALMP are fine tuned to the needs of the weakest groups: targeting and evaluation are necessary;
4   if households do not bear all the cost of youth unemployment.

The Lisbon strategy, as defined by the Special EU Council of March 2000, further re-launched at the EU Council of 2010, suggests the importance for young people of investing in human capital accumulation for the future of Europe as "the most competitive and dynamic knowledge-based economy in the world capable of sustainable economic growth with more and better jobs and greater social cohesion". Under the pressure of the economic crisis, the 2013 EU council held in Brussels launched the Youth Guarantee, a scheme that ensures that all young people under 25 – whether registered with employment services or not – get a good-quality, concrete offer within 4 months of them leaving formal education or becoming unemployed. The good-quality offer should be for a job, apprenticeship, traineeship, or continued education and be adapted to each individual need and situation.

The analysis carried out in this chapter suggests that the Lisbon strategy and the Youth Guarantee are good guides for EU governments to fight youth unemployment. Nonetheless, it also suggests that they are difficult to implement due to important institutional and historical differences across EU members, and also very costly to implement especially for countries where youth unemployment is very high and the institutions regulating the labour market are very weak, such as the Southern Mediterranean and transition countries.

Notes

1 The previous enlightening surveys of the literature (such as, for instance, Freeman and Wise, 1982; Blanchflower and Freeman, 2000; Ryan, 2001; O'Higgins, 2001; Hammer, 2003; Quintini, Martin and Martin, 2007) do not cover the period of the recent crisis.
2 Several former Yugoslavian countries and China also adopt the dual educational system.
3 For brevity's sake, the most part of the discussion is based on Italy.
4 According to the OECD (2013), the proportion of young people who could be expected to enter a university-level programme during their lifetime increased from 39 per cent in 2000 to 50 per cent in 2002 and 56 per cent in 2006, before dropping back to 48 per cent in 2011 (OECD average: 60 per cent).

References

Aghion, Phlippe and Olivier Blanchard (1994), "On the Speed of Transition in Central Europe", *NBER Macroeconomics Annual*, 283–320.

AlmaLaurea (2008, ed.), *IX Profilo dei laureati italiani. La riforma allo specchio*, Bologna: Il Mulino.

Becker, G. (1962), "Investment in Human Capital. A Theoretical Analysis", *Journal of Political Economy*, 70(5): 9–49.

Beleva, I., A. Ivanov, N. O'Higgins and F. Pastore (2001), "Targeting Youth Employment Policy in Bulgaria", *Economic and Business Review*, 3(2): 113–135.

Bell, D.N.F. and D.G. Blanchflower (2011), "Youth Unemployment in Europe and the United States", *Nordic Economic Policy Review*, 1: 11–37.

Bentolila, S. and J. Dolado (1994), "Labour flexibility and Wages: Lessons from Spain", *Economic Policy*, 9(18): 53–99.

Bentolila, S., J.J. Dolado and J.F. Jimeno (2012), "Reforming an Insider-Outsider Labor Market: The Spanish Experience", *IZA Journal of European Labor Studies*, 1(4), 1–29.

Bertola, G., T. Boeri and G. Nicoletti (2001), *Welfare and Employment in a United Europe*, Boston, MA: MIT Press.

Berton, F., F. Devicienti and L. Pacelli (2011), "Are Temporary Jobs a Port of Entry into Permanent Employment? Evidence from Matched Employer-Employee", *International Journal of Manpower*, 32(8): 879–899.

Blanchard, O.J. and P. Diamond (1994), "Ranking, Unemployment Duration and Wages", *Review of Economic Studies*, 61(208): 417–434.

Blanchard, O.J. and A. Landier (2002), "The Perverse Effects of Partial Labour Market Reforms: Fixed-Term Contracts in France", *Economic Journal*, 112(480): F214–F244.

Blanchflower, D.G. and R. Freeman (2000), *Youth Employment and Joblessness*, Chicago, IL: University of Chicago Press.

Boeri, T. (2000), *Structural Change, Welfare Systems, and Labour Reallocation. Lessons from the Transition of Formerly Planned Economies*, Oxford: Oxford University Press.

Booth, A.L., M. Francesconi and J. Frank (2002), "Temporary Jobs: Stepping Stones or Dead Ends?", *Economic Journal*, 112(480): F189–F213.

Bratti, M., D. Checchi and G. de Blasio (2008), "Does the Expansion of Higher Education Increase the Equality of Educational Opportunities? Evidence from Italy", *Labour*, 22(special issue): 53–88.

Büchel, F. (2002), "Successful Apprenticeship-to-Work Transitions. On the Long-Term Change in Significance of the German School-Living Certificate", *International Journal of Manpower*, 23(5): 394–410.

Burlacu, I. (2007), "Welfare State Regimes in Transition Countries: Romania and Moldova Compared", *CEU Political Science Journal*, 2(3): 302–318.

Caroleo F.E. and F. Pastore (2003), "Youth Participation in the Labour Market in Germany, Spain and Sweden", in T. Hammer (ed.) *outh Unemployment and Social Exclusion in Europe*, Bristol: Policy Press.

Caroleo F.E. and F. Pastore (2005), "La disoccupazione giovanile in Italia. La riforma della formazione come alternativa alla flessibilità", *Economia e Lavoro*, 39(2): 49–66.

Caroleo F.E. and F. Pastore (2012), "Talking about the Pigou Paradox: Socio-Educational Background and Educational Outcomes of AlmaLaurea", *International Journal of Manpower*, 33(1): 27–50.

Cazes, S. and A. Nesporova (2007), *Flexicurity: A Relevant Approach in Central and Eastern Europe*, Geneva: International Labour Organization.

Checchi, D., A. Ichino and A. Rustichini (1999), "More Equal but Less Mobile? Education Financing and Intergenerational Mobility in Italy and in the US", *Journal of Public Economics*, 74(3): 351–393.

Choudhry, Misbah Tanveer, Enrico Marelli and Marcello Signorelli (2012), "Youth unemployment rate and impact of financial crises," *International Journal of Manpower*, 33(1): 76–95.

Cicciomessere, R. and M. Sorcioni (2007), "La collaborazione fra gli operatori pubblici e privati", Rome: Italia Lavoro.

Clark, K.B. and L.H. Summers (1982), "The Dynamics of Youth Unemployment", in R.B. Freeman, and D.A. Wise (eds), *The Youth Labour Market Problem: Its Nature, Causes and Consequences*, Chicago, IL: University of Chicago Press/NBER (also available in Summers, L.H. (1990), *Understanding Unemployment*, Cambridge, MA: MIT Press).

Dietrich, H. (2007), "Leaving school but not prepared for work? School to work transitions and labour market policy for young people in Germany", IAB, mimeo.

Dolado, J.J., C. García-Serrano and J.F. Jimeno (2002), "Drawing Lessons from the Boom of Temporary Jobs in Spain", *Economic Journal*, 112(480): F270–F295.

Domadenik, P. and F. Pastore, F. (2006), "Influence of Education and Training Systems on Participation of Young People in Labour Market of CEE Economies. A Comparison of Poland and Slovenia", *International Review of Entrepreneurship and Small Business*, 3(1): 640–666.

Esping-Andersen, G. (1990), *The Three Worlds of Welfare Capitalism*, Cambridge: Polity Press.

Farčnik, D. and Domadenik, P. (2012), "Has the Bologna Reform Enhanced the Employability of Graduates? Early Evidence from Slovenia". *International Journal of Manpower*, 33(1), 51–75.

Fenger, H.J.M. (2007), "Welfare Regimes in Central and Eastern Europe: Incorporating Post-Communist Countries in a Welfare Regime Typology", *Contemporary Issues and Ideas in Social Sciences*, 3(2): 1–30.

Ferrera, M. (1996), "Southern Model of Welfare in Social Europe", *Journal of European Social Policy*, 6(1): 17–37.

Flora, P. and A. Heidenheimer (2003), *The Development of Welfare States in Europe and America*. New Brunswick, NJ : Transaction Books.

Freeman, R. and D. Wise (1982, eds), *The Youth Labour Market Problem: Its Nature, Causes and Consequences*, Chicago, IL: University of Chicago Press.

Gelmini, P.R. and M. Tiraboschi (2006), *Scuola, università e mercato del lavoro dopo la Riforma Biagi*, Milan: Giuffrè.

Giubileo, F. (2011), "Uno o più modelli di politiche del lavoro in Europa? I servizi al lavoro in Italia, Germania, Francia, Svezia e Regno Unito", *Rivista del diritto della sicurezza sociale*, 11(3): 760–777.

Hammer, T. (2003), *Youth Unemployment and Social Exclusion in Europe*, Bristol: Policy Press.

Heckman, James J. and George J. Borjas (1980), "Does Unemployment Cause Future Unemployment? Definitions, Questions and Answers from a Continuous Time Model of Heterogeneity and State Dependence", *Economica*, 47(187): 247–83.

Heckman, J. J. and B. Singer (1984), "A Method of Minimizing the Impact of Distributional Assumptions for Duration Data", *Econometrica* 52, 271–320.

Hennan, D.F., D. Raffe and E. Smyth (1996), "Cross-National Research on School-to-Work Transitions: An Analytical Framework", paper commissioned by the OECD secretariat to provide background for the Transition Thematic Review, Paris: OECD.

ILO (2004), "Starting Right: Decent Work for Young People", Background paper prepared for the Tripartite Meeting on Youth Employment: The Way Forward, Geneva: ILO.

Kornai, J. (1992), *The Socialist System: The Political Economy of Communism*. Oxford: Oxford University Press.

Krugman, P. (1994), "Past and Prospective Causes of High Unemployment," *Economic Review, Federal Reserve Bank of Kansas City*, IV(1): 23–43.

Leibfried, S. and S. Mau (2008), *Welfare States: Construction, Deconstruction and Reconstruction*, Cheltenham: Edward Elgar.

Mandrone, E. (2011), "La ricerca del lavoro in Italia: l'intermediazione pubblica, privata e informale", *Politica Economica*, 27(1): 83–124.

Meliciani, V. and D. Radicchia (2011), "The Informal Recruitment Channel and the Quality of the Job-Worker Matches: An Analysis on Italian Survey data", *Industrial and Corporate Change*, 20(2): 511–554.

Micklewright, J. and G. Nagy (1999), "Living Standards and Incentives in Transition: The Implications of Exhausting UI Entitlement in Hungary", *Journal of Public Economics*, 73(3): 297–319.

Micklewright, J. and G. Nagy (2002), "The Informational Value of Job Search Data and the Dynamics of Job Search: Evidence from Hungary", *Acta Oeconomica*, 52(4): 3999–419.

Mitani, N. (2008), "Youth Employment in Japan after the 1990s Bubble Burst", in G. De Freitas (ed.), *Young Workers in the Global Economy. Job Challenges in North America, Europe and Japan*, Cheltenham: Edward Elgar.

Newell, A. and F. Pastore (1999), "Structural Change and Structural Unemployment in Pole", *Studi Economici*, 54(69/3): 81–99.

OECD (1994), *The OECD Jobs Study*, Paris: OECD Publications.

OECD (2013), *Education at a Glance: Country note on Italy*, Paris: OECD Publications.

O'Higgins, N. (2001), *Youth Unemployment and Employment Policy: A Global Perspective*, Geneva: ILO.

Pastore, F. (2009), "School-to-work Transitions in Italy. A steeplechase with no Winner?", XXIV AIEL Conference, University of Sassari, Sassari.

Pastore, F. (2012a), "Le difficili transizioni scuola lavoro in Italia. Una chiave di interpretazione", *Economia dei servizi*, 7(1): 109–128.

Pastore, F. (2012b), "To Study or to Work? Education and Labor Market Participation of Young People in Poland", *Eastern European Economics*, 50(3): 47–77.

Pastore, F. (2013), *Employment Services in View of the School-to-Work Transition. A Comparative Analysis*, Rome: FORMEZ and European Social Fund.

Pistaferri, L. (1999), "Informal Networks in the Italian Labor Market', *Giornale degli Economisti e Annali di Economia*, 58(3–4): 355–375.

Quintini, G., J.P. Martin and S. Martin (2007), *The Changing Nature of the School-to-Work Transition Process in OECD Countries*, IZA discussion paper 2582

Raffe, D. (2008), "The Concept of Transition System", *Journal of Education and Work* 21(4): 277–296.

Rhodes, M. (2009), "South-European Welfare States: Identity, Problems and Prospects for Reform", *South European Society and Politics*, 1(3): 1–22.

Ryan, P. (2001), "The School-to-work Transition. A Cross-National Perspective", *Journal of Economic Literature*, 39(1): 34–92.

Skans, O.N. (2007), "School-to-Work Transitions in Sweden", *Transition Support Policy for Young People with Low Educational Background*, JILTP Report 5.

Sianesi, B. (2004), "An Evaluation of the Swedish System of Active Labour Market Programmes in the 1990s", *Review of Economics and Statistics*, 86(1): 133–155.

Steedman, H. (1993), "The Economics of Youth Training in Germany", *Economic Journal*, 103(420): 1279–91.

Tiraboschi, M. (2011), *Il testo unico dell'apprendistato e le nuove regole sui tirocini*, Milan: Giuffrè.

Titmus, R.M. (1958), *Essays on the Welfare State*, London: Allen and Unwin.

van Ours, J.C. (2004), "The Locking-in of Subsidized Jobs", *Journal of Comparative Economics*, 32(1): 37–48.

Vogel, J. (2002), "European Welfare Regimes and the Transition to Adulthood: A Comparative and Longitudinal Perspective", *Social Indicators Research*, 59(3): 275–299.

Webster, E. and G. Harding (2001), "Outsourcing Public Employment Services: The Australian Experience", *The Australian Economic Review*, 34(2): 231–242.

Weishaupt, J.T. (2011), *Social Partners and the Governance of Public Employment Services: Trends and Experiences from Western Europe*, ILO working document 17.

10 Youth unemployment and the disadvantages of the young in the labour market

Enrico Marelli and Marcello Signorelli

Introduction

Economic inequality is one of the key issues concerning economic performance and development. The "distribution" aspects were considered crucial by classical economists, who focused not only on the causes of the wealth of nations, but also on how wealth (and income) is distributed. Later, Keynes argued that unemployment and bad income distribution are the major failures of market economies, that require appropriate public policies.

Concerning the "classical" distribution between the factors of production – capital and labour – it is known that after World War II workers have been able to gain, in most Western countries, an increasing share of income as well as a mounting power, also in the industrial relations; this was also the effect of "Keynesian" policies and the extension of the "Welfare state". Since the 1980s, however, the labour share began to decrease, as a consequence of many factors: the declining role of the State (due to the diffusion of neoliberal approaches and the stricter constraints on public budgets), the globalization and internationalization of production, the "biased" technical change (that harmed unskilled labour), etc.

Labour markets have become increasingly "flexible", but this was not enough to reduce the unemployment rate, that has been particularly responsive to the economic cycle and to severe economic crises (e.g. the global crisis started in 2007–2008); in some cases (especially in Europe) it has also been persistent over time. Within the labour market, young workers have been especially injured, for many reasons (some of them will be discussed in the next section). The consequence of recent trends is that the unemployment risk is persistently higher among the young cohorts; also when the youth are able to find a job, in many cases this is a temporary, low-quality, poorly remunerated and – in general – "precarious" job.

The difficulties of young people in the labour market (lower wages, precarious jobs, higher and more persistent unemployment) have deep consequences on the income and job opportunity distributions across generations. Even the expected future gains are contained, because of the insecure jobs, the slighter career opportunities, the low (expected) amount of old-age pensions. This causes greater difficulties also in the credit market, e.g. the chance to receive loans for buying houses or other durables. So, a new type of inequality refers to the relative position of different generations on the labour market.

All this worse condition for young people also bears psychological (e.g., Headey, 2002)[1], medical (e.g., Taylor and Morrell, 2002) and social effects.[2] Unemployed young people progressively postpone marriage or the decision to leave the parents' home; this has negative effects on birth rates too. Despite generally high education levels, social mobility is impaired by the difficulty of finding stable jobs; this also matches low geographical mobility.

Labour mobility of educated people has recently increased at the international level (e.g., young graduates of Southern Europe moving Northward), but this corresponds to a waste of resources for the sending country.

Thus, the rising "intergenerational inequality" should be wisely considered by policymakers, in view of its economic, social and even political costs. Young people are a "minority" in modern societies[3] and as such are (in a certain sense) discriminated; but it is an ample minority and the long-run impact of the mentioned trends may be troublesome. Youngsters are a new category of "disadvantaged" workers, like women[4], immigrants and people with disabilities (see Malo and Sciulli, 2014).

This chapter continues in the next section with a review of the key literature on the causes of high(er) youth unemployment rates. The third section presents and discusses various labour market indicators concerning young people, in a comparison across the EU countries. The final section concludes offering some policy implications.

The causes of high youth unemployment

In most countries, youth unemployment is much higher, at least double, than the adult unemployment rate.[5] The main reason for this is that young people, despite possessing, on average, higher educational levels, are endowed with fewer skills, and are less experienced than adult workers. Moreover, youth unemployment is persistent over time, since about one-third of youth unemployment is long term. In addition, in the case of young people, unemployment is a more serious problem since it erodes human capital, it prevents the accumulation of work experience, thus it produces negative effects on lifetime income and career possibilities. All this raises the risk of young people being excluded from the labour market for a long time (Bell and Blanchflower, 2011), leading to what has been called a "lost generation", i.e., people who never enter the labour market (Scarpetta et al., 2010) or who enter it in bad conditions. In many countries, youth unemployment refers to individuals aged 15–24 years, although other ages are sometimes considered. An alternative indicator has been recently proposed: the number of young people who are "neither employed nor in education or training" (NEET): see O'Higgins (2012) and Bruno et al. (2014c).

First of all, it should be noted that significantly high (cross-countries and over time) correlations exist between youth and total unemployment rates, i.e., some important common factors at the national level affect the real job opportunities of the whole working-age population. In this respect, three ample groups of common determinants can be identified to explain (country's differences and trends) overall and youth unemployment rates (see Marelli et al., 2013). A first group of causes includes macroeconomic cyclical conditions. A second group of variables determining unemployment and labour market performance includes demographic, individual, social and structural conditions. A third group of variables includes policies and institutions. It is particularly relevant, since almost two-thirds of non-cyclical unemployment changes over time are explained by changes in those variables (OECD, 2006).

Let us focus now on youth unemployment rates. A specific strand of literature investigates the particular reasons for the worse labour market performance of youths compared with adults; some studies derive key institutional and policy implications. For example, a key issue is that, although young people are generally more highly educated than adults, they often lack the other two components of human capital: generic and job-specific work experience. This adds to another problem, i.e., the mismatch between knowledge acquired through formal education and the skills required by the labour market.[6] Thus, it is the existence of a "youth experience gap" that especially harms the employability of young people. A good match between labour demand and supply mainly depends on school-to-work transition (STWT) processes, which are quite heterogeneous among countries and change over time.[7]

Regarding the institutional variables specifically affecting youth unemployment, in empirical studies emerged the role played by minimum wages and by the extent to which temporary contracts may be used. Moreover, while employment protection legislation (EPL) and lay-off regulations affect worker turnover and duration of unemployment more than influencing the unemployment level, such regulations are more significant for younger than for older people.[8] Turning back to the macroeconomic determinants, most empirical studies have confirmed the greater cyclical sensitivity of the youth unemployment rate compared to the total unemployment rate, especially because of the weaker work contracts among young workers than among older workers.[9] As a matter of fact, following severe recessions, hardships for young people in both acquiring a job as a new entrant and remaining employed are enhanced; in fact, being discouraged by high YUR, many young people give up job search altogether; in such circumstances, they decide to postpone job search and continue their stay in the education system, but in other cases the outcome is even worse, since they join the NEET group.

In addition to the greater immediate impact of economic crisis, especially financial crises[10], on YUR than on adult unemployment rates, further evidence concerns the persistence of unemployment over time and the increasing share of long-term unemployment (e.g., Caporale and Gil-Alana, 2014; Bruno et al., 2014b and 2014c). As a matter of fact, long periods of unemployment erode the skills of young workers, reduce their employability, cause a permanent loss of human capital and make unemployment persistent. Even before the recent crisis, OECD (2005) stressed that young people in general – and in particular youngsters with low human capital and few skills – are particularly exposed to long-term unemployment, unstable and low quality jobs, and perhaps social exclusion.

A point to be stressed is that the crises exacerbated structural problems existing in many countries, especially problems concerning the transition from school to work; in fact, owing to the reduction in labour demand, school-leavers compete with more jobseekers for fewer vacancies (see Scarpetta et al., 2010). O'Higgins (2012) observes that not only young people are more vulnerable to a crisis's effects than older adults but also that such effects are more long-lasting for the young; making unemployment more persistent.

Some features of youth unemployment and labour in Europe

In Europe, particularly high YURs have been recorded in different areas: some Mediterranean countries (Spain, Italy, Greece), certain new EU member states (Hungary and Slovakia), but also some Northern countries (where YUR are not very high, but higher than TUR). After the recent crisis, the increase in the YUR has generally been larger than the rise in TUR, confirming the above mentioned greater sensitivity to the cycle; furthermore, the average duration of unemployment is also increasing.

A worsening situation concerns many other labour market indicators specific to young people. One of this is the NEET indicator, whose importance has been recognized also by international institutions.[11] Then, it has become a key statistical indicator, now collected also by Eurostat. A recent investigation on the characteristics of NEET in Europe, the institutional and structural determinants, the distribution across EU countries, the consequences (economic and social costs), and suggested policies, has been proposed by the "European Foundation for the Improvement of Living and Working Conditions" (Eurofound, 2012).

Table 10.1 Youth and total unemployment rates

| | Total unemployment rate (15–74 years) | | | | | | | Youth unemployment rate (15–24 years) | | | | | | |
| | Total | | | Male | | Female | | Total | | | Male | | Female | |
	2002	2007	2014	2002	2014	2002	2014	2002	2007	2014	2002	2014	2002	2014
EU-28	9.0	7.2	10.2	8.3	10.1	9.9	10.3	18.1	15.6	22.2	17.9	22.8	18.3	21.4
Eurozone-19	8.6	7.5	11.6	7.6	11.5	10.0	11.8	16.6	15.0	23.8	15.6	24.2	17.8	23.2
Belgium	6.9	7.5	8.5	6.3	9.0	7.8	7.9	15.7	18.8	23.2	16.0	24.0	15.2	22.3
Bulgaria	18.1	6.9	11.4	18.8	12.3	17.4	10.4	35.6	15.1	23.8	39.0	23.8	31.5	23.7
Czech Republic	7.0	5.3	6.1	5.8	5.1	8.6	7.4	15.4	10.7	15.9	15.7	15.0	15.0	17.1
Denmark	4.3	3.8	6.6	4.2	6.4	4.3	6.8	7.1	7.5	12.6	8.8	13.7	5.2	11.5
Germany	8.5	8.7	5.0	8.7	5.3	8.2	4.6	9.3	11.9	7.7	11.1	8.3	7.2	7.1
Estonia	10.0	4.6	7.4	11.3	7.9	8.7	6.8	20.2	10.1	15.0	17.2	19.3	24.7	10.0
Ireland	4.2	4.7	11.3	4.6	12.9	3.8	9.4	7.8	9.1	23.9	8.8	26.6	6.6	20.9
Greece	10.0	8.4	26.5	6.4	23.7	15.4	30.2	25.8	22.7	52.4	18.7	47.4	34.5	58.1
Spain	11.2	8.2	24.5	7.9	23.6	16.0	25.4	21.5	18.1	53.2	16.8	53.4	27.7	52.9
France	8.7	8.0	10.3	7.8	10.5	9.8	10.0	18.9	19.1	24.2	17.5	25.1	20.8	23.1
Croatia	15.1	9.9	17.3	13.2	16.5	17.3	18.3	36.3	25.2	45.5	34.3	44.9	38.9	46.4
Italy	9.2	6.1	12.7	7.0	11.9	12.6	13.8	27.1	20.4	42.7	23.7	41.3	31.5	44.7
Cyprus	3.3	3.9	16.1	2.6	17.1	4.2	15.1	7.7	10.2	36.0	8.0	37.4	7.6	34.6
Latvia	13.8	6.1	10.8	14.9	11.8	12.8	9.8	25.3	10.6	19.6	25.2	19.4	25.4	20.0
Lithuania	13.0	4.3	10.7	13.2	12.2	12.8	9.2	20.4	8.4	19.3	19.6	19.6	21.6	18.7
Luxembourg	2.6	4.1	5.9	1.9	5.9	3.6	5.8	7.0	15.2	22.6	5.3	26.1	9.0	18.1
Hungary	5.6	7.4	7.7	6.0	7.6	5.1	7.9	11.4	18.0	20.4	12.3	20.0	10.2	20.9
Malta	6.9	6.5	5.9	6.3	6.2	8.3	5.4	15.3	13.5	11.8	16.5	13.8	14.0	9.6
Netherlands	2.6	3.2	7.4	2.3	7.2	2.9	7.8	4.6	5.9	12.7	4.3	12.4	4.8	13.1

Austria	4.9	4.9	5.6	5.1	5.9	4.5	5.4	7.2	9.4	10.3	7.7	10.6	6.6	9.9
Poland	20.0	9.6	9.0	19.3	8.5	20.7	9.6	41.6	21.7	23.9	41.0	22.7	42.4	25.5
Portugal	4.6	8.1	14.1	3.9	13.7	5.4	14.5	10.5	16.7	34.8	9.2	34.2	12.1	35.4
Romania	8.3	6.4	6.8	8.7	7.3	7.8	6.1	22.2	20.1	24.0	22.4	23.6	22.0	24.7
Slovenia	6.0	4.9	9.7	5.7	9.0	6.3	10.6	14.8	10.1	20.2	13.5	19.4	16.7	21.3
Slovakia	18.7	11.1	13.2	18.7	12.8	18.8	13.6	37.7	20.3	29.7	38.8	29.5	36.3	30.1
Finland	10.4	6.9	8.7	10.7	9.3	10.2	8.0	28.2	16.5	20.5	28.6	22.8	27.8	18.4
Sweden	5.0	6.2	8.0	5.3	8.2	4.6	7.7	12.9	19.3	22.9	13.4	24.2	12.4	21.5
United Kingdom	5.0	5.3	6.1	5.6	6.4	4.4	5.8	10.9	14.3	16.9	12.8	18.9	8.8	14.8

Source: Eurostat database

Bruno et al. (2014c) found that NEET rates are persistent and that persistence increases during crisis periods.

After this introduction concerning previous empirical studies, let us look now at some recent data concerning youth unemployment and other labour market indicators for the European countries (all data are elaborations from Eurostat). We now consider both youth unemployment rates and the ratios between such rates (YUR) and total unemployment rates (TUR); the age classes refer to 15–24 years and 15–74 years respectively (see Table 10.1). We compare the initial year for which comparable data for most countries are available (2002) with the final year (2014); below we shall give some hints about the post-crisis period (2008–2014). We can see that in the EU as a whole both TUR and YUR in the final year is higher than the corresponding initial figures; however, the increase in YUR – from 18.1 per cent to 22.2 per cent – is comparatively greater.

While for TUR particularly high values are found, in 2014, in Greece, Spain, Croatia, Cyprus, Portugal, Slovakia, in the case of YUR top values are recorded in Spain (53.2 per cent), Greece (52.4 per cent), Croatia (45.5 per cent), Italy (42.7 per cent), Cyprus (36 per cent), Portugal (34.8 per cent). The only country exhibiting a YUR well below 10 per cent is Germany (7.7 per cent). While, in general, female and male unemployment rates in 2014 are almost identical (10.3 per cent and 10.1 per cent in the EU), in the case of young people the performance of males is now little worse (22.8 per cent) compared to the one of females (21.4 per cent); on the contrary, in 2002 there was a gap in the opposite direction. Considering the individual countries, female YUR are higher than the male ones in all countries with high YUR in general (above mentioned), but Spain.

Considering the long-run dynamics of the TUR (i.e. every single year), the best year in the 2002–2014 period was 2008, when TUR was equal to 7 per cent in the EU as a whole; the worst one was 2013, being TUR equal to 10.8% (data not shown in the table). In the case of YUR, we can detect a similar cyclical behaviour: a minimum of 15.6 per cent in 2007–2008 and a maximum of 23.6 per cent in 2013.[12]

The relative disadvantage of young people compared to the total population slightly increased in the period 2002–2014, as shown by the ratios between YUR and TUR (see Table 10.2): the ratio was equal to 2 in the initial year and 2.2 in the final one. A dire position for young people can be detected, in 2014, in countries such as Luxembourg (ratio 3.8, but the YUR is close to average), Romania (3.5), Italy (3.4), but also Sweden (2.9), the UK (2.8), Belgium and Poland (2.7 in both countries).

Thus a first conclusion is that the relative position of young people is bad in two types of countries: (i) where generally adverse economic conditions, especially after the recent crises, are reflected in high unemployment rates, TUR and even more YUR (countries like Greece, Spain, etc.); (ii) in countries that, despite the generally better economic conditions, are characterized by structural or institutional features that are not particularly favourable to young people (countries like the UK, Sweden, Belgium, Luxembourg, Poland, etc.).

In addition to unemployment, another important labour market indicator is the employment rate, from many points of view more thorough than the unemployment rate. Even the EU institutions have included the employment rate in the policy agenda, initially in the Lisbon Strategy of 2000 and more recently in the "Europe 2020" plan approved in 2010: a 75 per cent of employment is the target for people (males and female) of 20–64 years. Despite huge variations across the EU countries, the employment rates were generally increasing and converging up to the beginning of the crisis (2007–2008). Since then there has been a widespread reduction and a new divergence. The differentiation within the EU is even greater for young employment rates (Table 10.3). In 2014 the total rate for the

Table 10.2 Ratios between youth unemplyment rate (15–24) and total unemployment rate (15–74)

	2002	2003	2004	2005	2006	2007	2008	2009	2010	2011	2012	2013	2014
EU-28	2.0	2.0	2.0	2.1	2.1	2.2	2.2	2.2	2.2	2.2	2.2	2.2	2.2
Eurozone-19	1.9	1.9	1.9	2.0	2.0	2.0	2.1	2.1	2.0	2.1	2.1	2.0	2.1
Belgium	2.3	2.5	2.4	2.5	2.5	2.5	2.6	2.8	2.7	2.6	2.6	2.8	2.7
Bulgaria	2.0	2.0	2.0	2.2	2.2	2.2	2.3	2.4	2.3	2.2	2.3	2.2	2.1
Czech Rep.	2.2	2.2	2.4	2.4	2.4	2.0	2.3	2.5	2.5	2.7	2.8	2.7	2.6
Denmark	1.7	1.8	1.5	1.8	2.0	2.0	2.4	2.0	1.9	1.9	1.9	1.9	1.9
Germany	1.1	1.1	1.2	1.4	1.3	1.4	1.4	1.4	1.4	1.5	1.5	1.5	1.5
Estonia	2.0	2.4	2.5	1.9	2.1	2.2	2.2	2.0	2.0	1.8	2.1	2.2	2.0
Ireland	1.9	1.8	1.8	2.0	2.0	1.9	2.1	2.0	2.0	2.0	2.1	2.0	2.1
Greece	2.6	2.7	2.5	2.6	2.8	2.7	2.8	2.7	2.6	2.5	2.3	2.1	2.0
Spain	1.9	2.0	2.0	2.1	2.1	2.2	2.2	2.1	2.1	2.2	2.1	2.1	2.2
France	2.2	2.0	2.2	2.3	2.5	2.4	2.5	2.5	2.5	2.4	2.4	2.4	2.3
Croatia	2.4	2.6	2.4	2.5	2.6	2.5	2.8	2.7	2.8	2.7	2.6	2.9	2.6
Italy	2.9	3.0	3.1	3.1	3.2	3.3	3.2	3.2	3.3	3.5	3.3	3.3	3.4
Cyprus	2.3	2.1	2.0	2.6	2.2	2.6	2.4	2.6	2.6	2.8	2.3	2.4	2.2
Latvia	1.8	1.7	1.9	1.5	1.9	1.7	1.8	1.9	1.9	1.9	1.9	1.9	1.8
Lithuania	1.6	2.1	1.9	1.9	1.7	2.0	2.3	2.1	2.0	2.1	2.0	1.9	1.8
Luxembourg	2.7	2.9	3.3	3.0	3.4	3.7	3.5	3.4	3.2	3.4	3.7	2.6	3.8
Hungary	2.0	2.2	2.5	2.7	2.5	2.4	2.5	2.6	2.4	2.4	2.6	2.6	2.6
Malta	2.2	2.3	2.5	2.3	2.3	2.1	2.0	2.1	1.9	2.1	2.2	2.0	2.0
Netherlands	1.8	1.8	1.7	1.7	1.7	1.8	1.9	1.9	1.9	2.0	2.0	1.8	1.7
Austria	1.5	1.6	2.1	2.0	1.8	1.9	2.1	2.0	2.0	1.9	1.9	1.8	1.8
Poland	2.1	2.1	2.1	2.1	2.1	2.3	2.4	2.5	2.4	2.7	2.6	2.7	2.7
Portugal	2.3	2.2	2.2	2.1	2.1	2.1	2.2	2.1	2.1	2.3	2.4	2.3	2.5
Romania	2.7	2.8	2.9	2.8	2.9	3.1	3.2	3.0	3.2	3.3	3.3	3.3	3.5
Slovenia	2.5	2.4	2.3	2.4	2.3	2.1	2.4	2.3	2.0	1.9	2.3	2.1	2.1
Slovakia	2.0	1.9	1.8	1.8	2.0	1.8	2.0	2.3	2.3	2.5	2.4	2.4	2.3
Finland	2.7	2.6	2.6	2.4	2.4	2.4	2.6	2.6	2.5	2.6	2.5	2.4	2.4
Sweden	2.6	2.6	2.8	2.9	3.0	3.1	3.3	3.0	2.9	2.9	3.0	2.9	2.9
UK	2.2	2.4	2.3	2.7	2.6	2.7	2.7	2.5	2.6	2.6	2.7	2.7	2.8

Source: Eurostat database.

15–24 years age cohort was 32.4 per cent. Much higher values are found in Northern and Central Europe countries: the Netherlands[13] (58.8 per cent), Denmark (53.7 per cent), Austria (52.1 per cent), the UK (48.1 per cent); on the contrary, the lowest figures are recorded in Greece (13.3 per cent), Italy (15.6 per cent), Spain (16.7 per cent), Croatia (18.3 per cent).

Notice that the average EU employment rate is 4 percentage points (p.p.) below the figure of the initial year (2002) and almost 5 p.p. below the maximum value (recorded in 2007 before the crisis). The reduction has been larger in countries where the employment rate is now very low: for example minus 23 p.p. in Spain (2014 vs. 2007), 10 p.p. in Greece, 9 p.p. in Italy; but also minus 23 p.p. in Ireland, 12 p.p. in Denmark, 10 p.p. in the Netherlands. At the opposite, not surprising, there is one country where the youth employment rate has increased: Germany (from 45.4 per cent to 46.1 per cent).

While before the crisis the employment rate of young males was about 6 p.p. higher than the one of young females, for the EU as a whole, in 2014 the difference was less than 4 p.p. The lowest female rates are found, once more, in the mentioned countries: Greece, Italy, Spain, Croatia. However, the "gender gap" (in term of employment of young people) is even greater in Austria, the Czeck Republic, Bulgaria, Romania, Slovakia, Latvia, Lithuania. Denmark is the only country where the employment rate of young females is even greater than the one of young males.

With reference to NEET rates (Table 10.4), for the 15–24 cohort the average rate did not exhibit significant variations from 2004 to 2014 in the EU[14]: 12.9 per cent in the initial year vs. 12.4 per cent in the final year; the complete time-series dynamics (not shown in the table), however, exhibits a dip of 10.9 per cent in 2007–2008 and a peak of 13.1 per cent in 2012. The female rates are little higher than the male rates. If we now consider the age class 25–29 years, the NEET rate is significantly higher: in fact, it is less likely that young people in this group are in education or training, so youngsters not working are more likely in the NEET group; moreover, for this age class there was in the EU a small increase over time, from 19.6 per cent in 2004 to 20.3 per cent in 2014 (close to the top value of 21 per cent in 2013). For this age class the female rate is much higher (in 2004 double than the male rate), although decreasing over time.

By considering the same table, let us focus on the cross-country variations. While the best performance is shown by countries such as the Netherlands, Denmark, Luxembourg, Germany, high values in the age class 15–24 years are recorded in 2014 (all sexes) in Bulgaria (20.2 per cent), Italy (22.1 per cent), Croatia (19.3 per cent), Greece (19.1 per cent), followed by Spain, Cyprus, Romania; in all these countries (but Bulgaria and Romania) the NEET rates have been increasing over time; the ranking are generally the same for both males and females. In the age class 25–29 years, the NEET rates reach top figures incredibly high as 39.5 per cent in Greece, 33.8 per cent in Italy, 29.6 per cent in Bulgaria, 27.1 per cent in Slovakia, 26.7 per cent in Spain, 26.2 per cent in Croatia, with the female rates even higher (for example 44.1 per cent in Greece and 39 per cent in Italy). These figures testify the waste of human resources that has become a big social problem, especially after the recent crises, for the reasons we shall explain in the next section.

We have seen in the previous section that a major problem with YUR is that they tend to persist over time, so this type of unemployment – once turned into structural – cannot be tackled only with expansionary macroeconomic policies. Also from the social point of view, long-term unemployment is worrisome because unemployment benefits generally have, in most countries, a maximum duration. Many studies have shown that the risk of poverty is high when one of the parents is unemployed and such risk increases with the length of unemployment conditions.[15]

Table 10.3 Employment rate (15–24 years)

	Total			Males			Females		
	2002	*2007*	*2014*	*2002*	*2007*	*2014*	*2002*	*2007*	*2014*
EU-28	36.6	37.2	32.4	39.7	40.2	34.2	33.5	34.1	30.5
Eurozone-19	36.6	37.5	30.5	40.2	40.8	32.3	32.9	34.1	28.7
Belgium	28.5	27.5	23.2	31.3	29.9	24.5	25.7	25.0	21.8
Bulgaria	20.5	24.5	20.7	21.4	27.1	24.0	19.6	21.8	17.3
Czech Rep.	32.4	28.5	27.1	35.7	32.8	32.3	29.2	23.9	21.6
Denmark	64.0	65.3	53.7	64.4	66.5	52.7	63.5	64.0	54.9
Germany	45.4	45.4	46.1	46.9	47.2	47.7	43.8	43.5	44.3
Estonia	25.4	34.1	33.3	31.0	38.2	33.4	19.7	29.8	33.3
Ireland	44.9	51.0	28.4	48.1	53.7	28.5	41.6	48.3	28.4
Greece	26.9	24.0	13.3	31.9	29.1	15.8	21.7	18.8	10.9
Spain	34.3	39.2	16.7	40.4	44.2	17.4	27.8	34.0	16.0
France	29.9	31.0	27.9	33.9	34.1	30.1	25.9	27.9	25.7
Croatia	25.7	27.4	18.3	29.6	32.4	21.2	21.8	22.3	15.3
Italy	25.7	24.5	15.6	30.2	29.4	18.2	21.1	19.5	12.8
Cyprus	36.7	37.4	25.8	37.7	39.1	25.8	35.8	36.0	25.9
Latvia	28.3	38.1	32.5	31.2	43.8	36.5	25.3	32.2	28.3
Lithuania	25.2	24.8	27.6	28.9	29.4	31.0	21.5	20.0	24.1
Luxembourg	32.3	22.5	20.4	36.1	26.5	21.9	28.4	18.4	18.8
Hungary	28.6	21.1	23.5	31.7	24.4	26.4	25.6	17.7	20.5
Malta	51.1	46.8	46.1	52.2	48.9	45.6	49.9	44.5	46.7
Netherlands	70.5	68.4	58.8	71.8	68.9	58.7	69.2	67.9	58.8
Austria	51.8	53.8	52.1	55.9	57.0	54.3	47.7	50.6	49.9
Poland	22.0	25.8	25.8	24.4	29.2	30.0	19.6	22.4	21.3
Portugal	42.2	34.4	22.4	47.6	38.5	22.9	36.7	30.1	21.9
Romania	29.1	24.4	22.5	32.3	28.3	26.6	25.8	20.2	18.0
Slovenia	31.1	37.6	26.8	34.8	43.2	29.5	27.2	31.4	24.0
Slovakia	26.7	27.6	21.8	28.4	30.9	26.8	24.9	24.1	16.5
Finland	44.8	44.6	41.4	45.4	44.5	39.8	44.1	44.7	43.0
Sweden	44.0	42.2	42.8	43.7	42.0	41.6	44.3	42.3	44.0
UK	55.5	52.6	48.1	57.1	54.0	48.3	54.0	51.3	47.8

Source: Eurostat database.

Table 10.4 NEET rates

	15–24 years						25–29 years					
	Total		Male		Female		Total		Male		Female	
	2004	2014	2004	2014	2004	2014	2004	2014	2004	2014	2004	2014
EU-28	12.9	12.4	11.8	12.2	14.0	12.6	19.6	20.3	13.2	15.8	26.2	24.9
Eurozone-17	11.9	12.5	10.9	12.6	13.0	12.4	18.6	21.1	12.4	17.5	25.0	24.7
Belgium	15.4	12.0	14.7	12.6	16.0	11.5	18.0	17.9	14.0	16.5	22.2	19.3
Bulgaria	26.4	20.2	26.2	19.2	26.7	21.4	33.4	29.6	27.1	24.5	40.0	35.0
Czech Republic	13.7	8.1	12.0	6.5	15.5	9.9	23.8	18.4	9.0	8.0	39.2	29.3
Denmark	5.1	5.8	4.8	6.2	5.5	5.4	8.6	10.4	6.5	8.0	10.7	12.8
Germany	10.1	6.4	9.9	5.5	10.3	7.2	18.9	12.6	13.7	8.7	24.3	16.7
Estonia	12.5	11.7	10.5	11.8	14.7	11.6	21.2	16.8	13.9	10.5	28.7	23.6
Ireland	11.9	15.2	10.7	14.9	13.1	15.5	14.5	23.0	9.7	21.2	19.2	24.8
Greece	16.6	19.1	12.2	18.7	21.0	19.6	25.0	39.5	13.5	35.1	36.7	44.1
Spain	12.5	17.1	10.8	18.0	14.3	16.2	17.1	26.7	11.2	24.9	23.3	28.6
France	10.6	10.7	9.9	11.0	11.2	10.3	17.8	19.0	12.1	15.1	23.4	22.7
Croatia	17.1	19.3	15.9	21.9	18.3	16.7	23.9	26.2	18.2	23.3	29.9	29.2
Italy	16.8	22.1	14.9	22.7	18.7	21.4	23.8	33.8	15.1	28.7	32.4	39.0
Cyprus	9.4	17.0	6.3	19.0	12.2	15.3	11.6	23.0	3.7	22.7	19.2	23.2
Latvia	12.4	12.0	9.7	11.3	15.1	12.8	23.1	19.9	17.3	14.5	28.8	25.6
Lithuania	10.6	9.9	9.8	9.5	11.3	10.3	18.1	19.1	14.7	15.6	21.8	22.8
Luxembourg	6.3	6.3	4.6	7.8	7.9	4.6	11.2	6.9	6.7	6.6	15.7	7.2
Hungary	12.7	13.6	10.9	12.0	14.5	15.3	23.3	21.7	12.6	12.6	34.2	31.2
Malta	13.1	11.5	11.0	9.9	15.3	13.1	20.9	14.2	7.9	8.9	35.9	19.9
Netherlands	5.3	5.0	5.0	4.6	5.6	5.5	9.1	11.6	5.8	10.0	12.5	13.2

Austria	9.1	7.7	9.0	8.0	9.2	7.4	12.6	12.2	7.5	9.1	17.8	15.4
Poland	15.0	12.0	14.4	12.0	15.6	12.0	28.8	21.2	22.2	14.8	35.6	28.1
Portugal	11.2	12.3	10.3	12.3	12.0	12.3	13.3	19.2	9.7	17.4	16.8	21.0
Romania	19.8	17.0	18.9	15.3	20.8	18.8	23.8	24.6	17.2	18.3	30.7	31.3
Slovenia	7.5	9.4	7.0	9.7	8.1	9.2	9.4	18.5	7.0	13.7	12.0	23.6
Slovakia	17.9	12.8	16.9	12.8	18.8	12.8	27.6	27.1	17.6	18.4	38.0	36.1
Finland	9.1	10.2	8.8	11.9	9.3	8.5	13.7	14.8	9.2	11.8	18.5	17.9
Sweden	7.6	7.2	8.3	7.5	6.8	6.8	8.6	9.0	6.8	7.5	10.4	10.6
UK	8.4	11.9	7.2	10.7	9.6	13.1	9.8	16.2	6.2	10.2	13.5	22.2

Source: Eurostat database.

Considering long-term unemployment (longer than 12 months) as percentage of labour force (LTU), we find very high values for young cohorts (15–24 and 25–29) and a significant increase during crisis years. In 2014, LTU was particularly high in Greece (31.5 per cent the total rate for 15–24 years and 28.2 per cent for 25–29 years), Italy (25.1 per cent and 13.8 per cent respectively), Croatia (22.6 per cent and 12.3 per cent), Spain (21.5 per cent and 13.4 per cent), Slovakia (17 per cent and 10.2 per cent), as compared to the average EU figures (7.8 per cent and 6 per cent for the two cohorts). Very low LTU for young people are recorded in Denmark, Finland, Sweden, Germany, Austria.

The relative position of young people in the labour market depends not only on the probability to find a job and on the length of the unemployment condition, but also on the type of work and its remuneration. In fact, economists and sociologists have deeply debated about the "working poor" (e.g., Bazen et al., 1998; Peña-Casas and Latta, 2004; Fraser et al., 2011). Furthermore, the policies for the labour market – even in the EU following the Lisbon Agenda of 2000 – have set the aim to create "more and better jobs". A discussion about human capital, the skill content of jobs, the importance (and incidence) of work in innovative occupations and in the R&D sector would be interesting, but beyond the scope of this chapter.

Some data, however, can be presented and are important since have an immediate impact on the distribution of income between different working groups. As we have seen in the previous section, one strand in the literature maintains the young people exhibit a disproportionately larger incidence of "temporary" jobs, especially in countries that have adopted a flexibility approach oriented to remove restrictions to the entry into the labour market (rather than acting on dismissals, EPL, etc.). Many authors argue that youngsters, in this way, tend to hold "precarious" jobs, that often become a "trap", leading also to higher risk of unemployment.

Table 10.5 refers to the incidence of temporary employment out of total employees. The key evidence is the following: (i) the incidence is very high for the youngest cohort (15–24 years), reaching over 43 per cent in the EU as a whole: i.e. about half of young workers in Europe hold temporary jobs; (ii) the incidence decreases with the age of the workers: it is about 23 per cent for 25–29 workers (and even less for subsequent age classes, although not shown in the table); (iii) the incidence has increased over time (it was less than 36 per cent in 2002); (iv) there are no significant differences between male and female workers. The highest incidences of temporary employment are found in Slovenia (72.7 per cent in 2014 for the youngest cohort), Poland (71.2 per cent), Spain (69.1 per cent), Portugal (63 per cent); the lowest ones in Bulgaria, Romania, the three Baltic states and also in the U.K. The ranking is rather similar also for the subsequent cohort (25–29 years).

Concerning part-time employment, in the EU the incidence over total employment is significantly higher for young people (31.8 per cent in 2014) compared to all workers (20.3 per cent); moreover, it is increasing over time: in 2002, it was 21.4 per cent for young people, i.e. one-third smaller. As expected, the incidence is even greater for females: 40 per cent for young females 15–24 years old (up from 28 per cent of 2002), slightly greater than 38.5 per cent recorded by female workers of all ages (15–74 years). Considering the differences across countries, part-time employment is particularly important for young workers (all sexes) in the Netherlands (78.9 per cent in 2014), Denmark (66.9 per cent), Sweden (49.5 per cent), Ireland (45.2 per cent). Thus we can say that in Northern European countries, especially where the "flexicurity model" is prevailing, young people exhibit a better performance in the labour market – i.e. lower YUR and NEET rates; however, they are penalized by different working conditions, for instance shorter working hours and consequently lower incomes. This can be to some extent a voluntary choice, e.g. in order to reconcile working and education choices (or family duties in case of less young female workers, according to a traditional view), but in some other cases it might be another type of discrimination (it is staggering that in the Netherlands more than 87 per cent of young female workers are part-time workers). It is also remarkable that in all countries, also where the incidences of temporary and part-time employment were initially very low, there has been an increase over time.

A final comment refers to the earnings received by young workers compared to mature workers. In some countries, wages and compensations are much lower for young workers, although there are possibilities to increase over time, also thanks to the "seniority"; in some countries, the chances of career progression are high, thus productive and skilled young workers can quickly achieve good positions also from the point of view of compensations.

The available information (Eurostat data) is lacking for the generality of workers, employed in all firms. Thus it is proper to focus on the firms with at least 10 employees, for which data are more complete. Table 10.6 shows that the hourly earnings for young workers (less than 30 years) was in 2010, in the EU as a whole, around 10 euros, compared to 14 euros for all workers, hence about one-third less. It is also interesting that the wage discrimination of women is sizeable for all ages (12.6 euros vs. 15.4 for males), while it is very small in case of young workers.

The previously mentioned "gap" between the wages of young workers and all employees – about one third less – is more or less confirmed in all EU countries, both Continental, Northern or Southern; it seems a bit smaller in Eastern countries, including the Baltic and Balkan states, where of course the absolute level of hourly wages is much lower compared to the EU average or the other countries.

The 2008–2009 financial crisis, the following Great Recession, the subsequent Eurozone sovereign debt crisis and the ensuing austerity measures have caused a deep impact on the European labour markets. The most exposed segments of the labour market have been young people, old workers, vulnerable employment in general. The economic crises abruptly ended the gradual decline in global youth unemployment rates recorded before 2007 (ILO, 2012, 2014).

In many European countries, the situation is particularly serious. This is related to the greater sensitivity of youth unemployment to cyclical conditions (see p.197). According to many empirical studies, there are two characteristics of the Great Recession that have been particularly detrimental to young people: the financial origin of the crisis and the protracted recessions or stagnation, especially in the Eurozone. As a matter of fact, in the EU we had a double-dip and even triple-dip recession in the 2007–2014 period; a key reason is that the austerity measures imposed by EU institutions to overcome the Eurozone debt crisis have been too deep and widespread, with harmful effects on employment and disproportionate consequences for youth unemployment. The situation is even more worrying since, although a feeble recovery has commenced in many European countries, the risk is that it will be a "jobless" recovery (see ILO, 2014).

The employment and unemployment impact of the crisis has been, however, differentiated across countries. Germany's case is outstanding, since unemployment has decreased even in crisis years. In Europe, there have been two main types of adjustments: (i) in the most 'flexible' countries (such as Ireland, the Baltic states, Spain, that have followed an adjustment similar to the US), employment was cut rapidly and deeply, helping to maintain labour productivity, but at the cost of high and sudden increases in unemployment; (ii) in some other countries (not only Germany but also Japan, the Netherlands, Denmark, and Italy), labour hoarding practices, working hour adjustments and specific policy measures

Table 10.5 Temporary employment (percentage of total employees)

| | 15–24 years | | | | | | | 25–29 years | | | | | | |
| | Total | | | Male | | Female | | Total | | | Male | | Female | |
	2002	2007	2014	2002	2014	2002	2014	2002	2007	2014	2002	2014	2002	2014
EU–28	35.8	41.4	43.4	36.2	43.2	35.4	43.5	17.6	21.3	22.9	16.4	21.6	18.9	24.3
Eurozone–19	44.5	49.8	52.4	44.7	52.0	44.2	52.8	21.3	24.3	26.1	19.9	24.8	23.0	27.5
Belgium	27.4	31.6	34.2	25.9	30.8	29.4	38.1	11.3	12.9	14.9	8.4	12.9	14.6	16.9
Bulgaria	12.9	10.3	14.5	14.2	15.6	11.6	12.8	7.7	5.5	6.5	8.3	6.2	7.1	7.0
Czech Rep.	14.2	17.4	32.3	14.1	29.0	14.4	37.4	7.5	8.2	14.4	5.7	12.0	10.1	17.5
Denmark	25.0	22.5	21.3	26.2	25.6	23.9	17.2	12.5	14.0	16.1	8.5	13.3	16.8	19.1
Germany	51.4	57.4	53.4	53.9	54.6	48.7	52.1	15.2	21.5	22.1	16.3	22.2	14.0	21.9
Estonia	–	6.6	11.2	–	10.4	–	12.1	–	1.9	4.5	–	4.0	–	5.2
Ireland	12.5	21.2	33.9	11.7	31.2	13.4	36.5	3.7	8.2	11.7	3.6	10.5	3.8	12.7
Greece	25.5	26.5	29.4	24.7	31.4	26.6	27.1	15.1	15.7	20.8	13.9	19.2	16.6	22.5
Spain	65.2	62.7	69.1	64.8	69.4	65.7	68.8	43.9	43.5	43.9	41.9	43.5	46.4	44.3
France	48.5	53.5	57.3	47.3	55.6	50.1	59.3	22.7	20.7	24.7	18.9	22.5	27.0	27.0
Croatia	31.2	39.9	57.2	33.7	53.8	27.9	62.0	15.4	21.7	31.4	16.4	27.3	14.2	36.3
Italy	27.3	42.2	56.0	25.2	54.3	30.1	58.6	15.1	22.3	32.0	13.2	29.0	17.5	35.5
Cyprus	12.0	23.3	31.1	8.7	27.4	15.0	34.3	11.3	17.6	25.1	9.1	21.7	13.4	28.1
Latvia	21.0	9.0	8.4	24.3	9.2	17.0	7.3	14.0	3.8	3.1	19.0	3.9	–	–
Lithuania	14.5	10.5	8.5	17.3	9.9	–	–	7.1	4.4	–	9.3	–	–	–
Luxembourg	16.6	34.1	45.4	20.3	41.2	11.9	50.3	7.9	12.4	14.0	7.3	13.1	8.6	14.9
Hungary	14.6	18.9	25.1	13.9	24.6	15.4	25.8	8.4	9.0	13.5	8.6	13.6	8.1	13.3
Malta	8.8	11.1	19.0	–	20.6	–	17.3	–	5.2	7.7	–	7.0	–	8.4
Netherlands	36.4	45.1	55.5	36.7	53.7	36.1	57.4	17.0	24.3	33.1	16.5	32.9	17.6	33.4

Austria	35.0	34.8	35.1	39.2	38.5	30.1	31.4	5.5	8.8	10.4	3.9	8.9	7.0	11.9
Poland	45.1	65.7	71.2	44.5	68.4	45.8	75.1	21.0	39.1	43.5	21.1	40.9	20.9	46.7
Portugal	46.2	53.1	63.0	43.7	62.6	49.5	63.4	30.5	36.0	40.7	27.5	37.9	33.8	43.7
Romania	2.8	4.6	7.0	2.8	7.5	2.8	6.4	1.3	2.1	2.6	1.5	3.2	1.1	2.0
Slovenia	52.9	68.3	72.7	44.1	62.2	64.8	86.4	27.2	33.5	37.1	23.1	31.6	31.6	44.0
Slovakia	10.7	13.7	28.2	10.7	26.4	10.6	31.0	4.5	5.8	11.9	4.4	12.3	4.7	11.4
Finland	49.4	42.4	42.5	46.9	38.9	51.8	45.7	28.3	25.2	26.6	20.5	19.4	37.1	35.0
Sweden	51.3	57.1	56.2	44.3	49.9	58.4	62.4	22.0	27.8	27.2	16.6	23.3	27.9	31.5
UK	12.0	13.3	15.2	12.0	15.2	12.0	15.2	6.3	6.3	6.9	6.4	7.0	6.0	6.7

Source: Eurostat database

Table 10.6 Hourly earnings (in euros) – 2010 (firms with 10 employees or more)

	Total ages			Less than 30		
	Total	Male	Female	Total	Male	Female
EU-28	14.08	15.37	12.62	10.04	10.18	9.88
Eurozone-19	15.20	16.49	13.67	10.50	10.69	10.29
Belgium	18.92	19.80	17.78	14.31	14.43	14.17
Bulgaria	2.04	2.18	1.89	1.83	1.89	1.76
Czech Republic	5.43	6.00	4.73	4.56	4.70	4.39
Denmark	25.37	27.76	23.2	17.33	18.07	16.67
Germany	16.95	18.81	14.62	10.68	10.96	10.33
Estonia	4.84	5.73	4.17	4.55	5.06	4.04
Ireland	22.23	23.94	20.62	15.14	14.84	15.38
Greece	10.97	11.81	10.03	7.28	7.30	7.25
Spain	11.50	12.43	10.41	8.78	9.05	8.52
France	16.27	17.54	14.8	11.79	11.81	11.76
Croatia	5.87	6.03	5.69	4.64	4.59	4.71
Italy	14.48	14.82	14.04	9.87	10.04	9.64
Cyprus	12.08	13.12	10.91	7.71	7.84	7.56
Latvia	3.78	4.14	3.5	3.63	3.82	3.43
Lithuania	3.44	3.68	3.24	3.27	3.31	3.21
Luxembourg	21.95	22.64	20.67	15.59	15.37	15.93
Hungary	4.49	4.91	4.04	3.82	3.85	3.79
Malta	8.46	8.71	8.08	7.21	7.19	7.22
Netherlands	17.25	18.85	15.56	11.29	11.29	11.30
Austria	14.77	16.37	12.45	10.55	11.02	9.88
Poland	5.21	5.32	5.08	4.04	4.08	3.99
Portugal	7.71	8.23	7.18	5.16	5.3	5.00
Romania	2.63	2.74	2.5	2.26	2.26	2.26
Slovenia	9.10	9.13	9.07	7.02	6.75	7.43
Slovakia	4.74	5.24	4.21	4.18	4.34	3.98
Finland	18.12	20.35	16.22	14.34	15.18	13.57
Sweden	17.77	19.33	16.31	14.28	14.88	13.69
United Kingdom	16.98	19.20	14.72	11.79	12.23	11.34

Source: Eurostat database.

caused a small immediate reaction; however, these strategies and policies have been much less effective (but for Germany) and the persistence of the impact is much higher.

The impact of the crisis on youth unemployment has been impressive. YUR were in 2014 higher by half compared to 2007 values in the EU-28 (22.2 per cent versus 15.6 per cent). Some countries exhibit exceptionally high values in 2014, including Greece (52.4 per cent), Spain (55.2 per cent), Croatia (45.5 per cent), and Italy (42.7 per cent). Also, the NEET rate has increased in the EU: from 10.9 per cent in 2007 to 12.3 per cent in 2014; exceptionally high values can be found in Italy, where the NEET is above 22 per cent, Bulgaria (20 per cent), Greece and Croatia (about 19 per cent), Spain, Cyprus and Romania (17 per cent).

Conclusions and policy implications

As shown in the previous section with vast empirical evidence, a clear "disadvantage" of young people in the labour market emerged, with remarkable differences across the EU countries. Thus, a new type of inequality refers to the relative position of different generations in the labour market (in terms of quantity and quality of job opportunities and as regards life-cycle income). While in most developed economies the "old generation" is continuously getting an increasing share of income, due to demographic (the "ageing" society) and institutional (public expenditure for old-age pensions, health, etc.) reasons, the currently "young generation" receives a thin slice of production and income. The relative position of young people further worsened after the recent crises.

The key policy implications refer to both macroeconomic policies and specific policies for young people in the labour market. At the first level, there is a need to: stimulate economic growth and, of course, to avoid financial crises. Both suggestions are not trivial. Economic growth should be sustained, especially in Europe, because austerity measures have been too profound. As to financial crises, despite the numerous proposals at different levels (G-20, EU, individual countries) to reform the international financial systems, little progress has been made to date.

In particular, in the EU, in addition to indispensable changes in the institutional governance of the EU, economic policies should become more expansionary in order to stimulate economic growth in the short as well as in the long run.[16] The fiscal rules (Fiscal Compact, Stability Pact, etc.) should be enforced in a more flexible way, otherwise the austerity measures compulsory for many countries at the same time contribute to the current stagnation situation. Monetary policy since 2012 has been able to calm financial markets[17]. Unconventional monetary policy is even more important in this moment when deflationary conditions tend to prevail: the "quantitative easing" launched by the European Central Bank in March 2015 is a right move in this direction.

Of course, labour policies are also needed to reduce high unemployment and, especially, the high and rising YUR. Generous active labour policies and a reform of unemployment benefits could help. More specifically, age-targeted policies to tackle the YUR, including for example reforms of school-to-work institutions, may be more successful than a uniform policy. New school-to-work transition institutions, should include innovative educational, placement and training schemes. Generous active policies for the labour market should be integrated with the necessary passive labour market policies. In particular, the need for effective active labour market policies aimed at preventing short-term unemployment from becoming structural or long-term. The above mentioned policies can reduce the disadvantages of young people in the labour market, especially in the countries showing a high intergenerational inequality.

Notes

1 The lack of job stability is the most serious cause of lower satisfaction of temporary workers (see Bruno et al., 2014a, for an empirical investigation on the Italian case).
2 The relationship between youth unemployment and social exclusion has been analysed by Hammer (2003).
3 We refer to developed countries, while a different demographic situation tends to persist in less developed economies.
4 The different types of "disadvantage" can interact: for instance, Baussola and Mussida (2014) found for the Italian case that the disadvantage experienced by women in the labour market (i.e. the "gender gap" in terms of employment opportunities) is particularly significant for young and low-educated women.
5 This fact has attracted a number of empirical investigations (Freeman and Wise, 1982; Blanchflower and Freeman, 2000; Ryan, 2001; Quintini, Martin and Martin, 2007; Brada et al., 2014).
6 In this respect, the characteristics of educational systems and the different processes of human capital formation are of particular importance. For example, a dual educational system such as the one implemented in Germany where apprenticeship plays a key role together with formal education, is probably the best strategy to reduce the youth experience gap and improve the employability of young workers (Brunello et al. 2007).
7 See Caroleo and Pastore (2007), Quintini and Manfredi (2009) and Ryan (2001).
8 For a recent account of labour market institutions see European Economic Advisory Group (2013).
9 See Arpaia and Curci (2010), who produced a broad analysis of labour market adjustments in the EU-27 after the 2008–09 recession in terms of employment, unemployment, hours worked and wages.
10 The greater impact on YUR has been found in the case of financial crises, in an empirical analysis including a long period (starting 1980) and a large sample of countries in the world: see Choudhry et al. (2012). As for the joint impact of labour policies and the Great Recession on YUR, see Dal Bianco et al. (2015).
11 The initiative "Youth on the Move" within the Europe 2020 programme of the EU (European Commission, 2010) emphasises the importance of focusing on the NEET problem.
12 This was the worst year also for Greece and Spain, where TUR reached 58.3 per cent and 55.5 per cent respectively.
13 As we shall see below, the high incidence of part-time work favours the high employment of young people, who frequently are students and workers at the same time.
14 2004 is the initial year for which we dispose of Eurostat data.
15 As for the effect of unemployment on poverty and inequality, see Saunders (2002).
16 As for the main reasons of the Eurozone crisis and on the necessary innovative institutional and economic policies, see Marelli and Signorelli (2016).
17 After President Draghi's declaration "we shall save euro whatever it takes" and the launch of the "Outright monetary transactions" plan.

References

Arpaia, A. and Curci, N. (2010), *EU Labour Market Behaviour during the Great Recession*, Economic Papers 405, Brussels: European Economy, European Commission, Economic and Financial Affairs.
Baussola, M. and Mussida, C. (2014), Disadvantaged Workers in the Italian Labour Market: Gender and Regional Gaps, in M. A. Malo and D. Sciulli (eds) *Disadvantaged Workers: Empirical Evidence and Labour Policies*, Heidelberg: Springer.
Bazen, S., Gregory, M. and Salverda, W. (eds) (1998), *Low-wage Employment in Europe*, Cheltenham: Edward Elgar.
Bell, D.N.F. and Blanchflower, D.G. (2011), Youth Unemployment in Europe and the United States, *Nordic Economic Policy Review*, 1, 11–37.
Blanchflower, D.G. and Freeman, R. (eds) (2000), *Youth Employment and Joblessness*, Chicago, IL: University of Chicago Press.

Brada, J.C., Marelli, E. and Signorelli, M. (2014), Young People and the Labor Market: Key Determinants and New Evidences, *Comparative Economic Studies*, 56(4): 556–566.

Brunello, G., Garibaldi, P. and Wasmer, E. (2007), *Education and Training in Europe*, New York: Oxford University Press.

Bruno, G.S.F., Caroleo, F.E. and Dessy, O. (2014a), Temporary Contracts and Young Workers' Job Satisfaction in Italy, in M. A. Malo and D. Sciulli (eds) *Disadvantaged Workers: Empirical Evidence and Labour Policies*, Heidelberg: Springer.

Bruno, G.S.F., Choudhry, M., Marelli, E. and Signorelli, M. (2014b), Youth Unemployment: Key Determinants and the Impact of Crises, in M. A. Malo and D. Sciulli (eds) *Disadvantaged Workers: Empirical Evidence and Labour Policies*, Heidelberg: Springer.

Caporale, G.M. and Gil-Alana, L. (2014), Youth Unemployment in Europe: Persistence and Macroeconomic Determinants, *Comparative Economic Studies*, 56(4): 581–591.

Caroleo, F.E. and Pastore, F. (2007), The Youth Experience Gap: Explaining Differences Across EU Countries, *Quaderni del Dipartimento di Economia, Finanza e Statistica, Università di Perugia*, 41. Available online at http://www.ec.unipg.it/DEFS/uploads/quaderno41web_001.pdf (accessed December 4 2015).

Choudhry, M., Marelli, E. and Signorelli, M. (2012), Youth Unemployment Rate and Impact of Financial Crises, *International Journal of Manpower*, 33(1): 76–95.

Dal Bianco, S., Bruno, R. and Signorelli, M. (2015), The Joint Impact of Labour Policies and the "Great Recession" on Unemployment in Europe, *Economic Systems*, 39(1): 3–26.

Eurofound (2012), *NEETs – Young People Not in Employment, Education or Training: Characteristics, Costs and Policy Responses in Europe*, Luxembourg: Publications Office of the European Union.

European Commission (2010), *Youth on the Move*, Luxembourg: Publications Office of the European Union.

European Economic Advisory Group (2013), *The EEAG Report on the European Economy*, Munich: CESifo.

Fraser, N., Gutierrez, R. and Pena Casas, R. (eds) (2011), *Working Poverty in Europe: A Comparative Approach*, Basingstoke: Palgrave.

Freeman, R. and Wise, D. (1982), *The Youth Labor Market Problem: Its Nature, Causes and Consequences*, Chicago, IL: University of Chicago Press.

Headey, B. (2002), The Psychological Impact of Unemployment, in P. Saunders, and R. Taylor, (eds), *The Price of Prosperity. The Economic and Social Costs of Unemployment*, Sydney: University of New South Wales Press.

ILO (2012), *Global Employment Trends for Youth 2012,* Geneva: ILO.

ILO (2014), *Global Employment Trends 2014: Risks of a Jobless Recovery?*, Geneva: ILO.

Malo, M.A. and Sciulli, D. (eds) (2014), *Disadvantaged Workers: Empirical Evidence and Labour Policies*, Heidelberg: Springer.

Marelli, E. and Signorelli, M. (2016), The Eurozone Crisis, The Defective Policy Response and the Need for Institutional Innovation, in T. Eisenberg and G.B. Ramello (eds.) *Research Handbook in Comparative Law and Economics*, Cheltenham: Edward Elgar.

Marelli, E., Choudhry, M.T. and Signorelli, M. (2013), Youth and the Total Unemployment Rate: The Impact of Policies and Institutions, *Rivista Internazionale di Scienze Sociali*, 121(1): 63–86.

OECD (2005), *Education at Glance*, Paris: OECD.

OECD (2006), *Employment Outlook,* Paris: OECD.

O'Higgins N. (2012), This Time It's Different? Youth Labour Markets during 'The Great Recession', *Comparative Economic Studies*, 54(3): 395–412.

Peña-Casas, R. and Latta, M. (2004), *Working Poor in the European Union*, Luxembourg: European Foundation for the Improvement of Living and Working Conditions, Office for Official Publications of the European Communities.

Quintini, G., Martin, J.P. and Martin, S. (2007), *The Changing Nature of the School-to-Work Transition Process in OECD Countries*, Discussion Paper 2582, Institute for Study of Labor, Bonn: IZA.

Ryan, P. (2001), The School-to-Work Transition: A Cross-National Perspective, *Journal of Economic Literature*, 39(1): 34–92.

Saunders, P. (2002), *The Direct and Indirect Effects of Unemployment on Poverty and Inequality*, SPRC Discussion Paper 118.

Scarpetta, S., Sonnet, A. and Manfredi, T. (2010), *Rising Youth Unemployment During the Crisis: How to Prevent Negative Long-term Consequences on a Generation?*, OECD Social, Employment and Migration Working Papers 6.

Taylor, R. and Morrell, S. (2002), The Health Effects of Unemployment', in P. Saunders, and R. Taylor, (eds), *The Price of Prosperity. The Economic and Social Costs of Unemployment*, Sydney: University of New South Wales Press.

Index